SERENA WILLIAMS

SERENA WILLIAMS

Tennis Champion, Sports Legend, and Cultural Heroine

Merlisa Lawrence Corbett

ROWMAN & LITTLEFIELD
Lanham • Boulder • New York • London

Published by Rowman & Littlefield
An imprint of The Rowman & Littlefield Publishing Group, Inc.
4501 Forbes Boulevard, Suite 200, Lanham, Maryland 20706
www.rowman.com

6 Tinworth Street, London SE11 5AL

British Library Cataloguing in Publication Information Available

Library of Congress Cataloging-in-Publication Data

Names: Corbett, Merlisa Lawrence, 1965– author.
Title: Serena Williams : tennis champion, sports legend, and cultural heroine / Merlisa Lawrence
    Corbett.
Description: Lanham, Maryland : Rowman & Littlefield, 2020. | Includes bibliographical references
    and index. | Summary: "Record-breaking, trend-setting, and controversial, tennis star Serena
    Williams often sparks conversation and debate. She's one of the most intriguing figures in sports,
    and this book offers insight not only into her impact on tennis and popular culture but also into
    how she has challenged race and gender norms"— Provided by publisher.
Identifiers: LCCN 2019038838 (print) | LCCN 2019038839 (ebook) | ISBN 9781538109663 (cloth) |
    ISBN 9781538109670 (ebook)
Subjects: LCSH: Williams, Serena, 1981– | Women tennis players—United States—Biography. |
    African American women tennis players—Biography. | Celebrities—United States—Biography.
    | African American celebrities—Biography.
Classification: LCC GV994.W55 C67 2020 (print) | LCC GV994.W55 (ebook) | DDC 796.342092
    [B]—dc23
LC record available at https://lccn.loc.gov/2019038838
LC ebook record available at https://lccn.loc.gov/2019038839

To my father,
the late Robinson Louis Lawrence,
who read the *Lakeland Ledger* every day
before heading off to work.
He was always thoughtful enough to
leave behind the sports section for his daughters.

CONTENTS

ACKNOWLEDGMENTS

Steering a book from idea to completion is impossible without the support of family, friends, colleagues, and professionals. I especially want to thank the following folks who helped make this trip a rewarding ride.

Thank you to the professionals at Rowman & Littlefield, the driving force behind transforming me from writer to author. Thank you, Christen Karniski, editor extraordinaire. Your patience and guidance made even the potholes and pitfalls enjoyable.

Tracey Reavis, thanks so much. Your friendship and advice are always appreciated.

Thank you to my siblings, a built-in support system. This includes my brothers, Ranney and Selwyn, whose encouragement and unconditional love kept me from veering off the road.

Camille Mosley, a tireless crusader, thank you. Your passion for promoting and preserving the history of African Americans in tennis continues to inspire me.

To my mom, Esther, thank you for modeling creativity and an entrepreneurial spirit.

To Marvin, thanks for being pleasant and supportive over the years.

A special thank-you to Sara, Nicky, and Gregory, the three amigos. I love you guys.

Finally, thank you to the baristas at N+1 Coffee. Your mochas fueled much of this book.

INTRODUCTION

Less than two weeks after coming into this world on September 1, 2017, Alexis Olympia Ohanian Jr. had more than 60,000 Instagram followers. By February 2018, she had 259,000. She had 590,000 followers before she reached her second birthday. Olympia's Instagram account followed four people: her aunt, Venus Williams; her father, Alexis Ohanian Sr.; her doll Qai Qai; and her mother, Serena Williams, one of the greatest athletes of all time.

Serena is such an icon that her daughter and her daughter's doll have amassed social media followings. "Alexis" arrived during a headline-making month for Mommy. Maria Sharapova, 2–19 against Serena and 0–17 in the last 14 years, released a memoir entitled *Unstoppable: My Life So Far,* in which she characterized the 23-time Grand Slam champion as intimidating in size.

"First of all her physical presence is much stronger and bigger than you realize watching TV. She has thick arms and thick legs and is so intimidating and strong. It's the whole thing—her presence, her confidence, her personality. . . . Even now, she can make me feel like a little girl," wrote Sharapova, who is almost 6-foot-3 and can see over Serena's head when they stand side by side.

A *Daily Beast* columnist called Sharapova's language vile and racially tinged. The drama played out on social media as fans and media personalities debated whether Sharapova was body-shaming Serena to sell books. That all took a backseat when baby Ohanian arrived.

Serena gave birth and changed the subject. Similar to the way she grabs victory from pending defeat, Serena snatches the media spotlight away from all others. Whether on the court, on the runway, on the red carpet, or in the boardroom, Serena puts an exclamation point on almost everything she touches.

Record-breaking, trend-setting, polarizing, and controversial, Serena sparks conversation. Her failures are almost as epic as her triumphs. Her presence permeates so many aspects of mainstream culture—sports, fashion, celebrity, business—she's like a living piece of Americana.

She's one of the most intriguing figures in sports. This book offers a comprehensive look at Serena's life, including her impact on tennis, gender equality, racial issues, and popular culture.

The four-time Olympic gold medalist has a team, an entourage, celebrity groupies, and a band of fans who call themselves "Serena's army." She also has almost 11 million Twitter followers. She's in that first-name recognition club with Oprah, Beyoncé, Cher, Rafa, and Rihanna.

When not winning titles and making cameos in motion pictures, Serena is building her brand or funding schools for girls in Africa and Jamaica.

Her life is more than a sports story. "Professional athlete" is far too minuscule a title for someone whose impact on society leaps off the sports pages and into business publications, fashion magazines, and academic journals.

Serena is a tennis champion, sports legend, and cultural heroine. Still unfolding, her life's story is the ultimate American dream, filled with hope, anger, love, sadness, aspiration, perspiration, and perseverance.

I

SERENA'S COUNTRY CLUB UPBRINGING

Serena Williams's straight-out-of-Compton life story is a fascinating fairy tale. While her family did live in the rough neighborhood, Serena spent more of her childhood at country clubs in Florida than on the mean streets of South Central Los Angeles.

The story of a little black girl from the ghetto who reaches international superstardom makes a hell of a rags-to-riches tale, however. Indeed, Serena's journey from Compton to center court is the inspirational story of an American family with an influential father figure whose children survive, thrive, and persevere despite racism, sexism, and classism.

Serena was born in Saginaw, Michigan, her mother's hometown. Even though Michigan's Women's Hall of Fame inducted her in 2012, Serena has no memory of living in the state. The family moved back to California, where Venus was born, before Serena's second birthday.

Before Serena's father, Richard Williams, entered the picture, her mother, Oracene Price, married Yuseff A. K. Rasheed. The couple had three girls, Yetunde, Lyndrea, and Isha. Little is known about Rasheed, except that he was an attorney and died before Oracene married Richard in 1980.

In his autobiography, *Black and White: The Way I See It*, Richard called meeting Oracene the best thing that ever happened to him. "As a child, I had lived with my mother and three sisters," Richard wrote. "Here I was again, living in a house filled with four women—and I loved it."[1]

Richard and his new family of five moved into a house a few blocks from the beach in Long Beach, California. He said the idea to "raise champions" came to him while watching television in their Long Beach living room, before Serena and Venus were born. They weren't watching anything in particular, so Richard asked seven-year-old Yetunde to turn the remote-less television dial until landing on something interesting. When she turned past the end of a tennis match, Richard jumped out of his chair and turned back. He stood there amazed at the site of a 25-year-old Romanian tennis player receiving a check for $40,000. He couldn't believe his ears when late legendary tennis announcer Bud Collins told the player, "That's not bad for four days' work."

A serial entrepreneur, Richard decided to launch a new business, raising tennis stars. He approached this idea to raise champions the same way he did his cement business and security company. He developed a business plan, a 75-page manifesto. It was more than a wish list. Richard created a company called Richard Williams Tennis Associates.[2]

"I went into my office and began to plan for the day my daughters would dominate tennis," wrote Richard.[3] Until that point, Richard hadn't been interested in tennis—he did not even know how to keep score. So he immersed himself in the game. He bought books, magazines, and instructional videos. He purchased a racket and started taking lessons.

After Oracene agreed to have more children and Venus and Serena arrived, Richard put his plan into action. His security business allowed him to make his own hours. When he was not running the business, Richard focused on developing Venus's and Serena's tennis games. Serena started playing when she was only three.

Richard claims to have modeled his parenting and coaching philosophy after his mother. Her mantra: "Be tough." In *Black and White*, Richard said he chose to move his family from Long Beach to Compton as part of his plan to develop the girls into champions:

> What led me to Compton was my belief that the greatest champions
> came out of the ghetto. I had studied sports successes like Muhammad
> Ali and great thinkers like Malcolm X. I saw where they came from.
> As part of my plan, I decided it was where the girls were going to grow
> up, too. It would make them tough, give them a fighter's mentality.[4]

Living in a ghetto is not a prerequisite for all black champions. Michael Jordan, Tiger Woods, and Jerry Rice had typical suburban upbringings. Steph Curry grew up the son of a wealthy NBA player. But maybe Richard was onto something, because Tiger, Jordan, and Rice never took up the activist and social justice mantle in the way that Ali did—the way Serena and Venus have.

The house in Compton was a step down from the place they lived in near the beach. Oracene objected to the move at first, frowning upon the drug and gang scene in the new neighborhood. Even Richard had a few doubts about the move, especially after a fight with seven gang members left him hospitalized and missing 10 teeth.[5]

Gang warfare was a fixture at what Richard called the "East Compton Hills Country Club," a raggedy blacktop tennis court located at the intersection of Compton Boulevard and Lime Avenue. A different kind of country club, East Compton Hills is where Richard introduced his daughters to tennis.[6] East Compton country club lacked the amenities found at the facilities Serena would grow accustomed to in Florida. The sisters were more likely to come across crack vials and liquor bottles than lux hand lotions. Winos and weirdos were among the regular patrons. James Pyles, a part-time employee at the Compton Park Recreation Center, remembered, "When a gunfight broke out, those playing tennis would drop to the ground. When the shooting stopped, they would simply rise and continue."[7]

The courts were not far from 1117 East Stockton Street in Compton, the Williams family house, where the girls played handball in the front yard. Their family now consisted of six females—mom Oracene Price and sisters Serena, Venus, Yetunde, Lyndrea, and Isha—and Richard.

Determined to follow his plan, Richard tried to create a tennis center regimen with the girls. They kept a regular practice schedule, and their training included fitness. Surrounded by litter and various forms of urban decay, the tennis courts were where Serena's parents, self-taught players, laid the foundation for what would become two Hall of Fame–worthy careers.

Richard's plan to raise champions included more than tennis training. They still had to study as hard as they practiced, and Richard would take them to work with him as part the Job Development and Education Preparation (JDEP) program. Venus and Serena earned money delivering telephone books when they were three and two, respectively. Some of the Williams's neighbors and friends were so concerned about how hard Richard pushed his daughters that they called the police, alleging child abuse.

Early on, Richard decided it was more important that he lead the girls as a father, instead of a coach. He noted, "Approaching the girls' upbringing as a parent and not a coach, I could see that success in life was the union of three fundamental elements: confidence, courage, and commitment."[8]

Initially, Richard spent most of his time focused on Venus, the older, longer, and leaner of the two sisters. Meanwhile, Serena would get instruction from her mother and others, one of them being James Pyles.

Serena entered her first tournament at age four and a half.[9] She and Venus were entered in the under-12 tournaments in California, and according to Richard, Serena won 46 of 49 tournaments before turning 10. Word of the sisters' talent and prowess spread throughout the tennis community. People wanted to know just who and how good the girls were.

They would be invited to play at area country clubs, something Richard considered a possible stumbling block in his quest to keep his girls humble and hungry. Even with their early success, their parents remained steadfast in their desire to raise daughters who never forgot where they came from. One day, when Serena and Venus were playing at the Pacific Palisades Country Club, which they had been invited to, Richard approached them while they were eating hamburgers, fries, and ice cream. Aware that he hadn't given them any money, he asked, "How did you get these?" Serena responded, "It's on my tab."

Worried about the girls becoming spoiled, Richard reminded them, "We were Compton not country club." He told them that he had prepared peanut butter and jelly for them and demanded that they reject their newfound sense of entitlement.[10]

Except for local tournaments in California, the sisters bypassed the traditional United States Tennis Association (USTA) route through juniors play, in which young children traveled from region to region competing with the best players in their age groups from throughout the country.

Serena and Venus would remain a mystery, and mainly a family project, until May 1991. Richard and Oracene realized that because they had no formal tennis training, they would not be enough to take Venus and Serena to the next level. They decided to seek outside help, a pivotal move in Richard's plan. That's when Richard placed a call to Rick Macci, one of the top teaching pros in tennis. At the time, Macci ran a tennis academy at Grenelefe Golf and Tennis Resort in Haines City, Florida, a small town located about 20 miles south of the Walt Disney World Resort. Before the Williams sisters arrived, Macci's most notable pupils had been Tommy Ho and Jennifer Capriati. Both had reached number one in juniors, and Capriati was already making noise on the professional tour.

The call from Richard came out of the blue. Macci was intrigued. "Well, most of the time kids that are supposed to be special are nationally ranked, or they've achieved something, I see them at junior tournaments. But these girls never played any tournaments, and I did see an article in the *New York Times* about this girl name Venus," Macci said.[11]

After the call from Richard, Macci hopped on a flight to Los Angeles. "I remember it like it was yesterday," said Macci. "I figured out a weekend, and it's the first time ever I got on a plane and went to see someone play other than if I went to a junior tournament. So it was definitely a unique and different experience for sure."

Venus was a hot commodity. Even though she hadn't played in any major junior tournaments, sports agents and coaches were making inquiries. They wanted in on what could be the next big thing in tennis.

After the *New York Times* ran a feature on the girls, Venus enjoyed celebrity-like status in Compton. Gang members who otherwise used the courts as a battleground now came out to watch her play. The talk of a future star convinced Macci to give her a look.

Macci arrived in Los Angeles carrying a substantial bag of skepticism, but he was excited about getting a look at the buzzed-about Venus. "A lot of people were putting a lot of helium in the balloon. There was a lot of hype about this girl that had potential. She was playing 10-under tournaments in Southern Cal and supposedly didn't lose a match," he said.

This was the early 1990s. The legendary rivalry between Chris Evert and Martina Navratilova was over. By the end of 1991, 18-year-old Monica Seles had already won four Grand Slam singles titles and posed a threat to Steffi Graf and Gabriela Sabatini, a perennial Slam semifinalist. Graf and Sabatini were still in their early 20s.

Meanwhile, Macci had a hand in producing perhaps the most controversial teen prodigy in tennis history—Capriati. Having spent three years training Capriati, who turned pro at age 13, Macci knew what greatness looked like. It wouldn't take him long to figure out if the Williams sisters were the real deal.

Macci's first meeting with Richard was a family affair. Richard brought the girls to the hotel where Macci was staying. "We talked for three hours. Well, it was more like an interrogation," said Macci. "Venus sat on one leg of Richard and Serena sat on the other, and then Oracene was there. We just talked. Richard asked so many questions I almost felt like I was in a deposition."

Richard didn't want to entrust just anyone with his girls. After all, he was following a detailed plan and remained wary of outside influence on his daughters.

The day after that first meeting, Richard picked up Macci in the family's beat-up Volkswagen Beetle van and took him to Compton.

"They picked me up at the hotel, and we went to the tennis courts. He said it was the East Compton Hills Country Club," said Macci.

When they arrived at Compton's country club, Macci ran some drills with the girls to assess their movement, groundstrokes, and general tennis acumen. His first impression? Not impressed.

"I thought they were good little athletes. Venus was quite tall already. Serena was not that tall. I thought they were good athletes, but they were raw. You know, arms, legs, hair, feet flying everywhere."

After observing the girls for several minutes, Macci thought he'd seen enough to know Venus and Serena "would make a nice little project, but certainly weren't anything special," he said.

"So I'm thinking, 'Wow, what am I doing in Compton, California, for the weekend?' Because they were just like any other kids. There wasn't anything that blew me away."

That was until he asked the girls to play for points, keep score. "But then we changed the drill to where we were going to be competitive, we were going to play points. That's when the stock of both girls changed dramatically and went through the roof," Macci reflected. All of a sudden, the footwork got better, preparation got better, the focus got better, consistency got better, everything changed the minute they said, "Game on!"

Macci considers this a cautionary tale for coaches and parents. "You can't judge a book by its cover," he continued, "I can evaluate talent better than anybody. I just wasn't blown away because I was looking cosmetically. The minute we kept score, both of them changed dramatically. And so it was like they were gamers. They knew how to compete. It meant something."

After watching the girls play for points, Macci got excited. He knew he had stumbled onto something special. Macci stated, "So I'm sitting there [watching], and I go to Richard and ask, 'How tall is Venus going to be?' He said, she might be 6-foot-1, 160 pounds. Serena's probably going to be 5-foot-11. Because when we started playing, I thought right then and there, these two girls, with the right instruction, could transcend the game."

By transcending the game, Macci meant he could envision a day when the Williams sisters would usher in what tennis commentator Mary Carillo called "Big Babe tennis," an era in which players would merge the athleticism of Navratilova with the height and size of Lindsay Davenport.

"I didn't think they could be number two or number one in the world. I knew they could, right then," said Macci.

> Because in the 90s, the early 90s, if you were big and strong, you weren't fast. These girls were going to be big, strong, fast, quick, and competitive, like a lion that hadn't eaten for a week. . . . So even though they were rough around the edges and raw, with that package I thought they would transcend the game.

The first clue? Venus's athleticism. While Macci evaluated their talent, Venus asked her father if she could go to the restroom. With little effort, she walked to the restroom, on her hands.

"Then the next set, she kind of did these backward cartwheels," Macci remembered. "I told Richard, let me tell you something, 'You got the next Michael Jordan on your hands.' Then he put his arm around me and said, 'No brother man, I got the next two.'"

Convinced that he'd hit the jackpot, Macci invited the girls to train at Grenelefe. It was the chance Richard had been waiting for. The girls would no longer have to play on make-believe country club courts. They could take lessons at a world-class facility.

Still, Serena's parents struggled with the idea of uprooting the family and moving to Florida. "We liked California well enough," Serena wrote in her book *On the Line*. "But once everyone started talking about moving, Florida was the Promised Land."[12]

Richard and Oracene liked the idea of exposing their children to a better life. So they discarded the beat-up Volkswagen, packed up a Winnebago, and headed east.

The only family member who remained, their eldest sister Yetunde, would be murdered in a drive-by shooting in 2003. In his autobiography,

Richard lamented about leaving Yetunde behind, writing, "She wanted to stay in California and, bless her soul, that's where she's buried."[13]

GRENELEFE LIFE

According to Serena, the most memorable part of the coast-to-coast trip was that it was the longest stretch the family had gone without playing tennis. Not that Richard didn't try to work in a few drills at rest stops along the way.[14]

Macci's tennis academy was just one aspect of life at Grenelefe, a planned community like many others sprouting up throughout the country in the early 1990s. More than a collection of cul-de-sacs and tree-lined entrances, planned communities offered homeowners an upscale lifestyle, with golf courses, tennis courts, country clubs, and shopping. When the Williams family moved to Grenelefe, the community featured a spa, a conference center, and four restaurants.

Grenelefe life was nothing like the way most kids in Haines City lived. Nestled in Polk County, among the most rural in Florida, Haines City had a larger than average African American population. The schools Serena and Venus attended—Alta Vista Elementary and Shelley Boone Middle—had a large percentage of poor whites, migrant Hispanics, and Haitian students. Blacks made up 24 percent of the student body, double the percentage of African Americans in the country.[15]

Serena spent her mornings surrounded by mostly low-income minority students and then would be whisked away to the mostly white confines of Grenelefe, where she would practice four to five hours a day. Although Compton was majority minority, it was urban. Polk County is one of the reddest political regions of Florida. Rednecks and trailer parks were the norm before the Grenelefe development began sprouting in the 1970s. By the 1980s, Grenelefe was a world-class resort. It's where the Williams clan, a family of six, plus a couple of dogs Serena oversaw as pets, settled into their first home in Florida.

Imagine the cultural dexterity it took for 10-year-old Serena to play fierce with her white male coaches at Grenelefe, attend ballet lessons, and then go to school every day with country kids and migrants whose parents picked fruit for a living.

Meanwhile, Richard sought ways to keep the girls from slipping into a country-club mentality. He would drive them to poorer neighbors in nearby Haines City and away from the manicured golf greens of Grenelefe. He enrolled them in local public schools and taught them early on about the importance of connecting with the community.

"They didn't go from Compton to center court. Believe me," Macci said. "They were in Polk County. They lived right there at the resort."

Richard and his Winnebago were fixtures at Grenelefe and area charitable events. He was a founding member of the local MADD Dad's chapter, an organization affiliated with Mothers against Drunk Drivers. In 1991, the local Polk County Sheriff Department's DARE program was struggling to stay afloat due to lack of funds. Richard convinced Reebok, then supplying the girls with shoes and other sporting goods, to donate $5,000 to the program. At the time, it was the largest single contribution to the county's program.[16] They held a ceremony for DARE, which Serena participated in at Alta Vista Elementary.

The Williams family approached practice like business development, just another part of Richard's plan. Oracene and Richard maintained a watchful eye, but they outsourced developing Serena and Venus's game to Macci, who would help to smooth out the sisters' rough edges.

Venus and Serena were enrolled in an accelerated academic program that allowed them to leave school by 1:00 p.m. and head to the courts for training. Richard and Oracene concentrated on instilling determination and focus. They counted on Macci and his team to address tennis technique and tactics.

One major change was the upgrade in the fitness regimen. Prior to Grenelefe, Richard incorporated calisthenics and stretching into the girls' tennis drills. At Grenelefe, workouts were additional. The girls had to run up hills, work out, and even lift weights.

"I hated it," Serena wrote in *On the Line*. "What little kid wants to be out there every day? Or working out in the gym?"[17]

Serena also hated the way she looked. She didn't focus on any one feature. Instead, she assumed everyone saw her as ugly and described waiting for mean-girl moments. "Little girls can be so mean to each other, only here it wasn't like they were especially mean to me," she wrote. "I was guarding against that meanness every day."[18]

Afraid she might be picked on because of her perceived ugliness, Serena kept to herself and said little during school.

The self-doubt seemed to melt away when she took to the court. Whatever insecurities Serena had about her looks didn't translate to her game. She found solace in her gradual mastery of tennis.

The family put their faith in Macci to transform the girls from promising to polished.

"With both girls, they were just flawed," said Macci.

> They had big swings and hit off balance a lot. They just needed a lot of technical help on the serve and on the volley. They were just athletes playing tennis. But when your hitting partners are ranked among the top 300 in the world, you're going to get better. They got the best training, and they got the most individualized instruction. Even though they were great athletes, I tried to make them better athletes. We did taekwondo, baseball, basketball, football, ballet, jazz.

Richard incorporated ball-throwing into the girls' training. They'd throw baseballs and footballs to create a natural hurling motion needed for fluid serves. This set Serena and Venus apart from other female players, many who grew up never playing sports in which they'd have to throw.

Soon, Serena and Venus were winners-in-waiting, just smoothing out flaws en route to what they believed would be championship careers. The media and tennis community waited too. Just how real were the stories of Serena and Venus's power and tennis acumen?

Macci knew. "I knew what was coming," he said. "It was just a lot of training, getting those groundstrokes, they could be solid, because they're gonna have power, they're gonna be big and strong, and they're going to have technically good serves, and I even knew at age 11 that Serena would probably have the best serve of all time."

Besides tossing balls, Macci and Richard introduced the girls to unorthodox tennis training. Serena and Venus had to jog in sand traps on the golf course with a super featherweight boxer from Winter Haven, Florida, named Amos "Sweat Pea" Cowart.

"I hired him, and he would box with them in a sandpit, and they had a bag in front of them and if they didn't move they'd get popped a little bit," said Macci. "Richard said, 'Hey, it's fine with me.' That's one thing I liked about Richard. He didn't care what I did, he was really cool about that."

With Richard's blessing, Macci kept expectations high and practices rigorous.

"Everything we always talked about was always about being number one in the world. They thought they were going to be number one in the world. They expected to be number one in the world."

Macci made practice as difficult as possible. He and Richard tried to create conditions worse than what Serena and Venus would see at the pro level. This included adult male hitting partners who could crush the ball at 100 miles per hour. Richard believed in simulated adversity as preparation for inevitable obstacles.

"So, everything was over the top," Macci said. "I mean Venus didn't win a match at the academy. I let her play matches, and she didn't win a match for two years. If that happened nowadays, the parents would go somewhere else, in a week."

Parents who coddled their children, Macci believed, would consider Richard's tactics a blow to a child's self-confidence.

"But Richard said, 'I want them to lose. Makes 'em tougher.'"

So they manufactured adversity and incorporated difficulty into the girls' training. This meant opting for used balls with less bounce. "He wanted the worst balls I had, so they'd be slower, the kids would have to bend more and be faster," Macci disclosed.

> He wanted kids to play his daughters and cheat all the time, to get them ready for the real world.
>
> If I gave old balls and had a kid here at the academy play a cheater, there would be such an argument; people would leave. You've got to understand, the world's a different place, but he understood. He knew a little bit about tennis, but he was a great dad. You know, I've been around [Mary] Pierce, Capriati, Sharapova, you know I've coached them all. Just a great dad.

Richard also knew Serena would be better than Venus because she was a little rougher and tougher. He would always call her his little pit bull.

Mean and hungry is how Richard wanted Serena and Venus to play on the court; however, when it came to nurturing their self-confidence, Richard guarded their psyches like a barnyard dog.

In a 1995 interview with John McKenzie for ABC News, Richard exploded in anger at a journalist who appeared to doubt Venus's assertion that she could defeat Martina Hingis. While Richard was off to the side, out of view of the camera, the reporter repeatedly questioned Venus about what made her so sure she could beat Hingis. Richard interrupted and shut down the interview. He shouted to the interviewer to respect Venus's belief that she could win and not mess with the confidence of a young black girl.

Macci contended that Richard always knew what he was doing. The ability to focus and tune out detractors would serve the girls well in hostile environments both on and off the court.

While Richard orchestrated training, Oracene modeled calm composure. They were the yin and yang in Serena's life. She enjoyed ample quality time with both. When they were in California, Serena spent more time alone with her mother. "When we were kids, it was mostly just me and my mom. She was working a lot, that's true, but almost all of my one-on-one training was with her," Williams said in her biography.[19] But when they moved to Florida, training the girls became more of a collaborative effort.

Contrary to the outward demeanor projected in public, Serena likened her mother's coaching style to more of that of drill sergeant, "barking out" orders on how to move. Her father, Serena said, took a calmer approach and preferred that the girls figure things out for themselves.

Oracene's impact off the court included her devotion to the Jehovah's Witness faith. The girls attended Jehovah's Witness services at Kingdom Hall on Tuesdays, Thursdays, and Sundays. Serena was raised a Jehovah's Witness and remains devoted to the faith to this day.

ROOTED IN SOUTH FLORIDA

About two years after they moved to Florida, Macci made a move of his own. He relocated his academy to Delray Beach, about two hours south of Grenelefe. Serena and her family settled in nearby Pompano Beach. Although the relocation of Macci's academy prompted the move, Serena wrote in her autobiography that her father thought the family could use a change.

Although their location changed, the girls' routine remained the same: school, practice, and enrichment programs. The tight-knit family did everything together. Practicing was part drills, part family gathering, and part meals. They lived on the court. While Venus and Serena worked with Macci, their parents retained the official title as coaches.

Two-time Grand Slam champion Mary Pierce told the *New York Times* she remembers being amazed by the amount of time the family spent on the court. In recounting her days in Delray Beach, Florida, in the early 1990s, Pierce told the *New York Times*,

> I was living in an apartment on the third floor, and right below me were some clay courts. And I'm telling you, I don't know how many mornings I would hear the ball being hit. And I was like, "Who are these people playing in the morning?"
>
> They'd wake me up, and I'd look out my window, and there they are: the Williams family. And they were all on the court. They were on the court all day long, from morning until night. They would sit on the court and eat lunch. All day, hitting balls and hitting balls and hitting balls.[20]

In Delray Beach, the girls split time between Macci's academy and public tennis courts at Pompey Park, a low-income area. Although not occupied by gangs like in Compton, Pompey Park courts had cracks and potholes. An African American tennis coach named William "Bill" Murray had been hired by the city to run a free tennis program for inner-city kids.[21]

Macci told the *Palm Beach Post* that Richard had the girls play at Pompey Park to keep them grounded and remind them of their roots in Compton.[22] "They kept it all very private," Murray said.[23]

As they grew from little girls to teenagers, their potential became evident. At the time, a number of promising teenagers, including Hingis and Capriati, were on the tour. Macci saw the competitive edge before Serena and Venus went pro. He says they maintain that inner fire even today.

"You can just feel it come through your TV set. Everybody is competitive or they wouldn't be in sports. Everybody's competitive or they wouldn't be a world-class athlete. But, this quality, along with these other attributes, makes them a package, and that's why Serena is going to be the greatest player of all time."

Serena's hunger and drive have always been there. She hates losing more than she enjoys winning. She's a perfectionist who is harder on herself than any critic could be.

"At the end of the day, you can't teach it," Macci said of that type of determination. "I said this, that they would be better than Capriati, that they would be number one in the world. I was saying this when they were 10 and 11."

Relentless practicing helped Serena perfect her legendary serve, which stood out from even Venus's. Today, Serena is credited with having the greatest serve in the history of the game.

Macci thinks genetics is the reason Serena developed a better serve than Venus.

"Her motion was a little more natural than Venus. She [Serena] just had a more natural shoulder turn. She was a little more rhythmic. Venus was a little more mechanical," said Macci.

To this day, despite having a faster serve on record than Serena's, Venus struggles with her ball toss during the serve. Her second serve is often a liability and far less reliable than Serena's.

TOURNAMENT TIME

As they developed into better players, the desire to see them compete grew stronger. But their father insisted that they were too young, not ready for the rigorous demands of a professional career. Besides, Richard told Serena, "Meeka, there wasn't any point in traveling all around the country to watch you and V beat up on all those little girls."[24]

Meanwhile, Capriati had already defeated Graf in the gold medal match at the 1992 Olympics and reached the top 10 at age 14. But after losing in the first round of the U.S. Open, she went on a 14-month break to address issues with drug abuse and shoplifting. If Richard had any doubts about his decision to keep the girls out of the spotlight a little while longer, Capriati's troubles might have affirmed his philosophy about postponing their professional debuts.

Then came a rules change that would hasten their entry into the pros. In January 1994, the Women's Tennis Council proposed changing the rule that allowed players to turn pro after their 14th birthday. Under mounting pressure from those in the tennis community, the proposed new rule would have prohibited anyone younger than 16 from turning pro.

New York Times sportswriter Robin Finn wrote a scathing article in support of the rule change. "It will happen too late to help protect imminent phenoms Martina Hingis and Venus Williams, both of whom will turn 14 in 1994, but the WTC cannot continue to justify 14 as an appropriate age for its freshman class," wrote Finn.

Finn continued, "If the tennis community has a conscience at all, there won't be any 13-year-old pigtailed, pinafored 'professionals' available for exploitation in 1995 and beyond."[25]

Macci told Richard that he had to decide to either allow Venus to turn pro at 14 or risk the Women's Tennis Association (WTA) dictating when his daughter could play on the pro circuit. Richard agreed. So, in 1994, Venus made her professional debut at the Bank of the West Classic in Oakland. Serena was merely an observer that day.

Venus stunned onlookers as she defeated the number 57 player in the first round. Venus was up a set and a break on the number two, Arantxa Sanchez Vicario, before losing that match. Despite the loss, Venus' performance put the tennis world on alert.

A year later, Serena sought to debut at the same tournament, but the WTA denied her entrance based on the new rule.

Serena filed an antitrust lawsuit against the WTA, challenging its age restriction; however, she later dropped the lawsuit and listened to her father, who recommended she wait eight months until she turned 15.[26]

Stubborn and ready to compete despite the age restriction, Serena sought and got a wild card to a tournament in Canada. She dreamed of a glorious debut, just like the one Venus had. Things didn't work out the way Serena planned. In fact, her professional debut was a disaster.

2

QUEEN OF THE COURT

Serena's professional career got off to an unimpressive start.

After Venus's successful professional debut, Serena decided it was time for her coming-out party. Her father discouraged the decision. He thought Serena needed more time to develop; however, Serena wanted to do everything her big sister did. So just as she bogarted her way into a tournament as a preteen, Serena sought to defy the WTA and its new age restrictions by taking a wild card into the competition in Quebec.

Ambitious, Serena researched the new restrictions and figured that if she played just once in 1995, she could establish herself as a pro and avoid having to wait until she was 16.

Her wild card got her into the qualifying round in Quebec, just two months after turning 14. She faced 18-year-old Annie Miller, a decent player, but nothing like the number 57 ranked player Venus took on in her debut.

She bombed. Serena's travel to her first professional tournament turned out to be more eventful than the actual match. Of the debut, Robin Finn of the *New York Times* wrote,

> After 10 years of practice and a harrowing 15-hour trip through stormy skies, Serena Williams, the last of the 14-year-olds to sneak onto the women's tennis circuit, touched down at an obscure tournament over the weekend and, ostensibly without the blessing of her parents or the WTA Tour, began her professional career. [1]

Miller defeated Serena 6–1, 6–1. Serena told reporters that she was embarrassed and that she did not play like a professional. She left the court humbled. "Playing in all those little-kid events out in California, I'd always expected to win—and I usually did," she wrote in *On the Line*. "Here, though, I could no longer expect to win. I'd have to earn it, fight for it."[2]

Serena left Quebec as she had arrived—a youngster with potential still playing in her big sister's shadow. Serena believed that the lopsided loss had more to do with her insecurities and inexperience than her game. She wrote in her autobiography, "I think the moment was a little too big for my fourteen-year-old self."[3]

Inexperienced and uncomfortable with losing, Serena committed to learning from her mistakes. Although she continued training in Florida, she did not play another professional match until 1997, when she was 15 years old. Of that period, Serena described herself as a "professional in name only."[4]

Meanwhile, Venus played in 15 tour events in 1996, and broke into the Top 100. The following year, Serena would get a second chance to make a different impression.

Serena's second professional match was almost as bad as the first. A French player named Alexia Dechaume-Balleret defeated Serena, 6–4, 6–0, in the first round of the 1997 Indian Wells tournament. But unlike in Quebec, this time Serena had Venus with her. They entered the doubles tournament and reached the quarterfinals before losing to Lindsay Davenport and Natasha Zvereva, 6–3, 6–0. Playing doubles with Venus established the rhythm of winning multiple matches. Some success in doubles also helped build Serena's confidence. Moreover, she got badly needed experience in managing day-to-day routines players develop during extended stays at tournaments. Although Serena lost in the first round of three tournaments that year, by the end of 1997, she had grown into her professional status. She notched upset wins over Mary Pierce, Monica Seles, and Davenport, and finished 1997 ranked number 99.

In 1998, Serena entered the Australian Open for her first Grand Slam main draw appearance. Most teenage players make their Grand Slam debuts on outer courts, away from the crowds and the media frenzy; however, as if the tournament organizers knew Serena belonged on the big stage, the 16-year-old American played her first Grand Slam match on Center Court.

Serena knocked off sixth-seeded Irina Spirlea, of Romania. A bit of controversy surrounded the match because of an incident between Spirlea and Venus at the 1997 U.S. Open. During a changeover, Spirlea refused to sidestep as she passed Venus and initiated a chest bump. Later, Spirlea apologized, but that was after she received a $5,000 fine.[5]

The win over Spirlea at the 1998 Aussie Open set up a second-round match against Venus. It would be the first Grand Slam showdown between the Williams sisters. Venus defeated Serena. After the match, in a memorable scene, the sisters locked hands and raised their arms together as if they had won the tournament. Venus described the experience as weird. "We're gonna make a pact and be number one and number two so we only meet in the finals, and then we won't care because we'll be playing for the title," she said.[6]

Although Serena lost her first professional encounter with Venus, 1998 would become a breakout year for the younger sister. She won her first professional title, albeit in doubles at a tournament in Oklahoma City. During the trophy ceremony, the sisters received a giant cardboard check for $4,500. That may be a tiny amount compared to the millions of dollars players get for winning Slams these days, but for Serena, it was not about the money. She wanted the spectacle of it all. "The check itself was for $4,500—a lot of money, absolutely, but hardly enough to justify all that paperboard for the fake check. And yet when they presented it to me and V it felt like we'd won a million dollars," Serena wrote in *On the Line*.[7]

That same year, Serena reached the fourth round at the French Open and the third round at Wimbledon, where she retired two games into the match due to a calf muscle injury. She also lost in the third round of the U.S. Open and won her first two Grand Slam titles—in mixed doubles with partner Max Mirnyi.

Serena finished the year ranked in the top 20 and ready to challenge the WTA's status quo.

THE NEW TEEN IN TOWN

By 1999, Steffi Graf's career was winding down. The great Martina Navratilova, in her 40s, had not officially retired. Martina Hingis held the record for the youngest female player to win a Grand Slam. Being just a year older than Serena and the same age as Venus, Hingis made for a natural rival. She would also serve as the standard-bearer and barrier the Williams sisters would have to clear.

Hingis began the year ranked number two. Davenport was number one. Meanwhile, fellow teens Kim Clijsters and Anna Kournikova were also vying for trophies, dollars, and sponsorships. Serena continued to play in Venus's shadow, although she did win her first WTA singles title at age 17, when she edged Amelie Mauresmo at the Open Gaz de France in Paris.

As the sisters moved swiftly up the rankings, fewer people questioned their potential. They were clearly on a trajectory toward amassing titles. But even with the tennis world bracing for their bright futures, Serena and Venus arrived ahead of schedule, in the final at the Lipton Championship, which would later become the Miami Open.

They were ranked in the top 20 and seeded (Venus number six and Serena number 16), with the tournament and tour still featuring such names as Graf, Hingis, and Seles. Venus beat legends Jana Novotna and Graf en route to the final. Serena defeated Seles and the number one, Hingis.

It was the first all-sister final in WTA history. Their jubilant father held up a homemade sign that read, "Welcome to the Williams Show!" Indeed, the teens put on a show, displaying what would become trademark groundstrokes. After Venus raced off to a 6–1 first-set win, Serena took the second set. But Venus prevailed, winning 6–1, 4–6, 6–4.

Following the match, Venus spoke with reporters about holding off her younger sister. "Serena always comes back and defeats people, and I didn't want to become another victim."[8]

Richard told reporters that Serena hadn't played up to her potential. Serena agreed and, in the postmatch press conference, said, "I was making way too many errors. Seems like I couldn't keep many balls in play. It just wasn't the same Serena like the rest of my 16 matches."[9]

Later that year, at the U.S. Open, Serena faced Clijsters, who had recently turned 16. Serena was about a month shy of her 18th birthday. Clijsters was only ranked number 98, but she was a gifted athlete. She moved as well as Serena and could hit just as hard. After each player took a set, Clijsters went up, 5–2, in the third set and seemed to be cruising toward a victory. After Serena held to make it 3–5, Clijsters was serving for the match. That is when Serena staged one of her biggest comebacks.

Clijsters's serve was the first thing to break down. She quickly fell behind, 0–30. One of her second serves dipped to 69 miles per hour. (In comparison, Serena's fastest serve tops 120 miles per hour, and she can go through an entire tournament serving 95 miles per hour.) Down 0–40, Clijsters double-faulted, putting the ball and the match back on Serena's racket.

Serving to level the match, Serena, perhaps sensing Clijsters tightening, became more aggressive. With Clijsters retreating, Serena took charge, hitting winners from both wings. The entire Williams clan, including Venus, in the players' box roared after each Serena winner. Serena leveled the match at 5–5.

Serena rattled off three straight games. Clijsters badly needed to regain her composure. Instead, she unraveled, panicked. Facing a game point, down 0–40, Clijsters did the inexplicable—she stopped play in the middle of a point. Serena hit a hard forehand that landed squarely on the baseline, and Clijsters froze. The match was before Hawk-Eye, so there was no way for her to challenge the call. The umpire didn't overrule a ball that landed inside the court. Back then, CBS used something called the "Mac Cam" replay, which also showed the ball inside the court. While a flustered Clijsters stood with her hands on her hips, Serena had already walked to her chair for the changeover. Now up 6–5, Serena closed out Clijsters, winning the match 4–6, 6–2, 7–5. She ended that match winning 16 of the last 17 points in one of her most remarkable comebacks.

Serena prevailed, but a more significant challenge remained. Hingis awaited.

Hingis had already defeated Venus in a Grand Slam final. She had won the Australian Open and reached the final at the French Open. Despite being a contemporary, Hingis already had five Grand Slams singles titles. The Williams sisters had none.

In the lead-up to the match, Hingis disparaged the Williams family by saying, "They have a big mouth."[10]

Serena went into the match as the underdog. Not only did Hingis have more championship experience, but also she was ranked number one and possessed what many considered to be the more all-around game. Most predicted Venus would be the first of the sisters to win a Slam. After all, she was the oldest.

"Richard always claimed that Serena would be the superior player, but when Venus made her spectacular run to the 1997 U.S. Open final, most observers dismissed such talk as another Richard hype job. It turns out that father knew best," wrote *Sports Illustrated*'s S. L. Price. [11]

With a win, Serena would be the first African American woman since Althea Gibson (1957) and the first African American since Arthur Ashe (1968) to win the U.S. Open. Perhaps threatened by the swift rise of the Williams sisters, Hingis took to trash talking. Mike Lupica of the *New York Daily News* called Hingis a "very bad girl," adding that she seemed to "relish her role as Martina the Teenage Witch." [12]

After taking the first set, 6–3, Serena held off Hingis in the tiebreak in the second to send Hingis packing in straight sets, 6–3, 7–4. Serena teamed up with Venus to win the U.S. Open doubles title.

In a postmatch interview, Serena responded to Hingis's comments about her family: "She's always been the type of person that . . . says things, just speaks her mind. . . . I guess it has a little bit to do with not having a formal education. But you just have to somehow think more; you have to use your brain a little more in the tennis world." [13]

It was a pivotal moment in Serena's career. She not only made history but also made it clear to the media that she would not back down on the court or remain silent when it came to defending her family.

What looked like the beginning of an Evert/Navratilova-style long-term rivalry turned out to be a seismic shift in women's tennis. Serena's power overwhelmed Hingis, who would never win another Grand Slam singles title. The phenom, Hingis won all five of her Grand Slam singles titles before reaching her 19th birthday. Hingis finished 1999 and 2001 ranked number one; however, tennis was now the Williams show.

Serena finished 1999 ranked number four. In only her second full year on tour, Serena had caught up with and, in some respects, surpassed her big sister. Venus ended the season ranked number three.

Like most first-time Grand Slam winners, Serena struggled with the newfound pressure. In 2000, she lost in the fourth round of the Australian Open. She lost in the finals of the Open Gaz de France and the quarterfinals at Indian Wells. After failing to defend her titles at those two tournaments, Serena hoped to perform better in Miami, now the Ericsson Open. She was seeded fifth but lost in the fourth round to Jennifer Capriati, seeded number 13.

After the match, Serena shrugged off questions about whether she was struggling with no longer being the underdog. She told reporters, "People were always gunning for me. I don't know. I mean, they always played me real hard than I've ever seen them play other people. You know, whenever I go out there, I know people are going to play me extremely hard, whereas they might go a little easy on other people."[14]

She withdrew from the French Open with a leg injury but returned for Wimbledon, where she lost to Venus in the semifinals. Serena did capture another doubles title with Venus, who went on to win Wimbledon, her first Grand Slam singles title. The highlight of that year was winning a gold medal in doubles at the Summer Olympics in Sydney. Venus also won the gold medal in singles. That year, Venus was the bigger story, having rebounded from missing the first five months of the season with tendinitis in both wrists. It appeared that once again, Serena was back to being Venus's sidekick. Venus finished the year ranked number three and Serena number six.

Serena would end 2001 Slam-less and still ranked number six; however, that year will be forever marred by what happened at Indian Wells. In one of the ugliest scenes in tennis history, the Indian Wells crowd heckled Serena to tears. This incident would leave a black eye on the tournament for years.

The Williams sisters were the hottest ticket in tennis, and many of the affluent attendees at Indian Wells wanted to see them play. They were scheduled to meet in the semifinals, but Venus withdrew just four minutes before the match, citing an injury. Withdrawals happen at tournaments all the time,[15] but the patrons at Indian Wells decided to punish Serena for Venus's injury. Unsubstantiated rumors that Richard orchestrated and manipulated his daughters' schedules fed the frenzy.

The crowd behaved more like an angry mob. Many fans booed Serena's winners and cheered her unforced errors and double faults. They buoyantly backed the Belgian over the California-raised American. Venus and Richard would comment that someone called her a "nigger." After dropping the first set, Serena fought to hold back tears but managed to defeat Clijsters, 4–6, 6–4, 6–2.

After the match, Serena told reporters, "At first, obviously, I wasn't happy. I don't think mentally I was ready for that. To be honest, what I literally did on a changeover, I prayed to God to help me be strong, not even to win, but to be strong, not listen to the crowd."[16]

The incident would lead to Serena and Venus boycotting the premier mandatory event for more than 15 years.

PRIME TIME

Going into the 2001 U.S. Open, Indian Wells was the lowlight and highlight of Serena's season. It was her biggest tournament win in an otherwise disappointing run that saw her lose three consecutive quarterfinals to Capriati. Her ranking dipped from number six to number 10. She was seeded number 10 and Venus number four.

The 2001 U.S. Open was the first Grand Slam final meeting between two sisters since 1884, when Maud and Lilian Watson faced off at Wimbledon.[17] The match ushered in the prime-time spotlight for women's tennis. It was Williams versus Williams at Arthur Ashe Stadium for the U.S. Open title, the first women's slam singles final ever played at night.

It wasn't the best-played match. Serena committed 36 unforced errors and fell to her big sister, 6–2, 6–4. But the atmosphere was electric, and the 69-minute match drew higher ratings than a Nebraska–Notre Dame football game in the same slot.

The high ratings turned out to be the best evidence in the fight to get equal pay at Grand Slams. Billie Jean King and others had lobbied for equal prize money for years. Now they had the ratings from the Williams sisters' match to bolster their argument. Later, Venus would give a speech in London in which she would cite the ratings. That speech helped women gain equal prize money at Grand Slams.

Going into 2002, Serena and Venus had reached a celebrity status that transcended sports. Serena defeated Jennifer Capriati in the semifinals at the 2002 French Open en route to her first final at Roland-Garros. Failing to win on the red clay at Roland-Garros left Serena with a deficiency on her resume that she sought to remedy. The French Open was like a hex that cursed so many American greats. Pete Sampras, John McEnroe, and Jimmy Connors never won the tournament. Thus, with Venus and Serena in the final, another American French Open champion was in the bag. But which sister would claim a clay-court Slam title first?

Serena beat Venus, 6–4, 7–2, to capture her second Grand Slam title. Venus and Serena would leave the tournament ranked number one and number two, respectively.[18]

Serena told *Sports Illustrated*'s Jon Wertheim, "History is definitely being made."[19] Wertheim, who was in Paris to cover the French Open, captured the sisters' transition from novelty to respected champions. He wrote,

> Yet the Williamses have entered a new phase. The beads are gone. Their dresses and tresses no longer have much shock value. . . . In Paris, they ripped through the draw like tornadoes through a trailer park. Both have games built on power, but they complemented their force with depth and leavened it with feathery touch shots and clever angles. Even established players such as Monica Seles and the resurgent Mary Pierce could offer only scant resistance.[20]

After the historic final, Wertheim wrote,

> In reaching the final Venus and Serena fulfilled their father's longtime divination and achieved the number one and number two world rankings, respectively. It's fitting that sisters who are so close that they share a South Florida mansion also share a penthouse atop the rankings.[21]

The sister act rolled into Wimbledon with Venus and Serena as favorites. Venus entered the match as the two-time defending Wimbledon champion; however, Serena bested big sister, 7–6, 6–3, to win her second Wimbledon trophy and second Grand Slam title that year in her popularly dubbed "Serena Slam." Furthermore, Serena would claim the number-one ranking for the first time. It was a turning point in their sibling rivalry, and the confidence we identify with Serena today was beginning to surface. It would be the last year Venus would hold more Grand Slam titles than Serena.

The 2002 U.S. Open featured the third consecutive major final between the Williams sisters. While many fans enjoyed the sibling rivalry, several tennis writers complained about the sister act and wondered if two people so close could ever produce the intensity customary in finals contests. Still, Venus and Serena insisted they didn't rig their matches. Instead, they pointed to the awkward situation in having to play your sister and best friend, and the struggle against an opponent who understands your game that well.

It was a breakout tournament for Serena in more ways than one. She wore the infamous catsuit, a tight, leather-like, curves-clinging one-piece bodysuit that would later land in a fashion museum. Wearing the outrageous catsuit, Serena dominated Venus, the two-time defending champion, and left the match as a bona fide superstar. Serena, who won 32 consecutive sets in Grand Slam competition in 2002, became the first woman to win three straight majors in the same season since Steffi Graf in 1996.

Serena entered 2003 vying to hold all four major titles at the same time. She wasted no time in backing up her 2002 season. At the 2003 Australian Open, Serena needed to get past Kim Clijsters in the seminal to set up a fourth consecutive all-Williams final. Venus had already booked a spot in the final and was sitting in Rod Laver Arena looking on as her younger sister, now ranked number one, took to the court.

After splitting the first two sets, Clijsters got off to a commanding 5–1 lead in the final set before Serena mounted an epic comeback. She saved two match points and won six straight games to defeat Clijsters.

When a reporter asked Serena how she knew she could win, she responded, "I kept fighting. I thought, 'I don't want to lose 6–1.' Then I said, 'I don't want to lose 6–2.' So I just kept fighting. Next thing I know, I came back. It was just an unbelievable battle out there."[22]

Following the match, the Williams sisters would post another entry into the history books. The *New York Times'* Christopher Clarey wrote,

> When Serena Williams's compelling comeback against Kim Clijsters in the Australian Open semifinals ended in bright sunlight, with Venus Williams watching from the stands, the history-making sisters had added another achievement to their collective résumé. No other two players in the 35-year history of Open tennis have played each other in four consecutive Grand Slam finals: not Martina Navratilova and Chris Evert; not Steffi Graf and Monica Seles.[23]

Serena defeated Venus in the final in three tight sets to win her fourth consecutive Grand Slam title and hold all four Grand Slam titles at once. It was Serena's fifth Grand Slam title. She now had a Career Grand Slam.

At the time, it seemed that the sisters might trade Grand Slam titles and, eventually, Venus too would hold trophies from each Slam; however, despite winning seven Grand Slam titles, Venus has yet to win an Australian Open or French Open. The last time she won a U.S. Open title was in 2002.

Going into the French Open, Serena seemed unstoppable. Instead, the match dubbed the "hand incident" at Roland-Garros sparked what would become one of Serena's most intense rivalries. Serena and Justine Henin met in the semifinals. Henin was married at the time and went by the last name Henin-Hardenne. Before 2003, Henin was 1–4 against Serena, and that one win was on clay in Charleston.

Serena took the first set, 6–2. Henin evened the match, taking the second set, 6–4. Up in the decisive third set, Serena was serving to take a commanding 5–2 lead. During the seventh game, however, the match took a hostile and divisive turn. The pro-Belgian crowd became anti-Serena. Fans booed contested calls and cheered Serena's unforced errors.

Serena went to serve but thought she saw Henin lift her hand, a signal opposing players use to halt when they are not ready. Serena's serve went out, but she argued that Henin raised her hand. The chair umpire, Jorge Dias, did not see it, so he turned to Henin to ask her if she did. The good-faith etiquette expected in tennis would oblige Henin to admit that she had indeed raised her hand. But she did not. On Serena's slower second serve, Henin won the point and went on to break Serena.

The remainder of the match, the French crowd mercilessly booed Serena. After the match, a tearful Serena told reporters, "I was a little disappointed with her. . . . I probably still should have won the game. It definitely didn't turn around the match. But I think to start lying and fabricating, it's not fair."[24]

A few months later, Serena learned of her sister's murder, and her career began to unravel.

Serena entered the 2004 Wimbledon final tournament ranked number one and the two-time defending champion. Seeded number 13, Maria Sharapova, 17, was a known entity, but she was certainly not expected to win a Wimbledon field packed with Grand Slam champions. This included Jennifer Capriati; Lindsay Davenport; Conchita Martinez; Mary Pierce; Venus Williams; and Martina Navratilova, who, at 47, had taken a wild card to play in her final Wimbledon singles draw.

Although she represented Russia, Sharapova's tennis background was similar to Serena's. Both were products of a Florida tennis academy, and Sharapova's father, Yuri, oversaw her career.

Serena's inept performance was as startling as Sharapova's relentless ball striking. The *Guardian*'s Jon Henderson wrote of Serena's demise,

Williams's last stand came in the ninth game of that second set, a 14-point drama in which she successfully staved off three break points, snorting high-decibel defiance as she realized the end might be close, before succumbing to the fourth, when, symbolically, she slipped to the ground as she chased a typically forthright Sharapova return. Cool as you like, Sharapova then served out the match, Williams's last, lame return suitably representative of what had preceded it.[25]

The win would catapult Sharapova to superstardom. Although she would eclipse Serena in endorsement earnings, Sharapova would get just one more win against Serena, later in 2004. Serena is 19–0 against Sharapova since 2004.

After dropping out of the top 10 for the first time since 1999, Serena was ranked number 11 but seeded third at the 2004 U.S. Open. Her quarterfinals opponent, Capriati, had defeated Serena in the semifinals of the French Open earlier that year. Capriati defeated Serena, 2–6, 6–4, 6–4, in a match marred by controversial calls that resulted in USTA officials issuing an apology.[26]

During the last set, chair umpire Mariana Alves made four questionable calls against Serena. The most glaring bad call came in the first game of the second set, when Serena hit what appeared to be a clean backhand winner. The line judge called it in, but Alves overruled. Upon realizing the call had been overruled, Serena walked over to the chair umpire, waved her finger, and pleaded with Alves, saying, "What's going on. . . . Excuse me. That ball was so in."

A stunned crowd booed. Even tennis commentator John McEnroe expressed disbelief. After the match, Serena told reporters, "I'd really prefer if she not umpire my courts anymore because she's obviously anti-Serena. . . . I'm extremely angry. I feel cheated. Should I keep going? I just feel robbed."[27]

The USTA suspended Alves for the rest of the tournament. The controversy is considered the reason professional tennis finally instituted video replay known as Hawk-Eye.[28]

REDEMPTION

The 2005 Australian Open semifinal win over Sharapova would be Serena's first victory in a winning streak that has reached 15 years. Sharapova had two consecutive victories against Serena. She had become the darling and face of women's tennis. Sharapova was seeded number four and Serena number seven. Davenport had regained the number-one ranking. Sharapova jumped out in front, taking the first set. She took an early lead in the second set. Serena fought off three set points and won, 2–6, 7–5, 8–6.[29] Serena went on to defeat Lindsay Davenport, 2–6, 6–3, 6–0, to capture a second Australian Open title.

Plagued by injuries and personal setbacks, Serena hobbled through the 2006 season and dropped out of the top 50. Meanwhile, Sharapova, the media darling, had ascended to the number-one ranking.

Serena entered the 2007 Australian Open out of shape and ranked number 85. She had dropped in the rankings after struggling to recover from a series of knee injuries and personal issues. Before the match, retired-Australian-tennis-player-turned-tennis-commentator Pat Cash wrote a scathing column about Serena's chances at the Australian Open. Cash declared Serena "delusional" and "washed up":

> If anybody is qualified to make deluded statements about tennis, it is a former world number one and winner of seven Grand Slam titles. But when Serena Williams arrives in Australia on her first foreign playing trip in a year and announces that it is only a matter of time before she is again dominating the sport, it's time to tell her to get real.
>
> The Williams sisters changed the face of women's tennis, taking power play to previously unimaginable levels. They blazed everybody else out of their path; however, Serena has a limited attention span. At her peak, she had no patience in the way she played her tennis. Now she does not appear to have the fortitude to stick at what she is trying to do . . . but to make such a crass statement on her arrival in Australia was an insult to Amelie Mauresmo and Maria Sharapova, who have risen to the top of the game in her absence.[30]

Serena came out on fire, blasting winners from every area on the court. Sharapova looked overwhelmed. Serena won, 6–1, 6–2, to become the first unseeded player to win the Australian Open since 1978.[31]

Serena finished 2007 ranked number seven, after reaching the quarter-finals or better at all four Grand Slams for the first time in two years.

Although Serena made a comeback in 2007, 2008 was when she finally clawed her way back into form. She was more consistent, in better shape, and focused. Her season began with a title at the Hopman Cup with Mardy Fish. Serena suffered a minor setback at the Australian Open when Jelena Jankovic ended her 18-match winning streak. She rebounded at the Miami Open, where she won a fifth title in Miami, matching Steffi Graf.

Serena faced Venus in the Wimbledon final that year. It was their first Grand Slam finals showdown since 2003, which was also the last time Serena won at Wimbledon. Venus proved to be the better grass-court player and defeated Serena in straight sets. The pair would team up to win their sixth Grand Slam doubles title.

One of the highlights of Serena's 2008 season came in the quarterfinals of the U.S. Open. In arguably the best match the sisters ever played against one another, Serena broke the tie in their head-to-head record. Serena trailed in both sets. She fought off 10 set points and came back from being down 3–6 in the second-set tiebreaker to win her third consecutive U.S. Open title, 7–6, 7–6.

"I felt like I was always in control. . . . If it was someone else, I definitely feel like I would have won the match," Venus told the Associated Press.[32]

Serena would go on to defeat Jankovic in the final and regain the number-one ranking.

By 2009, Serena overshadowed Venus in terms of accomplishments and celebrity status. In the 2009 Wimbledon semifinals against Elena Dementieva, Serena entered the match the favorite. But Dementieva had won three of their four previous matches. At the time, Dementieva was considered one of the best female players to have never won a Grand Slam. Getting by Serena would be a mega step in that direction. Playing at the peak of their athletic prowess, Serena and Dementieva moved seamlessly from miraculous defensive saves to stunning winners. The two combined to produce 72 winners. [33]

They would trade sets. Dementieva entered the decisive set with the momentum. When she reached match point, the Wimbledon crowd roared with excitement. But with just one stealth volley at the net, Serena erased a match point and Dementieva's dreams. Once Serena climbed out of the hole to even the match, everyone on Centre Court and those watching at home knew it was over.

Serena won 6–7 (4–7), 7–5, 8–6. After the match, a disappointed Dementieva said it was the best match she ever played on grass. Yet, her best was not good enough to keep Serena from reaching another Grand Slam final against Venus.

Serena's next Grand Slam run ended in a rant that damaged her image. What was an otherwise well-played contest between friends erupted into a stain on Serena's career. Down a set against Clijsters and trailing, 5–6, Serena was serving to stay in the match, 15–30. Serena misfired on her first serve. On the second serve, the line judge called a foot fault. Suddenly, Serena faced match point.

Annoyed and angry, Serena walked over to the line judge and reportedly threatened to shove a ball down the judge's throat.[34] The profanity-laced tirade cost Serena a code violation and ultimately the match. Serena had already been assessed a violation for racket abuse when she slammed her racket to the court in frustration. After the match's abrupt end, Serena walked over to the net, shook Clijsters's hand, and congratulated her on the win.

The USTA fined Serena a record $82,000 and put her on probation. Serena issued an apology via a written statement and personally apologized to the line judge.[35]

When the 2010 Australian Open rolled around, Serena continued to face questions about her behavior at the U.S. Open. She was determined to let her play answer her critics. Serena faced Henin in the final. Of all her contemporaries not named Venus, Henin presented the biggest challenge. She once defeated Serena in three straight majors. The Belgian was to Serena what Nadal was to Federer, a clay-court master and Slam nemesis. Serena enjoyed a winning record against Henin on every surface, except clay.

Serena got her revenge in the final meeting between the two with a 6–4, 3–6, 6–2 win. Williams owns an 8–6 career record against the now-retired Belgian, perhaps the closest person not named Venus to a true Serena rival. The win against Henin gave Williams her 12th major title, tying her with the legendary Billie Jean King.

That summer, Serena won her fourth Wimbledon title.

After winning Wimbledon, Serena was celebrating at a restaurant in Germany when she stepped on glass and cut her foot so severely that she needed surgery. The surgery and months with her foot in a boot contributed to a pulmonary embolism that threated her life.

She would be away from the game for another five months. After facing such a threat, many wondered if she would ever get back to being the dominant force she had become. Serena eased back into competition at the Aegon International in Eastbourne, on grass. She wanted a quick warm-up before the big test, Wimbledon. Although Williams was ranked number 24, Wimbledon officials seeded the two-time defending champion at number seven.

In her first match at Wimbledon, Serena struggled to defeat a promising young French player. After her win, Serena sat courtside with her face buried in a towel, sobbing, grateful to be back.

"I don't usually cry, and I don't understand it but I never dreamt it could be like this. I just wanted to win a match because it's been a disaster year and to come back at Wimbledon is awesome," she told the *Evening Standard*.[36]

In the second round, Serena faced up-and-coming 19-year-old Romanian star Simona Halep. The Romanian took the first set, as Serena struggled to hold serve. After taking the second set, Serena raced out to a 5–0 lead in the third. She won the match, 3–6, 6–2, 6–1. She went on to defeat Russian Maria Kirilenko in straight sets but lost to Frenchwoman Marion Bartoli in the fourth round.

Unable to defend her title and ranking points, Serena fell to number 175, her lowest ranking since 1997.[37]

Two months after Wimbledon, Serena fought her way to the finals of the 2011 U.S. Open. The match turned out to be probably Serena's most shocking defeat in a Grand Slam final since the loss to Sharapova at Wimbledon in 2004. Samantha Stosur dominated the match from start to finish, winning 6–2, 6–3.

Stosur was enjoying the best season of her career. Prior to 2010, she had been more of a doubles specialist. In 2007, she was diagnosed with Lyme disease and took most of the year off. Few expected this late-career surge.

The Australian could match Serena's groundstrokes and dictated play. After hitting what she thought was a clean winner, Serena yelled, "C'mon," while the ball was in play on Stosur's side of the court. Chair umpire Eva Asderaki charged Serena with a hindrance call and gave the point to Stosur. During the changeover, Serena let Asderaki know exactly how she felt. "Don't even look at me," she said. "You're a hater. You're very unattractive inside. I never complain. Who would do such a thing? You're punishing me for expressing my emotion."[38]

Glossed over in this controversy was the decision by ESPN to broadcast Serena's exchange with the umpire. Many players, notably Roger Federer, get into heated exchanges with chair umpires. But airing Serena's grievances played into the bad sportsmanship narrative and drew comparisons to her last appearance at the U.S. Open. Serena was fined $2,000 for expressing her displeasure with the official. [39]

Even after the defeat, Serena remained the player to beat. In 2012, she entered every tournament as the favorite, which magnified her upsets early in the season. She fell to Ekaterina Makarova in the fourth round of the Australian Open. While seeking a record-breaking sixth title in Miami, Serena lost to Caroline Wozniacki in straight sets.

But no defeat was as shocking as her first-round loss at the 2012 French Open to Virginie Razzano. Seeded fifth, Serena was one of the favorites going into the French Open. She had faced upsets before but never in the first round of a Grand Slam. The loss to Razzano, ranked number 111, reverberated throughout the sports world.

So much about Serena's performance was inexplicable. Up 5–1 in the second-set tiebreaker, Serena lost 13 consecutive points. She came within two points of closing out the match nine times; however, the game's best closer left the door open for the unsung, barely known Razzano. Serena saved seven match points but never looked entirely comfortable on the clay.

After the loss, Serena stayed in Paris and sought to improve her game with the guidance of Patrick Mouratoglou. [40] The partnership would later propel Serena back to the top of her game and into the record books.

Wimbledon would be the first test of the Mouratoglou partnership. Serena reached the final without dropping a set. She faced Agnieszka Radwanska, who was trying to become the first Polish player to reach number one. Serena was still seeking her first Grand Slam win since returning from an 11-month absence. The short two-week period between the French Open and Wimbledon left little time to recover from the embarrassing first-round loss at the French Open.

A crafty player, Radwanska had the kind of shot variety that could frustrate Serena. Nevertheless, she lacked power, and her serves to Serena were like target practice. When Serena took the first set, 6–1, the match appeared all but over. Then, it rained. The break cooled off Serena and allowed Radwanska back into the match. A few mishits and Serena found herself in a third set.

Radwanska was up, 2–1, with dreams of a Wimbledon title reachable, plausible. That was until Serena, nonchalantly, hit four aces in a row to even the set at 2–2. No fist pumps or "C'mon!" Serena shrugged her shoulders as if to send a message to Radwanska: I'm back in the zone, this match is over.

Radwanska would not win another game, and Serena bagged her fifth Wimbledon title. In her postmatch press conference, Serena told reporters, "It's the beginning of a great phase. Nice to have great people around you. You know, I feel amazing out there. This whole tournament I felt really great physically. So I think it's definitely the beginning of something great. I hope it is."[41]

Serena dominated the remainder of 2012. At the Summer Olympics, a few weeks after winning the Wimbledon title, Serena was back on Centre Court at the All England Club, this time going for the gold. She faced Russia's Sharapova, who was seeking her first gold medal. Conditions were horrible. Blustery winds swirled through Centre Court. Serena had a more difficult time keeping her skirt from flying up than she did dismantling Sharapova. The score, 6–1, 6–0, was not even that close. Serena dominated Sharapova from start to finish. She celebrated the win with a dance called the Crib Walk, named after a gang from Compton.

Critics would take issue with that; however, Serena's confidence and youthful exuberance signaled she had overcome her disastrous French Open and was playing fearless, carefree tennis. That first-round French Open loss was but a hiccup in an otherwise stellar year. Serena would go on to win the gold medal in doubles, the U.S. Open, and the WTA Finals. Serena finished the season 7–0 in finals and 16–1 against players ranked in the top 10 at season's end. The one loss came against Angelique Kerber.

As triumphant as her 2012 became, Serena's 2013 season would be even better. She began 2013 ranked number three, behind Victoria Azarenka and Sharapova. Her season did not get off to a strong start. A 19-year-old American, Sloane Stephens, upset Serena in the fourth round of the Australian Open. Although Serena was bothered by back spasms, the media overhyped the loss as a hint of the changing of the guard. Stephens is also African American, and before their match, the media reported on the relationship between Serena and Stephens as mentor–mentee or upstart against the idol. After the match, Stephens berated Serena and claimed they were never close. For her part, Serena never said a bad word about Stephens, at least not in public.

Serena won another title in Miami, a remarkable comeback against Sharapova in the finals. Serena arrived at the French Open undefeated on clay and seeking her first title at Roland-Garros since 2002. Like many American greats before her, Serena struggled to achieve on clay what she did on the grass and the hard courts.

Even if Serena wanted to forget about her shocking first-round defeat the prior year, the media kept reminding tennis fans. Nonetheless, a more fit, more focused Serena breezed through the field until the quarterfinals, where she faced 2008 French Open champion Svetlana Kuznetsova, who grew up on clay at the Sanchez-Casal Academy in Barcelona.[42] A two-time Grand Slam champion, Kuznetsova was always a tough matchup for Serena.

Serena quickly took the first set, 6–1. In the second set, Kuznetsova turned up her level of play as Serena's slipped. The Russian went up 5–1, closing out the second set 6–3. Serena found herself down 0–2 in the final set. She told the Associated Press (via ESPN), "I thought, you know, 'Can't go out like this again.'"[43] By "like this again," Serena meant she hadn't advanced to the semifinals at the French Open in a decade.[44]

At one point, Serena bent over and screamed to herself, "Fight! Fight!" With her intensity amped up, Serena became more aggressive, moving into the net and taking the ball out of the air. This seemed to unnerve Kuznetsova, who began committing unforced errors. Once Serena grabbed the lead, she closed out the match, 6–1, 3–6, 6–3.

Serena went on to win the French Open by defeating Sharapova in the finals. Serena also defended her titles at the U.S. Open and WTA Finals. Her $12,385,572 earnings made her the first female player to eclipse more than $10 million in a single season. She won 11 titles and finished the season 75–4, the best winning percentage of her career.

She entered 2014 just one win away from tying Americans Chris Evert and Martina Navratilova with 18 Grand Slams. Already considered one of the greatest of all time, Serena would join only a handful of women who had amassed so many Grand Slam titles. After her record-breaking season in 2013, many thought reaching 18 would be a cinch.

But 2014 turned out to be a challenging year in the Slams for Serena. Ana Ivanovic upset her in the fourth round of the Australian Open. Garbine Muguruza upended Serena's run in the third round at Roland-Garros.

At Wimbledon, Alize Cornet derailed the defending champion in the third round. After the loss to Cornet, Serena looked disoriented in a doubles match. The defending doubles champions were forced to retire.

Although Serena was ranked number one and the two-time defending champion, she entered the U.S. Open looking far less dominant than a year prior. An early exit at Flushing Meadows would leave Serena slam-less and still searching for answers. In the end, her victory in the final was pretty routine, 6–3, 6–3. Serena fell to the ground in disbelief, and per-haps a little relief, as she clinched her 18th Grand Slam title.

Navratilova and Evert joined Serena on the court for the trophy cere-mony and presented her with a Tiffany bracelet with a charm engraved with the number 18. "It is a pleasure for me to win my first Grand Slam here and then this number 18. . . . So I'm really emotional. I couldn't ask to do it at a better place."[45]

Because Serena won the points race in the U.S. Open Series, she earned a record $4 million in prize money. She became the first female athlete to surpass $60 million in prize money earnings.[46]

EXHALING AND EXCELLING

After finally reaching that 18th Grand Slam title, Serena seemed more relaxed. With only Graf ahead in terms of Slams won in the Open era, Serena appeared content with her place in history and focused on the task at hand, maintaining her status as the number one player on tour.

Fresh off winning the 2014 WTA Finals in November, Serena entered the Australian Open ranked number one. She reached the finals, another showdown with Sharapova. In characterizing the lopsided rivalry Serena enjoys against Sharapova, Wertheim wrote, "Though cast as rivals, they have rivalry the way a juicer has a rivalry with an orange. Their record is not a head-to-head, so much as it is a foot-to-backside."[47] Although more entertaining than some of their contests, Serena defeated Sharapova in straight sets to win her 19th Grand Slam title, making her the record holder for the American tennis player (male or female) with the most Grand Slams wins.

Following her Australian Open victory, Serena released a video that signaled she was ready to return to Indian Wells. After her first match at Indian Wells since the boycott, Serena admitted to being a bit nervous.

Still, she would call it one of the proudest moments of her life. Monica Niculescu, ranked number 68, was supposed to be a footnote in Serena's celebratory return; however, the Romanian, known for crafty play, frustrated Serena. Although Serena won in straight sets, 7–5, 7–5, Niculescu pushed the reigning Australian Open champion to a tense two-hour match.

An emotional and relieved Serena thanked the crowd for their support. The warmth was in stark contrast to the boos and jeers that had rained down on her in 2001. She withdrew from the tournament in the semifinals but went on to win another Miami Open title.

She followed up the Miami Open win with a successful clay-court season that ended with winning her third French Open title. After Serena won the French Open, there was some, but not much, talk about her finally winning a calendar-year Slam. Once she won Wimbledon, the calendar-year Slam was all anyone talked about.

Playing with unprecedented media hype for a tennis match, Serena tried to downplay the pressure she felt. She told reporters she had nothing to lose. Meanwhile, ticket prices for the women's final jumped 12 percent after Serena won Wimbledon.[48] Prices soared to more than $1,000 after Serena beat Venus in the quarterfinals.[49]

When Italian Flavia Pennetta took out 2014 runner-up Azarenka in the semifinals, Serena's coronation appeared inevitable. But an unseeded and less-heralded Italian, Roberta Vinci, stood in the way. Serena routinely took the first set, 6–2; however, Vinci, a veteran of slice-and-dice tennis, found ways to frustrate her opponent. Vinci crushed Serena's dreams, taking the match 2–6, 6–4, 6–4, ending Williams's bid to become the fourth woman to win the calendar-year Grand Slam. The calendar-year Slam remains the one major accomplishment missing from Williams's resume. At least for now.

Heartbroken, Serena would end her season early and not play again until 2016.

The crushing defeat in the 2015 U.S. Open left Serena still one Grand Slam shy of tying Graf. When she lost to Angelique Kerber in the final of the 2016 Australian Open, equaling 22 seemed as complicated as her quest for 18. Serena would reach the final at the French Open, only to finish runner-up to Spain's Garbine Muguruza. But now at Wimbledon she was on grass, where her serve proved more potent than on any other surface. Kerber entered the match with a Grand Slam defeat against Serena that year and in pursuit of the number-one ranking.

In one of the best-played matches in Wimbledon finals history, Kerber and Williams produced powerful crosscourt winners that had fans giving rousing applause and standing ovations. When she hit her final winner, Serena let go of her racket and fell back onto the grass as if she were floating into a pond of pillows. When she returned to her feet, she lifted her arms into the air waving two fingers on each hand signaling "22." Now tied for the most Grand Slams won in the Open era, Serena set her sights on breaking the record and chasing Margaret Court's all-time record of 24.

After another disappointing ouster at the U.S. Open, Serena took off the rest of the season, as she had done in 2015. Her next chance to break the record came at the 2017 Australian Open versus Venus. It had been years since the Williams sisters had met in a Grand Slam final. Serena was trying to take sole possession of the record for most Grand Slam titles in the Open era. Venus wished to win her first Australian Open title.

The match turned out to be uneventful and straightforward. Serena defeated Venus, 6–4, 6–4. Despite the close score, Serena dictated play throughout. The highlight happened after the match when Serena received her 23rd Grand Slam trophy, surpassing Graf for most Slam titles in the Open era.

Little did the public know that Serena was pregnant, carrying her first child. The pregnancy might explain Serena's muted celebration. She slowly sat back on the court, instead of the full collapse to the court, as she had done in the past. During her trophy ceremony speech, Serena acknowledged the impact Venus has had on both their careers. "She's the only reason I'm standing here today. She's the only reason the Williams sisters exist. Thank you for inspiring me. Every time you won this week, I felt like I got a win, too," Serena said of her sister.[50]

It would be the only Grand Slam Serena in which she would compete that season. Months later, she would announce her pregnancy.[51]

The birth of her daughter and postpartum complications kept Serena away from the game for longer than she expected. Her first attempt back at competition came at the 2018 Fed Cup rubber against the Netherlands. The rubber took place in Ashville, North Carolina. The U.S. Fed Cup team had already wrapped up a victory against the Netherlands. Venus won two singles matches, and CoCo Vandeweghe went 1–1. So when the

Williams sisters took the court to play doubles, the contest was all about Serena and her match readiness.

A heavier, less-agile version of Serena walked out with Venus. Serena was still breastfeeding at the time and lacked her trademark explosive speed. Fans did not seem to care. What they focused on was baby Olympia, dressed in red, white, and blue, sitting courtside on her father's lap. They dismissed the doubles match as an exhibition. Still, Serena and Venus getting thrashed in a doubles match served as a prelude to struggles to come.

Disappointing outings at Indian Wells and a first-round loss at the Miami Open, and Serena decided her comeback had been premature. She retreated to rigorous training and emerged again at the French Open.

Playing in her first Grand Slam since giving birth, Serena faced a first-round challenge against Kristyna Pliskova, the lower-ranked part of tennis's second-hottest sister act on tour. Like her older sister Karolina, Kristyna Pliskova has a powerful first serve and can unleash aces on opponents. She was ranked number 70. Serena was ranked 381 spots lower than her. None of that mattered. Everyone wanted to see where Serena's game was. How far off form had she gotten? The crowd on Court Philippe Chatrier oohed and awed at the sight of Serena's black bodysuit.

Pliskova fired off 10 aces in the opening set and took a 3–0 lead in the tiebreaker. But Serena battled back, rolling off six straight points. She won the match, 7–6 (4), 6–4. Serena went on to reach the fourth round before withdrawing due to injury.

A month later, Serena reached the 2018 Wimbledon final, her first since giving birth. She faced Angelique Kerber, her opponent in the 2016 Wimbledon final. Serena arrived on court having already exceeded expectations. Her friend Meghan, now the Duchess of Sussex, was in the Royal Box. Despite falling out of the top 100, Wimbledon officials seeded Serena number 25, based on a protected ranking system. Normally, being seeded number 25 would mean a clash with top 10 talent by round three; however, with top seeds having been upset in earlier rounds, Serena reached the finals without having to face any players seeded in the top 10. Her semifinals opponent, Julia Georges, was seeded number 13.

Now she faced a former number one and two-time Grand Slam champion. Immediately, Kerber demonstrated that she was playing at a level superior to the opponents Serena had beat on her way to the final. Kerber broke Serena's serve four times en route to a dominant 6–3, 6–3 win.

Serena was simply outmatched. She knew it, but that didn't keep tears away. Her voice cracked and she cried as she addressed the crowd, which included friends, family, and fans.

"It's obviously disappointing, but I can't be disappointed. I have so much to look forward to. I'm literally just getting started, so I look forward to it. . . . To all the moms out there, I was playing for you today. I tried."[52]

By the time the U.S. Open came around, Serena appeared to be in better shape. In the quarterfinals, Serena defeated number eight seed and former number one Karolina Pliskova, 6–3, 6–4, en route to the finals. Only Japan's Naomi Osaka stood in the way of Serena and a 24th Grand Slam title. Although Osaka represented Japan, she grew up in Florida and idolized Serena. Osaka also had Serena's former longtime hitting partner Sascha Bajin as a coach. Bajin, also known as "Big Sascha," had been Serena's hitting partner and close friend for eight years before he left in 2015, to work with two-time Grand Slam champion Victoria Azarenka.[53] If anyone knew Serena's game and in-match tendencies, it was Big Sascha.

Osaka played like an opponent who could anticipate Serena's every move. Hitting clean winners from both wings, she took the first set, 6–2, in just 33 minutes. Serena went up 1–0 in the second set and had two break points (15–40) against Osaka when chair umpire Carlos Ramos assessed a code violation for coaching. Osaka won the next two points and leveled the second set at 1–1.

Coaching is allowed in women's tennis, just not in Grand Slams. Even so, Serena never takes on-court coaching; however, her coach, Patrick Mouratoglou, tried to get her attention from the players' box, where he sat with her family and friends. Cameras showed him making hand gestures. Serena claims to have not seen him and was offended by the accusation that she was taking on-court coaching. She considered that the same as accusing her of cheating.

"I don't cheat to win. I'd rather lose. I'm just letting you know," Serena told Ramos.[54]

Serena managed to break Osaka and led the second set, 3–1. She was serving at 30–15 to go up 4–1, when she double-faulted twice, giving Osaka a break point. Osaka broke back to get back on serve. In frustration, Serena smashed her racket on the court. Ramos assessed a second code violation, which meant Osaka would be awarded a point. Osaka began her 2–3 service game already up 15–0.

A visibly angry Serena confronted Ramos about the first violation. She insisted she didn't cheat and that his assessment challenged her character. She demanded he apologize and tell the crowd that she does not cheat.

Meanwhile, Osaka remained focused and broke Serena again to take a 4–3 lead. Unable to get the first violation out of her head, Serena erupted. She called Ramos a "thief" and a "liar," for stealing a point from her. Serena lost her momentum and her cool. She pointed her finger at Ramos and accused him of mistreating her. Ramos levied a third violation, for verbal abuse, which cost Serena a game. She now faced a 3–5 deficit, and regardless of whether she could hold serve, Osaka would be serving for the championship.

Almost in tears, Serena demanded to speak with the U.S. Open tournament referee, Brian Earley, and WTA supervisor Donna Kelso. Serena pleaded with Earley for what she thought had been a history of wrongs waged against her at the U.S. Open, including the 2004 Jennifer Capriati incident, the loss to Kim Clijsters in 2009, and the hindrance point taken during a match against Sam Stosur in 2010. "This has happened to me too many times. . . . This is not fair," Serena said.[55]

Meanwhile, fans seated in Arthur Ashe Stadium booed and jeered as Serena fought back tears. Osaka served and closed out the match, 6–3, 6–4. Serena embraced Osaka amid a chorus of boos.

The outburst overshadowed Serena's accomplishments—making it to two Slam finals in her first year back since giving birth. Once again, heartbreak and controversy played out on her home turf. In her long, storied career, Serena never suffered as much ridicule or heartbreak at any other Slam as she has at the U.S. Open.

Four days after the final, Jon Wertheim wrote that Serena's outburst might have been avoided if Ramos had handled the situation differently:

> I still say this could have been avoided if the chair had first said, "I am not accusing you of cheating. It's your coach who was gesticulating. Unfortunately, it's a coaching violation not a 'receiving coaching violation.' So you are bearing the penalty for his actions." Serena seemed genuinely affronted by the idea that her integrity was being questioned. It wasn't. And this should have been articulated. Sometimes

tennis is a glorious global village. Other times it is a Tower of Babel, with two people speaking past each other.[56]

Serena didn't play in another tournament that year, opting to shut down her season, as she had in 2015 and 2016. She finished the year ranked number 16, up from number 481 in the spring. Two Grand Slam finals and a 400-plus surge in the rankings would be a champagne-popping season for most players. But for Serena, only four tournaments offered an opportunity to give her what she wanted, more Grand Slam titles and a chance to own the record books.

She'd get another chance at the 2019 Australian Open. Unfortunately, what looked like another dream run ended in one of her worst losses. Serena seemed headed to a rematch with Osaka when she held a 5–1 lead over Karolina Pliskova in the third set of the quarterfinals and appeared to roll her ankle. Her mobility, her serve, and the match vanished. Pliskova took advantage of whatever ailed Serena to win the match, although she went on to lose to Osaka in the final.

Serena left the Australian Open stunned and still in the hunt for the elusive 24th Grand Slam title.

She'd get another chance, at Wimbledon, where she reached the finals for the second consecutive year. This time, she was seeded number 11. Yet, again, she managed to reach the finals without having to play an opponent seeded in the top 10. She suffered a result similar to 2018. Simona Halep, playing in her first Wimbledon final, defeated Serena, 6–2, 6–2, in just 53 minutes. In a near-flawless performance, Halep committed just three unforced errors to Serena's 26. She broke Serena's serve four times.

Unlike after her finals loss in 2018, Serena shed no tears in her on-court interview. She praised Halep's performance. "She literally played out of her mind," Serena told the crowd, via an ESPN broadcast. "It was a little bit 'a deer in the headlights' for me."

Serena seemed a bit more reflective in her postmatch press conference. She contemplated whether she needed more match time or if too many matches might cause an injury setback.

Getting to three Grand Slam finals in the less than two years after giving birth would be career-resting laurels for most players. But Serena sought more. She vowed to keep working, tweaking her game and pursuing more titles.

Two days after the loss, journalist Alyssa Roenigk offered her perspective about Serena's outlook in an article she penned for ESPN.com. "Make no mistake: She wants to win another Slam and is going to continue to search for ways to get there," wrote Roenigk. "Since her return, Williams's coach, Patrick Mouratoglou, has said Williams doesn't want to reach Court's record. She wants to surpass it—to lift the bar Court placed at number 24 and set it down somewhere only Williams has been."[57]

3

SISTERLY LOVE

Tennis history includes several sibling success stories. Seven-time Grand Slam champion John McEnroe and his younger brother Patrick won a couple of doubles titles together and are now both color commentators for ESPN.[1] Murphy and Luke Jensen won the 1993 French Open, and identical twins Tim and Tom Gullikson won 10 doubles titles. Perhaps the greatest men's doubles duo of all time, twins Bob and Mike Bryan, have won 116 doubles titles, 16 of them majors.

Nevertheless, tennis, and indeed sports, has never witnessed a sibling duo like Venus and Serena, winners of a combined 30 Grand Slam singles titles, 14 Grand Slam doubles titles, and eight Olympic gold medals. Serena also won two Grand Slam mixed doubles titles with Max Mirnyi.

When Rick Macci told Richard Williams he had in Venus the next Michael Jordan, Richard responded he had two. While his response may have sounded like an unwarranted boast at the time, it turned out to be an understatement.

Venus and Serena's relationship transcends tennis. More than just a sports story, Venus and Serena's is a love story—sisterly love. Like all good love stories, the tale of the Williams sisters includes trials and tribulations, setbacks and comebacks, tension and triumph. They've taken on the world while contesting one another for the highest achievements in their profession.

Their bond is a knot woven into a family fabric created by their parents and nurtured by older sisters. Although Venus and Serena enjoy the highest profiles in their family, they are the babies in a sisterhood headed by Oracene. As the youngest of the ladies in the house, Serena benefited from a team of strong female role models.

During Serena's childhood, Oracene was the queen bee. Yetunde, nine years older than Serena, played the role of Oracene's understudy. When they were younger, Yetunde would often carry out such maternal duties as braiding Serena's hair and making sure her younger sisters got dressed for school. Isha and Lyndrea were the immediate supervisors, and Venus was Serena's best friend and sparring partner.

Richard embraced Oracene's daughters as his own; however, Serena and Venus were the only other people in the family that shared his last name. In a household of seven, they were also the only two who had Richard and Oracene as parents, which created a unique element within the larger family unit. Venus and Serena grew up with their mother's resolve and their father's bodacious, risk-taking approach to business.

Serena's relationship with Venus is a separate entity within the broad-er sisterhood. It's at the core of one of the greatest sports stories ever and contradicts stereotypes about female competition, catfighting, and sibling rivalries. Despite being less than two years older than her younger sister, Venus assumed many roles in Serena's life. Venus is Serena's mentor, role model, protector, cheerleader, and BFF. Serena often says there would be no Serena without Venus.

There is some science to support Serena's sentiment about her older sister. One Japanese study found that having an older sister made women more competitive.[2] Imagine having an older sister who is a world-class athlete as a pacesetter. Serena often admits to relishing her role as the baby in the family. She also credits Venus with stepping up big time in the big sister department. One day, when they were at school, Serena forgot her lunch money and faced being forced to eat the cafeteria-issued peanut butter and jelly sandwich. Kids who couldn't afford lunch or forgot their lunch money received these sandwiches. To make matters worse, it was "fried chicken day" at school, Serena's favorite. According to Serena, who has told this story on several occasions, Venus unselfishly went without a meal so that her little sister could enjoy her fried chicken.

Venus's benevolence neutralized Serena's supposed bratty behavior. In his book *Venus Envy*, Jon Wertheim recounted nightly conversations Serena and Venus had when they were kids. Afraid, Serena demanded that Venus stay awake until her little sister fell asleep. Tired, Venus tolerated the nagging and caved, depriving herself of sleep so Serena felt at ease.[3]

After they started playing tennis, they became competitive but somehow avoided combativeness with one another.

Venus as sidekick and exemplar created an amicable pressure-cooker environment for Serena. Her biggest competitor was her best friend. It may have also contributed to some insecurities Serena felt growing up. According to Sylvia Rimm, Ph.D., a noted psychologist and director of the Family Achievement Clinic in Cleveland,

> Where two close-aged, same-gender siblings are treated similarly, both children are likely to feel more competitive pressure. Because they are expected to act the same, the age difference typically puts stress on the younger one to keep up with the older one, causing the younger one to feel inadequate.[4]

Serena worshipped Venus; however, Serena wrote about feeling inadequate when compared to Venus when they were kids. She thought Venus was prettier, skinnier, and more confident. Mostly, however, Serena grew up in awe of her older sister and insisted on accomplishing all of Venus's achievements.

After Venus began entering tournaments, Serena was eager to follow suit. But like many younger siblings, Serena had to wait her turn. "Not yet Meeka. You're not ready," she recalled her father saying.[5]

That didn't stop an enterprising eight-year-old from entering herself in a tournament, without her parent's knowledge. It was a 10-under tournament in the Los Angeles area before they moved to Florida. Because she usually brought her racket along when traveling to Venus's events, no one suspected that she was in the competition. She was even smart enough to check the draw without giving herself away.

"I didn't think I was doing anything wrong. I just wanted what Venus had. That was all I ever wanted, to be just like Venus—my role model, then and still—so I went out and took my turn like I had it coming," she revealed.[6]

That would be the first time the Williams sisters faced off in a tournament. After her parents got over the initial shock, they grew excited as they realized their daughters would meet in the final. Serena remembers her parents feeling torn about who to root for and deciding they just wanted both girls to play well.

When they arrived at Grenelefe, Macci's coaching staff allocated more resources for Venus. Serena envied Venus's top-tier status. She wrote in *On the Line*, "These coaches wanted a chance to work with her and grow their reputations on the back of her success because everyone could see she'd be a champion. With me, nobody could really see that just yet. Daddy could see it, I think. V could see it. I could see it. My mom could see it, too."[7]

Serena spent much of her childhood spying on Venus. When they were in Compton, Serena envied the extra time Venus had with their father, as he focused on the elder sister's tennis. When they moved to Florida and Venus received more attention from Macci and the other coaches, Serena finally had her father to herself. Still, she wrote about craving the specialized coaching Venus was now getting. Serena reasoned that if these coaches were good enough for Venus, they had to be the best.

During most of their time at Grenelefe, Serena was relegated to second fiddle, the kid sister of the lanky tennis phenom. Perhaps because Serena experienced the embodiment of big sisterhood, her relationship with Venus always tilted toward reverence instead of rivalry. Keeping the family close was one of the reasons Richard insisted that Venus and Serena avoid the junior circuit.

When they turned pro, Venus had a smoother transition and garnered more attention. In 1997, Venus made her Wimbledon debut. Like so many times when they were younger, Serena tagged along. The girls were already making headlines, and speculation centered on how Venus might do against the top tier of the WTA. Well, at least that's what sports journalists were debating. Venus knew who her rival would be. She lived with her. While many reporters covering Wimbledon that year chose to focus on Venus, Nick Callow, a writer for the *Independent*, decided to introduce his readers to Serena. Callow wrote,

> But in the unlikely event that she is the ultimate winner in two weeks, Williams senses that her triumph will be devalued by the absence of her most significant rival—and we are not talking Steffi Graf here. Williams believes, moreover insists, that her main challenges will not come from the established order, but from a player yet to play a professional tournament—her younger sister Serena.[8]

Naturally, members of the media ran with the narrative of the sibling rivalry. It's a storyline too irresistible and easy. Serena and Venus refused to facilitate journalists in their quest to unearth some deep-seated division. The sisters were a team, raised to rely on each other.

When they started playing on tour, they kept to themselves. Given their unique situation—two black girls from the same ghetto, born just 18 months apart and playing in a predominantly white sport—they may have become allies, even if they weren't sisters. Early in their careers, they grew close to Alexandra Stevenson, another black female tennis player on the tour, who was also their age. Stevenson is the daughter of NBA Hall of Famer Julius Irving. She was among the few tennis players the sisters bonded with outside of the immediate family.

Some perceived the sisters' reluctance to assimilate into the mostly white tennis community as adversarial.

"Venus and I are very much loners when it comes down to tennis. . . . We tend to just hang out together. I say 'hi' and stuff to others players, but I'm not best friends with them. They are opponents and you have to remember you have to beat them," Serena told the *Independent*, as she accompanied Venus to her Wimbledon debut.[9]

Dave Rineberg was a hitting coach to Venus and Serena from 1992 to 1999. In his book *Venus and Serena: My Seven Years as Hitting Coach for the Williams Sisters*, he wrote, "Serena's path to the pros was a paved superhighway compared to Venus'. Venus had already broken down all the barriers, whether they were racial, social, critical, or economical. Venus had been the pioneer in the Williams family and had blazed a trail, creating a formula for success."[10]

Rineberg also noted that if you compared Serena's first year on the tour to Venus's, Serena accomplished much more.

It was as if Venus absorbed so much of the pressure that Serena could come through, untethered by the weighty expectations of being first up to bat. She could sit back, observe, take notes, and adjust accordingly.

In an interview with Oprah Winfrey in 2003, Serena talked about how difficult it was for her to establish an identity in the shadow of Venus. "There were two Venus Williamses in our family—it was crazy," Serena said.[11]

Serena went on to describe a time when she felt a need to order whatever Venus was having when they ate at a restaurant. "My parents would make me order first, but once she ordered, I'd change my mind. It was tough for me to stop being Venus and become the person I am."[12]

After they faced one another at the Lipton International Cup in 1999, Serena shrugged off the suggestion that being competitors on the court would ever interfere with their relationship.

"I can't necessarily say that our relationship is going to be affected by tennis," she said.

> We have a strong background; we're Jehovah's Witnesses, we really believe that family comes first, not a game that's going to last 10 years at the most. I don't know if I'm going to be playing 10 years. It can last. Why would I want that to [come] between someone who has always been around, always been a very special friend for me. I couldn't imagine that. I definitely don't think she could either. I don't think, no matter how many times we play each other, I could never say that it would affect my relationship with Venus.[13]

In her autobiography *On the Line*, Serena devoted a chapter to Venus, "Me and V." Serena described feeling overshadowed by an older sister she considered "taller, prettier, quicker, more athletic" than her.[14]

Even as Venus grabbed headlines and Serena entertained doubts about her game, she was determined to become as good as her older sister. She took chase of Venus's accomplishments in an "anything you can do I do better" manner. Sometimes, at night, when she'd slip into Venus's bed to talk, Serena sought counsel and encouragement from her big sister. "She just told me to work hard and to play my game. The rest will come. . . . Your time will come."[15]

The elder sister continued to cast an enormous shadow over Serena, one she would not completely shake until years later.

"Serena was the youngest; in her case, the youngest of five girls," said Rineberg. "Venus dominantly cast the shadow Serena faced, because of her tennis profession; however, add in the success of the other sisters and the shadow Serena was in might have seemed like Mt. Everest!"[16]

Although her father told the world that Serena might be better than Venus, the first solid evidence emerged in 1998, at the Sydney International in Sydney, Australia. Serena went through qualifying and reached the quarterfinals, where she was set to face Lindsay Davenport, who Venus referred to as the "Big L." Venus was 0–2 against Davenport, ranked number two at the time.

Davenport took the first set, 6–1, in just 20 minutes. She raced out to a 5–2 lead in the second set. Serena faced two match points before staging a comeback to defeat Davenport, 1–6, 7–5, 7–5. That match served as a preview of things to come. Serena would go 9–1 against Davenport in the next 10 matches. Venus would fall 1–8 against Davenport before turning things around. The results in Sydney also served notice to the rest of the tour that Venus's baby sister had the game to knock off top players. A prelude to the future, Serena's victory over Davenport would be the first of many times she would upstage Venus.

Serena "had accomplished something her big sister had never been able to do—she beat Davenport. She had stepped out of Venus' shadow and into the direct sunlight for everyone to notice," said Rineberg.[17]

Early in their careers, Venus outmatched Serena. In fact, Macci and Rineberg believed Venus was the better tennis player. Even now, Macci contends that Venus has the most technically sound game. In his book, Rineberg claimed that when the girls were younger, Venus sometimes let Serena win.

"Venus used to walk Serena to school, and as they approached a busy street they had to cross, Serena would not go without first reaching for Venus' hand. Venus was her protector, her defender, and sometimes her idol," wrote Rineberg. "Serena was the little sister that she had protected, consoled, and sympathized with all her life. She would have to give her baby sis a break every once in a while and let her win. I saw her do it in practices for five years."[18]

Years later, when the stakes were higher, their encounters would be described as boring, and even bad for the game. Sports journalist John Roberts wrote in the *Independent*, "Unity is the strength of the Williams sisters. . . . They perceive each other as one and the same person. Only when they compete against each other at the highest level does their unity appear to be a weakness."[19]

Roberts described their matches in Grand Slams as "anticlimactic." Rumors arose about whether their father predetermined the winner of their matches. Martina Hingis publicly accused them of match-fixing.

Following the Indian Wells incident, where Venus and Serena were mercilessly booed, *ESPN the Magazine* columnist Mark Kreidler speculated about whether there was enough evidence to convict the Williams sisters in the court of public opinion and perhaps even official WTA sanctions, writing,

> Depending upon how seriously you view the situation, the Williams family constitutes either a minor but ongoing annoyance; a hugely frustrating lost opportunity to expand the WTA's popularity into previously unmarked corners; or the most mortifying threat to the sport's legitimacy since wood rackets gave way to the Wilson T-2000.

While presenting himself as a neutral voice in the debate, Kreidler wrote that the first reaction of people who follow the game was that, "Richard had once again orchestrated the outcome of the match before it had a chance to be played."[20] Once again? This clearly implied that it was believed previous matches had been fixed.

The incident at Indian Wells generated open debate about whether there was match-fixing. When asked about this, Richard would respond angrily and point out that no one asked this of McEnroe or Chris Evert when they played their siblings.

A year before the dustup at Indian Wells, in 2000, Australian tennis player Pat Cash claimed that Richard would tell the girls who should win the match. Cash was not the only tennis player or journalist who believed the Williams family determined the outcome of the sisters' contests before the match began. These insinuations and accusations reinforced some of the lessons and lectures Serena and Venus heard at home—distrust those with an agenda and rely on family.

In 2000, Andy "Coach" Cotton, a columnist with the *Austin Chronicle*, took issue with the likes of Cash making such an incendiary yet baseless accusation. Cotton wrote, "Everyone with any tennis credentials was asked their opinion . . . was the match fixed? The absurd ramblings of a part-time Aussie journalist were repeated over and over until his irresponsible statement became, ex post facto, a supposed real occurrence."[21]

Cotton believed that by making the unfounded accusations public, journalists and tennis commentators were putting the Williams sisters in a lose–lose situation. He continued,

> How exactly was the Williams family supposed to respond to this accusation: that they participated and colluded in the most heinous crime a professional athlete could be accused of inside the lines of their sport? Talk about trying to disprove a negative! So instead of basking in a well-deserved glow of being in the finals at Wimbledon, having dispensed with the joyless task of having to beat a sibling to get

there, Venus Williams had to defend herself against outrageous accusations she can't *prove* are wrong. After all, if I say you killed your mother yesterday, you can call me a damn liar and prove it by trotting out old mom. How do you prove your baby sister didn't let you win? A tad unfair, I think.

They followed up an appearance in the 2001 U.S. Open final by reaching the finals at the French Open and Wimbledon in 2002. The locker room was abuzz with chatter about conspiracy theories. More players accused Richard of arranging the outcome of their matches. The *Telegraph*'s Robert Philip went as far to lament about the sisters' dominance. He wrote, "You just wish Mr. Williams would take his little darlings over to the local park tomorrow afternoon to play behind a private privet hedge and inform us of the result afterward rather than stage a repeat of the soulless 'final' in Paris."[22]

Serena and Venus dismissed the rumors, and as the *San Francisco Chronicle* detailed, they preferred to "let tennis do the talking."[23] Serena backed up her French Open and Wimbledon titles by winning the U.S. Open, for a third consecutive Grand Slam trophy. Venus was the runner-up in all three finals. By the end of 2002, Serena and Venus had taken turns at number one. Serena completed the "Serena Slam" by winning the 2003 Australian Open. Again, Venus was the runner-up.

As time would prove, the awkwardly played matches were due to two players who were as close as two people could be and knew one another's games. The older they got, the better their matches would become. Working through awkward situations is the hallmark of maturity.

Even before they turned pro and were still developing their skills, Rineberg noticed the ambiguous approach the sisters took to their matches.

"The girls did their best to act as if their matches against each other were like any other matches, but it was apparent to me, and many others, that their matches were not of the same quality," he wrote. "When practicing before playing Hingis or Graf, Venus and Serena were so focused. They would hit every ball at me or past me as if I was their opponent. Sometimes I would stop and say: 'Save it for the match, Venus,' or 'Don't waste it on the practice court, Serena.'"[24]

Serena and Venus ignored the accusations and continued starring in what their father called "The Williams Show."

After defeating Venus to win the 2002 U.S. Open, a reporter asked Serena if it was tougher playing against her sister than other opponents. "No, not at all," Serena said. "If anything I prefer to play Venus because that means that we have reached our maximum potential and that we'll both go home winners. So for me—I always want to see Venus do well. I never want to see Venus lose. For me, I'm happy to play her in the final."[25]

That the sisters were always so gracious to one another in defeat was a testament to their family's creed: Family first, in all things. Serena and Venus came onto a tennis scene filled with overbearing and even abusive parents. Jelena Dokic, Mirjana Lučić-Baroni, Mary Pierce, and Jennifer Capriati, contemporaries of Serena and Venus, suffered through embarrassing and sometimes frightening experiences with their fathers.[26] Lučić-Baroni had to flee Croatia to escape her abusive father.[27] According to the *Independent*, Dokic's father once called tournament officials "Nazis" and was thrown out of Wimbledon after stomping on a reporter's phone. He was also banned from the U.S. Open for arguing about the price of salmon.[28] Lučić-Baroni was still a teen when she came to the United States with her mother, fleeing her Croatian father, who reportedly beat her.[29] Pierce's father was so abusive that the WTA instituted the "Jim Pierce Rule," to curtail abusive behavior from tennis parents.

Richard was loud but never accused of abusing the girls. Many people considered him controlling, manipulative, and obnoxious. The media, however, rarely gave Serena's parents kudos for raising two responsible, intelligent women who excelled both on and off the court. Richard and Oracene taught the sisters to tap into their fiery competitive spirits while rejecting a natural inclination to compete with one another. Whatever nurturing tools Richard and Oracene used to raise their daughters, it's a method worthy of replication.

John McEnroe once marveled at how well Venus handled consecutive defeats by her younger sister. The ESPN commentator stated that he's not sure he could have handled losing so many big matches to his younger brother. Certainly not as well as Venus did. Perhaps that's because Patrick's game was never on par with John's. Although they shared the same last name and played doubles, they were never considered a package deal.

Serena and Venus, "The Williams Show," became a brand separate from the individuals. Venus and Serena even tried their hand at reality TV, starring in *Venus and Serena for Real*. The show ran on the ABC

Family network and followed the sisters as they played in tournaments and pursued careers in interior design and fashion.[30]

The Williams story was unfolding like a fairy tale. They made television appearances together, did "Got Milk" ads together, posed for photo shoots, and appeared on the covers of magazines and in books together. Still in their early 20s, they had a combined 10 Grand Slam titles and two Olympic gold medals before tragedy threatened to shatter them both.

In September 2003, their oldest sister was murdered.

In "Fatal Volley," *People* magazine's Bill Hewitt described how Venus and Serena learned of their sister's death.

"The mysterious murder sent shock waves through the close-knit Williams clan. Venus, 23, got the news in New York City, where she was visiting for Fashion Week. Serena, 22, was in Toronto shooting *Street Time*, a cable-TV show about urban crime, and by one account she became hysterical when she learned of her sister's death."[31]

Serena considered Yetunde a second mom. "There was such a big age difference between us—almost nine years—that she did kind of take that role. She even took us back-to-school shopping," Serena remembered.[32]

The news of Yetunde's death rocked the family. Serena continued, "I thought, 'Gone? Tunde?' It didn't make sense. I'd just spoken to her earlier in the day. She was so excited about this show I was working on and the progress I was making on my knee, how well Venus had played that summer, how beautifully her children were growing, and on and on."[33]

A sister, yes; however, Serena mourned Yetunde like a child mourns a mother. She relied on the remaining sisters to pull her through the worst moments of her life. Serena recalled a specific way she and her siblings would try to cope with Tunde's death: They played UNO, the card game. It was a game they played when they were in Compton, and in the days and weeks following Tunde's funeral, they played UNO, often. "For hours and hours, we'd play UNO. At Tunde's house. At my apartment, or Lyn's," wrote Serena. "Wherever we happened to be—and for the most part, we happened to be together. None of us could sleep, so it was a way to pass the time, a way to keep Tunde close."[34]

Their father, Richard, who remained outside during the funeral, said of the grieving sisters, "You can see it in the expression in their faces."[35]

Yetunde left behind three children, Jeffrey, Justus, and Jair, who at the time were 11, 9, and 5, respectively. Serena and Venus, barely adults themselves, supported their mother in her efforts to win custody of their niece and nephews.[36] Yetunde's second husband, a convicted felon and father of two of the kids, once accused the Williams family of orchestrating a kidnapping of his kids.[37] Oracene would eventually end up raising the kids.

While the custody battle played out, Serena and Venus had to get back to tennis. When asked about her grief, Serena told reporters, "I haven't really coped yet. I'm trying to figure out how to cope with it. But not a day goes by when I don't think of it, and I try to make sure I talk to all of my sisters every single day."[38]

When Serena was named *Sports Illustrated*'s 2015 Sportsperson of the Year, Venus introduced her at the ceremony in New York. After Serena finished speaking, her mother and sisters—Lyndrea, Isha, and Venus—gathered around the podium and posed for a family portrait.

Venus deserves credit for being mature and even-keeled enough to play mentor and cheerleader in Serena's life without any public indication of strife at home. The more volatile and moodier Serena might not have fared as well as the older sibling.

So much of Serena's success has come at Venus's expense. When she beats Venus, Serena mutes her victory dances. She doesn't leap quite as high or twirl. She realizes that her older sister has had to swallow humble pie, in public, often.

"I know that her career might have been different if she had had my health," Serena told *Vogue*.[39] "I know how hard she works," she told *Metro UK*'s George Bellshaw.[40]

"Most of their matches are decided mentally before play starts," said Vijay Freeman, editor of *Black Tennis Magazine*.

> Venus knows how bad her sister Serena wants it and what it means to her younger sister to win a major. Richard Williams mentioned several times earlier in their career that Serena would eventually become a better player than Venus. Richard knew Serena had the potential to be great and exceed the accomplishments of her older sister Venus due to her strong-willed personality.[41]

Serena has been so dominant that now she often overshadows Venus and her accomplishments. Despite not having won a Grand Slam title in a decade, Venus is still second only to Serena among active players. Venus is a great champion, but Serena is in a class by herself.

"Similar to the difference between Kobe Bryant and Michael Jordan—Venus will step on your neck to choke you, Serena will cut your throat," said Freeman. "Serena has the killer instinct during competition and has only one agenda—to win. . . . [Serena] has more desire to beat Venus to prove that she is the best; she simply wants it more."[42]

As they've aged, their relationship has matured, on and off the court. "I hate playing her because she gets this look on her face where she just looks sad if she's losing. Solemn. It breaks my heart," Serena told Bellshaw. "So when I play her now, I absolutely don't look at her, because if she gets that look, then I'll start feeling bad, and the next thing you know I'll be losing. I think that's when the turning point came in our rivalry, when I stopped looking at her."[43]

The older the sisters got, the more well-received they were. The public finally appears to be warming up to them. Once booed and jeered, for the most part, Serena and Venus are celebrated at tournaments.

After their fourth-round match at the 2016 U.S. Open, *Rolling Stone* writer Juan Jose Vallego noted that the sibling rivalry had taken a kinder, far gentler turn. "It's amazing to think that there was a time when these sisters, who have given tennis so much, were not particularly welcome within its confines," Vallego wrote. "When every move they made was greeted with controversy. When their guard had to be up at all times. When they could only count themselves and their family as a source of peace."[44]

After defeating Venus at the 2017 Australian Open, Serena told the crowd at Rod Lavar Arena,

> There's no way I'd be at 23 without her, there's no way I'd be at one without her. She's my inspiration, she's the only reason I'm standing here today, and the only reason the Williams sisters exist, so thank you, Venus, for inspiring me to be the best player that I could be and inspiring me to work hard.[45]

Following her victory, Serena posted a photo of her and Venus during the trophy ceremony on her Instagram page. She wrote, "The top is never lonely when your best friend @venuswilliams is there. Here's to #23. What a night for our family."[46] They post supportive messages and praise for one another on their social media pages.

Their mother, Oracene, told Jon Wertheim, "They love each other so much they're almost like a husband and wife."[47]

Venus and Serena have played one another 30 times, with Serena winning 18 of those matches. Yet, they remain one another's biggest cheerleaders.

4

GALVANIZING GIRL POWER AND BLACK GIRL MAGIC

Billie Jean King, Wilma Rudolph, Jackie Joyner-Kersee, and Mia Hamm are iconic female athletes who also served as role models to millions; however, none of them galvanized "girl power" like Serena, who changed the way female athletes are promoted, perceived, and paid.

During the early 1970s, Billie Jean King ruled women's tennis and was one of the most recognizable women in sports. In 1972, King won the French Open, Wimbledon, and the U.S. Open. That year, *Sports Illustrated* named her Sportswoman of the Year. She graced the cover of the year-end issue, but she appeared at the bottom, beneath a photo of legendary UCLA basketball coach John Wooden, named 1972 Sportsman of the Year.

A year later, King challenged the idea of male superiority in sports when she defeated Bobby Riggs in the "Battle of the Sexes" exhibition tennis match. Still, after the much-hyped event, few considered King the greatest athlete in sports. Her greatness largely remained segregated based on gender.

A mentor and role model to Serena, King dedicated her postplaying career to fighting for gender equality in tennis and sports in general. A generation later, Serena would go on to eclipse King's accomplishments on the court and ultimately become the face for gender equity in sports.

Serena's ability to overcome obstacles makes her an aspirational and inspirational role model. She demonstrated self-determination early on, as evidenced in the TransWorld video that stated, rather matter-of-factly, that she wanted people to want to be like her.

Whether hoisting her arms into the air with Venus after their first Grand Slam match or strutting through tournaments in jaw-dropping attire, Serena always seems to be sending the message, "I am who I am," which in turn allows girls to be as they are or wish to be.

Of course, Serena did not invent girl power. She did, however, provide a blueprint for how to sustain that power in the face of adversity and adversaries.

She modeled how to project physical strength and anger without apologizing for unabashed femininity. Her chiseled arms, power grunt, and death stare never seemed to clash with her dangling earrings, blinged-out nails, and match-time mascara. A girlie gladiator, Serena altered thinking that such competitive characteristics as aggression, power, and intimidation should be reserved for men.

Serena reshaped the conversation about body image. When she entered the 2007 Australian Open, she was not in peak condition. Injuries kept her away from the tour. Her ranking sank, and her weight gain became a topic for discussion. Other athletes, male and female, have battled weight gain. But the conversations about Serena's body appeared to be more personal. Some reporters labeled her overpaid and out of shape. Worse, they linked her weight gain to lack of professionalism and poor work ethic.

Serena took it in stride. After winning the 2007 Australian Open, she responded to public discussions about her weight in an interview with *People* magazine. "I know, I know, I have a big fat butt and big boobs, and there's nothing I can do about it," she said. "Generally, guys like butts and boobs, so it's not an issue for me."[1]

Even after she returned to the top 10, the body shaming continued. In 2009, sports columnist Jason Whitlock wrote a scathing article in which he deemed Serena's size and fitness as impediments to greatness. "With a reduction in glut, a little less butt, and a smidgen more guts, Serena Williams would easily be as big as Michael Jackson, dwarf Tiger Woods, and take a run at Rosa Parks."[2]

That Whitlock, an African American man who was obese by any standard, found it okay to publicly trash a black female athlete's body represented the antiblack misogyny Serena faced from all sides throughout her career.

The animosity and venom reserved for Serena have roots buried in slavery, according to Delia Douglas, Ph.D., a scholar who studies gender, race, and sexuality and teaches at the Social Justice Institute at the University of British Columbia in Vancouver, British Columbia. Douglas, whose work has been published in the *Journal of Black Studies*, *Gender Place and Culture*, the *Journal of Sport and Social Issues*, the *Sociology of Sports Journal*, and *Sports Education and Society*, finds Serena a fitting subject and sports the perfect setting to explore black misogyny, especially as it relates to body shaming.

"The denigration of black women and their bodies is so commonplace that it's not acknowledged. I mean, it's not even identified as that," she said.[3]

The intersectionality between race and gender also has a name, *misogynoir*, a term often cited by scholars who discuss Serena as a cultural heroine.

"Her skin, muscle tone, curves, and hair are fodder for public consumption," said Douglas.

Kim Golombisky, professor of women's studies at the University of South Florida and author of the book *Feminists, Feminisms, and Advertising: Some Restrictions Apply*, believes Serena is subjected to shaming mostly based on race.

"You can recall all those horrible stereotypes of the mammy, the sapphire, all those stereotypes play into people's interpretation of what's happening, constantly," said Golombisky, "and they don't even realize it."[4]

This type of ambivalence reached a crescendo in 2015, when the *New York Times* ran a story with the headline, "Tennis's Top Women Balance Body Image with Ambition." The article's author, Ben Rothenberg, led with Serena as an example. He wrote, "Williams has large biceps and a mold-breaking muscular frame, which packs the power and athleticism that have dominated women's tennis for years. Her rivals could try to emulate her physique, but most of them choose not to."[5]

That comparison alone might have been enough to draw backlash. After all, you had a white male making a black female athlete's body an issue for being—built like an athlete?

But Rothenberg ignited more controversy by including a quote from Tomasz Wiktorowski, coach of Agnieszka Radwanska, a slender Polish player: "It's our decision to keep her as the smallest player in the top 10 because, first of all, she's a woman, and she wants to be a woman."

Douglas said that quote harkened back to the days when some suggested that Althea Gibson undergo a chromosome test to prove she was not a man.

Women took to social media to express outrage about the article and the timing of its publication—right when Serena was going for a calendar-year Slam. *Seventeen* magazine ran an article entitled "Why This Article Body Shaming Serena Williams Has Twitter Raging," with the subhead, "Stop talking about her body already."[6]

Rothenberg's column drew such ire that the *New York Times* printed an apology and a rebuke of the freelance journalist. Under that headline, "Double Fault in Article on Serena Williams and Body Image," public editor Margaret Sullivan acknowledged that the *Times* had missed the mark in framing the conversation.[7]

Celebrities, friends, and fans came to Serena's defense. But the fact that the sports world was having this conversation yet again, about Serena's femininity or lack thereof, reinforced the themes of intersectionality.

Serena took the opportunity to encourage women to ignore the negative and accept their bodies as is. Meanwhile, she was chasing career goals, putting on a fashion show mere days after losing at the U.S. Open.

That summer, some of the biggest names in sports gathered in Los Angeles for ESPN's ESPYs, the network's annual sports award show. The show is mostly a popularity contest in which fans vote for their favorite sports stars, teams, and moments.

Serena was a shoo-in for best female tennis player and the favorite to win best female athlete; however, in the latter category, she lost to Ronda Rousey, a white female mixed martial arts fighter who competed in a professional sport that didn't even exist when Serena began her tennis career.

Rousey attended the ceremony. Serena did not. Rousey was being heralded as sexy. A professional fighter, Rousey is a muscular woman who fought, kicked, and beat people bloody. Yet, she had not endured the same accusations of being on steroids or a man in disguise.

The juxtaposition between Rousey and Serena was stark: two famous female athletes, both heralded for their strength and physique. But one was being glorified while the other was being vilified. Rousey's white privilege allowed her to move freely and flaunt her femininity, even as she bludgeoned people for a living. Meanwhile, critics sought to paint Serena as masculine, possibly not even female.

Regarding career accomplishments, Rousey seemed out of Serena's league. Chris Chase, then a writer for *USA Today*'s "For the Win" column, wrote about what he considered an upset.

> But, come on: For Ronda Rousey, an athlete in a sport devoid of any real competition who spent a total of 30 seconds playing her sport over the past year (she had two bouts, one lasted 16 seconds, the other 14 seconds), to win Best Female Athlete over Serena Williams, who won every single Grand Slam played in between ESPY shows (a 28–0 record), is like *Entourage*, which Rousey starred in this year—probably the most difficult thing she had to do—winning Best Picture over, I don't know, any other movie. It probably didn't hurt that Rousey was in attendance at the awards while Serena was doing something with which Rousey is mostly unfamiliar of late: competing (at a tournament in Sweden, specifically).[8]

Douglas believes the talk surrounding Serena's perceived masculinity is the result of what she calls the "'ungendering' of blackness as female." Because Serena is the victim of racism and sexism—intersectionality—her accomplishments are viewed with skepticism.

"Serena Williams, her engendered blackness, and heterosexuality are not simply unknowable, but they are deemed impossible. I link this to the historical denial of black humanness and the denial of black women having a gendered position," said Douglas, who cites scholar Hortense Spiller's explanation as to why Serena's femininity is called into question. Spiller wrote about "ungendering" that took place during the middle passage. "Black men and women were not distinguished," said Douglas. She continued,

> So I think that Serena continues to present a danger. Her presence, her success, and her agency and increasing visibility around her agency, that poses a threat to white-male domination and capitalism. Not only in tennis, but in society. And so even though she has economic stability, given in the context of antiblackness, the constant barrage she's subject to, the threats, the challenges to her emotional and physical identity and well-being, demonstrate the limited privileges and standing that are available to her as a black heterosexual woman even though society is heterocentric. She's a black heterosexual woman. So

I think what's interesting, in sport, which is patriarchal and heterocentric in North American structures, is that even though all female athletes have to navigate this idea that sport or that athletic competition masculinizes girls and women, for black women, the black female body and black female athletes have to be understood in the context that they have this history that they've inherited, of ungendering.

J. K. Rowling, author of the famed Harry Potter books, gave a humorous response to someone body-shaming Serena when she got into a Twitter tit for tat for a post claiming that Serena was "built like a man." A huge Serena fan, Rowling responded by posting a picture of Serena wearing a hip-hugging red dress and stilettos as she left the Ed Sullivan Studio after an appearance on the *Late Show with David Letterman*. Her comment: "Yeah, my husband looks just like this in a dress. You're an idiot."[9]

Serena has no problem defending herself; however, prominent female celebrities, authors, and athletes have also had her back. Just before the start of the 2015 U.S. Open, Claudia Rankine, a poet and essayist, wrote a feature for *New York Times Magazine* titled "The Meaning of Serena Williams." In her article, Rankine asked, "What does a victorious or defeated black woman's body in a historically white space look like?"

Rankine's article celebrated Serena as an individual and role model. Rankine praised Serena for plowing through the nonsense. "I want Serena to win, but I know better than to think her winning can end something she didn't start," wrote Rankine. "But Serena is providing a new script, one in which winning doesn't carry the burden of curing racism, in which we win just to win—knowing that it is simply her excellence, baby."[10]

Serena is a strong black woman who offers herself—imperfections and vulnerabilities—as a woman in full. Her strength is enhanced by her vulnerability, including crying on the court and expressing sadness and disappointment. Black female activists have long fought for the public to view them as human, as women.

By just being Serena, she has helped change the way black women are perceived. The angry black woman could also be the successful businesswoman and gal pal next door. She could be an athlete and also appear in the swimsuit issue of *Sports Illustrated* and grace the covers of news magazines.

Professor and political pundit Melissa Harris-Perry wrote a book about the mythology of the "strong black woman." On the one hand, it is a backhanded compliment. "The strong black woman myth makes black women particularly susceptible to dispositional explanations for inequality," wrote Perry.[11]

"Because black women's bodies have always been . . . [viewed as property], deemed expendable, disposable, because on the one hand sport is still claimed as a male space . . . you are navigating sexism and racism," Douglas said. "But to claim that all female athletes simply have to navigate sexism and heterosexism does not get at the specificity of the history of black women and black women's bodies, which are particular targets."

Golombisky agrees. "The women's body as an athlete is one thing, but the black woman's body as an athlete is something totally different," she said. "Some might argue it's not even really, if we understand womanhood . . . the black woman's body isn't really a woman's body if you're understanding all those horrible stereotypes."

If Serena is the poster child for misogynoir, she's equally the standard-bearer for "black girl magic." Similar to the "black is beautiful" mantras that emerged in the turbulence of the 1960s and the civil rights movements, the phrase "black girl magic" is used as affirmation.

In a *Los Angeles Times* article, journalist Dexter Thomas mentions Serena in an effort to explain the origins of the phrase "black girl magic." CaShawn Thompson reportedly coined the phrase. She told the *Los Angeles Times* that one of the reasons she calls it magic is that "sometimes our accomplishments might seem to come out of thin air, because a lot of times, the only people supporting us are other black women."[12]

Indeed, black girl magic, often used as a hashtag on Twitter, is a form of support. It's as if black women are reaching out to give one another a collective hug, a high five.

The least paid, the most likely to die during childbirth, and most often the target of violence, black women sometimes depend on black celebrities who can lend their voices to their message, hopes, and dreams. Serena is that person.

When Serena wins a match, expect to see the hashtag #BlackGirlMagic. When she posts photos of her and her daughter, there it is again, #BlackGirlMagic. When she's beating Maria Sharapova for the umpteenth time, #BlackGirlMagic.

Serena didn't start the black girl magic movement; however, more than any other woman, she's synonymous with its message. Serena is a proud black woman and, perhaps more than any other African American female, the answer to the question, What's black girl magic?

Black girl magic is more than a mantra or a cute catchphrase. It's an oasis in a desolate landscape infested with negative stereotypes about black women, especially deep, dark sisters like Serena. Whether dog-whistled or billboarded, black women are bombarded with messages saying they are too dark, their butts are too big, their lips are too full, or their hair is not quite right. So, when Serena wins a tournament or appears in a new television commercial, black women relish her win as a loss for the haters. Serena is the walking, twinkling, sparkling embodiment of black girl magic.

Nicole Monique, a sports journalist and owner/host of the *That's What SHE Said Sports: Sports Talk Her Way* radio show, blog, and podcast, said Serena is embraced by the sisterhood, an unincorporated club of black women. "When you are a black woman you are automatically part of the club," she said. "So just like any family—we can talk about her—but you better not say jack about her or we will come for you. When Serena wins as a black woman, I win; when she loses my heart breaks for her. That is the power of black girl magic."

Like so many black women, Monique feels a kinship with Serena and experiences the tennis player's ups and downs as if they were her own. She further commented,

> I remember watching Serena's U.S. Open meltdown live—it was not her greatest moment and I felt bad for her. But I also remember thinking—if she was a white guy would the media have been so mean? The king of famous tennis meltdowns, John McEnroe, is almost celebrated now. I've witnessed many male athletes have meltdowns—some worse than Serena's—but the way people came at Serena was cruel. She was called a sore loser over and over again, not to mention some other names that were not called for. I don't know what was going on with her at that time—she was obviously going through something. Threatening the line judge was totally unacceptable, but we had another thing at play here. This whole incident played into the "angry black woman" stereotype—so she was in a no-win situation. Even if she hadn't gone off on the line judge and just rolled her eyes—they would have still called her out. [13]

That passionate defense of Serena's behavior is common among black women who follow Serena's career. Monique's favorite black girl magic moment came at the 2012 Olympics in London, when Serena entered the final the favorite against Maria Sharapova. It was the United States versus Russia; however, more than anything, it was the sister versus the blond Russian who, through Madison Avenue, had co-opted the position as "America's sweetheart." The match was not close. On a blustering windy day, Serena dictated play from the start. She went on to crush Sharapova, 6–1, 6–1, to win the gold medal. She would later take gold in doubles with sister Venus.

"When Serena beat Maria Sharapova at Wimbledon at the 2012 Olympics and then did the crip walk after. . . . She was excited and she did the dance and it pissed people off. That black girl magic shined through, and Serena told the whole world—relax. Loved it!"[14]

For many black women, Serena represents a sort of psychological payback. She waves her racket and presto, black girl magic happens. She crushes the haters and naysayers. She rebukes those who relegate black women to the back of the bus, the end of the line, the lowest tiers of the payroll totem pole.

During Serena's run at the calendar-year Slam in 2015, Rankine joined many black women throughout the world in hoping and praying for Serena's triumph. Serena had held all four major titles before but never a calendar-year Slam. Steffi Graf had two, and for black women who sensed that whites would use any and all data to keep Serena from what they believed was her rightful place on the women's tennis throne, the calendar-year Slam was a must, not because they believed Serena needed it to prove she was the greatest, but because there was this collective desire for Serena to dismiss all doubt, clear all goalposts.

When she could not accomplish the feat, her fans mourned with her, but perhaps black women took the loss more personally.

Later that year, *Sports Illustrated* selected Serena as Sportsperson of the Year. The cover of the magazine showed Serena, dressed in a black leotard and black stilettoes, lounging with one leg draped over the arm of a throne. But this was not without controversy.

The staff at *Sports Illustrated* always selects Sportsperson of the Year; however, in recent years, the magazine had allowed readers and sports fans to weigh in via a reader's poll. In 2015, readers chose a horse, Triple Crown winner American Pharoah, over Serena. The *Los Angeles Times* decided to run a picture of Serena next to a picture of the horse (no mention of the jockey) and asked its readers to vote on who they thought should be *SI*'s Sportsperson of the Year. Serena's photo next to the horse set off a fury among many women, not just blacks. One Twitter follower responded, "You are actually comparing a black woman to a horse?" Like the *New York Times*, the *Los Angeles Times* decided to print an apology and an explanation. Meanwhile, legions of black women counter the body shaming with what they called black girl magic.

In a 2016 interview with Harris-Perry, published in *Glamour* magazine, Serena discussed her role as the icon of Black Girl Magic.

"You and Venus were the original black girl magic. People who do not know you feel a personal stake in every match you play," Harris-Perry told Serena.

"That's something. I meet people who say, 'Girl, I watch every match, and I pray for you,'" said Serena. "I feel that energy and those prayers. Sometimes when I'm down on the court, in the back of my mind, I'm thinking, 'They want me to win. Is there anything else I can give?' It encourages me to do better, to fight harder."[15]

After Serena defeated Angelique Kerber to win the 2016 Wimbledon final, Maya A. Jones, an associate editor for ESPN's *The Undefeated*, wrote, "It was a glorious day in the land of #BlackGirlMagic, thanks to Serena Williams' hard-fought 7–5, 6–3 Wimbledon victory over Germany's Angelique Kerber early this morning."[16]

Serena is that homegirl who made it big and never forgot where she came from. Her accessibility is appreciated. Serena is the epitome of black girl magic, according to Errin Whack, an award-winning journalist who wrote about Serena's black girl magic for ESPNW during Serena's run at a calendar-year Slam in 2015. "Before Beats by Dre and Nike were clamoring for her endorsement, or she was posing for paparazzi photos with Kim Kardashian, millions of black women knew and loved 'Rena,' 'ReRe,' or 'my girl,' their terms of endearment for Serena Williams," wrote Whack.

> Serena, in all her #BlackGirlMagic glory, was first worshipped by the legions of girls and women who saw themselves in the determined, hardworking, and charming phenom from Compton, California. It's these women who are among those cheering the loudest for Serena, because for them, she has already won.[17]

"Black girl magic is celebrating our greatness and what we find as great," said Monique.

> The magic behind black women has always seemed a mystery to others—but we know it's a multitude of things. On the surface, we are strong, fierce, and confident—but underneath we can be sensitive and vulnerable. That is Serena—she is all those things, and to black women, we want to protect her. [18]

There are black women who cared little about tennis until the Williams sisters arrived. As Serena's stature grew, so did the angst about defending her against black misogyny. Living life on the defensive gets old. It's draining. Perhaps that's why so many black women gravitate toward black girl magic. As is the case when Serena is hitting winners, it's far more fun to go on offense. There's energy in the positive.

"Sisters know she has to literally play the game—strong—but not too strong, outspoken but watch what you say, watch your face, smile even when you do not feel like it," said Monique. "We have all been there—so we admire her tenacity when having to deal with the tennis world, and we can relate when she's criticized, and we will defend her to the end if someone talks crazy about her." [19]

Black girl magic is an unapologetic bias in rooting for black female excellence. Serena's continued success permits black women to express unbridled pride.

That so many black women take on Serena's success and failures as their own is a testament to the athlete's impact on the collective, communal psyche born of a shared experience unique to African American women.

"As affirmation, as celebration, as recognition, to see yourself in a particular kind of way," said Douglas. "To see her dancing . . . to see her success is our success. Her joy is our joy. It's like we get to rejoice in her reaching her goals and her demonstrating excellence. And let's be clear, it also does matter when she's beating white girls."

Douglas's sentiment about how race factors into the way black women experience Serena's losses explains why so many black journalists took issue with Maria Sharapova's characterization of Serena in the memoir *Unstoppable*, published in 2018. Sharapova was set to return from a drug ban and was promoting the book.

Sharapova described feeling "intimidated" by Serena when they faced off at Wimbledon in 2004. Even though Sharapova doesn't mention race, "When Sharapova, a Russian with blond hair and devoid of curves, mentions Serena's physical attributes as being part of the intimidation factor, it does give one reason to pause," wrote Ricardo Hazell, for the Shadow League, an online sports blog.[20]

In an article for BuzzFeed entitled "Maria Sharapova's Rivalry with Serena Williams Is All in Her Head," writer Bim Adewunmi echoes the sentiments of many black women.

> In reading excerpts from Russian tennis player Maria Sharapova's new memoir, *Unstoppable*, it would be reasonable to see the reality of her situation: an athlete humiliated and angered by a far superior opponent over the years. But there is also an inescapable undercurrent of bitterness that relies on something more sinister when it comes to discussing the number one player in women's tennis, Serena Williams.
>
> But Sharapova's description has nothing to do with Serena's world-straddling skill and ability. It is about setting her up as "other," as superhuman (but in the detrimental way that curls into itself and reemerges as subhuman) and therefore unfair and unworthy to be in that space, on that court.
>
> Thick arms and thick legs (coded as masculine), in addition to being intimidating ("I felt threatened, officer") and strong (read: too strong, ergo masculine)? Well, that's too much. How could I, a slender blonde, be expected to play against this, and win? Never mind that at 6-foot-2, Maria Sharapova stands a clean five inches above Serena Williams's 5-foot-9 frame. Sharapova painted a shorthand cultural picture we have come to understand very well, in which a dainty white lady is menaced by a hulking black specter. It's fake news.[21]

Douglas explained why so many black women expend so much emotional capital on Serena and Venus. "They've never apologized for wanting what they want. They've never apologized for being. And that offends so many people," she said. "We just appreciate the challenges that are both spoken and unspoken. And knowing the unspoken because we know you can't always speak them."

"Regarding the black girl magic, we identify, it's recognition and celebration, like an embrace. There's just so few opportunities to witness—I mean we get to bear witness to expressions of her unbridled, like 'here I am and this is me. I'm here for this,'" Douglas added.

Unlike Tiger Woods, who, Douglas said, "grew up thinking 'I can be part of the boys club because I'm a boy,' Serena and Venus did not have the expectation . . . they weren't looking to be welcomed. They were just looking to compete. They were like, 'We're here and we're competing.' There wasn't even a question of, 'Please include us and we're looking to be included.' It was more like, 'We're here.'"

Whack's ESPNW story featured prominent black females expressing why they consider Serena the definition of black girl magic. The article included a quote from Brande Victorian, managing editor of Madame-Noire, who wrote of Serena,

> When her *New York Magazine* cover came out, I'd never seen that magazine shared by so many women. They aren't tennis fans, but they love what Serena represents: black woman excellence. And [she's a] dark-skinned black woman, which we don't get to see so often. She helps other black women be more comfortable with their bodies. It's an important moment.

Victorian further stated,

> We put on so much every day as black women, but she's carefree! She's like, "No, I get up, I have fun, I kill it, I go hang out with my boo." That's great to see that life doesn't always have to be, "Woe is me." We know the racial undertones of the way people critique her. At least, from the outside looking in, it doesn't appear to have a strong effect on her or make her hide her personality. That's what greatness is. When her name is trending, it's because of what she does. So many people trend because of controversy. We're talking about her because she's dominating. She's doing her job and being respected for it.[22]

Traci L. Green, head coach of the Harvard women's tennis team, led the Crimson to an Ivy League title in 2017. As an African American tennis coach at the most prestigious university in the country, Green can appreciate what Serena has accomplished. "Serena is a powerful black woman who embodies strength, beauty, and confidence. She is an icon at every level," she said. "Serena has an unbelievable will, strength, and resilience, in addition to incredible innate athletic ability. She is the ultimate competitor who's been blessed with the gift of longevity."[23]

So when Nike announces that the largest building on its new campus will be named after Serena, that's black girl magic.[24] When Serena makes the cover of a magazine, it's black girl magic. But more than anything, when Serena is on tour, taking on the world and rising above her competitors, every winner, ace, and overhead smash is black girl magic.

Undoubtedly an inspiration to black women, Serena is a role model to girls of various backgrounds because of the various ways in which she's succeeded. Her life story embodies so many feel-good themes. She's the commoner who reaches royal status, the comeback kid, the working mom, and the miracle who survived two near-death experiences.

On March 19, 2019, Brooklyn Nets guard Spencer Dinwiddie walked onto the court wearing a pair of basketball shoes bearing a picture of Serena, serving. On road trips, Dinwiddie often uses his sneakers as a canvas to honor iconic figures from the region in which his team is playing. On this day, the Nets were playing the Los Angeles Clippers, and Dinwiddie decided to pay homage to SoCal gal Serena.

Serena's life story, her career and journey, continue to have a transformative and inspirational impact on men and women from all walks of life; however, her influence on young black female tennis players has been profound. When Serena won the U.S. Open in 1998, she became the first black woman to win a Grand Slam since the 1950s. At the 2019 French Open, there were seven black women in the main draw. Four of those women held Grand Slam titles. Among active players, Serena held the record for most Grand Slams. Venus was second, with seven. Naomi Osaka had two and Sloane Stephens one. Madison Keys had already been to a Grand Slam final. African American Coco Gauff, 15, became the youngest player to win a match in the French Open qualifying round. [25]

Keys, Stephens, Osaka and Gauff all cite Serena as a role model. Gauff and Osaka claim to have patterned their games after Serena.

In an ad for dating site Bumble that ran during the 2019 Super Bowl, Serena said, "We're living in a world and society where people are starting to see differently and starting to understand that we are just as strong and just as smart and just as savvy and just as businesslike as any other male in this world." Serena has played a significant part in reshaping how men view women and how girls perceive themselves. "Don't wait to be given power," Williams says in the ad, "because here's what they won't tell you: We already have it." [26]

Serena Williams and sister Venus Williams flank their father, Richard Williams, at Rick Macci's Academy at Grenelefe Golf and Tennis Resort in Haines City, Florida, in 1991. *Charles Edward Denard*

Serena and Venus pose with their father, Richard Williams, while taking a break from practice at Grenelefe Golf and Tennis Resort in Haines City, Florida, in 1991. *Charles Edward Denard*

Tennis was always a family affair. Pictured at Grenelefe, Richard Williams sits with one of Serena's older sisters, Isha Price, who would later become a fixture in the players' box at tournaments. *Charles Edward Denard*

Rick Macci, who coached Venus and Serena when they first moved to Florida, sits at his tennis academy, located at Grenelefe Golf and Tennis Resort in Haines City, Florida, in 1991. *Charles Edward Denard*

Long before they turned pro, Serena and Venus got used to being in front of a camera. Here they are taking part in an interview at Rick Macci's Academy at Grenelefe Golf and Tennis Resort in 1991. *Charles Edward Denard*

Serena Williams prepares to serve during a match at the 2010 Australian Open in Melbourne. *Ann Kaguyutan*

Serena Williams during a match at the 2010 Australian Open. She would go on to win the tournament. *Ann Kaguyutan*

Serena Williams gets pumped up during a match at the 2010 Australian Open. *Ann Kaguyutan*

Serena Williams makes a play on the ball at the 2010 Australian Open. *Ann Kaguyutan*

Serena Williams practices as her coach, Patrick Mouratoglou, looks on at the 2016 BNP Paribas Open in Indian Wells, California. *Ann Kaguyutan*

Serena Williams during practice at the 2018 U.S. Open in Flushing Meadows, New York. *Ann Kaguyutan*

Serena Williams hits the practice court at the 2018 U.S. Open with Coach Patrick Mouratoglou. *Ann Kaguyutan*

Serena Williams hits a forehand at practice with Coach Patrick Mouratoglou during the 2018 U.S. Open. *Ann Kaguyutan*

5

DIGITAL AGE ACTIVIST

Serena turned pro in the mid-1990s, at about the same time mobile phones and online services went mainstream. Born in 1981, she straddles two generations: Generation X and the Millennials—generations that witnessed technological advances ranging from the advent of the Automatic Teller Machine to Twitter. Perhaps that is why Serena has been such a proactive force in using new media to promote old-fashioned activism.

Serena's activism is not as vociferous as Muhammad Ali's or as militant as Jim Brown's. Instead, Serena is the "light shiner" who uses her celebrity to bring attention to what she considers social injustice. A champion for women's rights and social justice, Serena leverages her social media presence to engage and mobilize followers. She is a digital age activist.

With social media followers topping 12 million, Serena has a built-in audience at her fingertips. She is not afraid to speak up on issues that divide people along racial, cultural, and political lines.

As a Jehovah's Witness, Serena refrains from voting; however, that has not kept her from weighing in on such hot-button subjects as police brutality, equal pay, gay rights, gun control, and racial bias. She manages to mesh activism with her tennis career, philanthropic endeavors, and entrepreneurial pursuits. She has created a seamless platform in which she equates truth with power, regardless of whether she is pitching a product, accepting another trophy, or working the red carpet.

It is the always-on persona associated with brand Serena that makes her digital activism effective. She has developed a savvy social media strategy when it comes to disseminating her messages. What begins on-line often ends with real action.

Earlier in her career, Serena let her father and Venus take the lead in handling controversial issues. Although she bore the brunt of the abuse of the Indian Wells crowd, Venus and Richard leveled accusations of racism, which became a flashpoint in Serena's first few years on the tour. The way the mostly white tennis fans treated Serena and Venus was a reflection of the underlying race relations in the United States. Circumstance thrust the sisters into their roles as black activists as a means to defend themselves against open hostility.

In 2003, the French Open crowd mercilessly booed Serena during a semifinal match against Justine Henin-Hardenne.[1] After the competition, Martin Jacques, a writer for the *Guardian*, penned an article entitled "Tennis Is Racist—It's Time We Do Something about It." In the article, Jacques cited the Henin-Hardenne hand incident, the reaction from fans at Roland-Garros, and a list of other racist acts aimed at Serena and Venus. He went on to write, "The extraordinary thing is that this is hardly ever written or said. As race courses through the veins of tennis, people pretend it doesn't exist. Instead the Williams sisters, together with their father, are subjected to a steady stream of criticism, denigration, accusation, and innuendo." As Jacques pointed out, Serena and Venus faced blatant racism while surrounded by people who seemed oblivious to it.[2]

When they were trading trophies and time atop the rankings, Venus and Serena gobbled up the headlines. The sister act was considered one of the hottest tickets in sports. Their popularity and dominance gave them more opportunities to speak out. Unlike some active athletes who feared alienating sponsors and fans, Venus and Serena spoke up about the disparity in prize money at the Grand Slams. They played a crucial role in righting that wrong.

In 2001, their U.S. Open final drew 10.7 million viewers and a 6.8 share in the ratings, the highest for a woman's match since 1995. "It was the first Grand Slam final between siblings in more than a century, the first major women's final televised in prime time and the first Grand Slam singles final between two black players," wrote tennis journalist Ravi Ubha about the historic nature of that first meeting.[3] The 2003 U.S. Open final, which featured future Hall of Famers Justine Henin and Kim Clijsters, dropped 52 percent in the television ratings compared to the epic Williams clash. Growing increasingly aware of her platform, Serena began to lend her name to the movement for equal pay for women in sports.

Her mentor, Billie Jean King, made unequal prize money an issue in 1970. That year, she won the Italia in Rome and made just $600. Ilie Nastase, the men's winner, received $3,500. A bona fide star, King threatened to boycott the 1973 U.S. Open if women did not receive equal pay. The U.S. Open was the first of the Slams to offer equal prize money. The Australian Open, which fluctuated in its pay to men and women, made equal prize money a standard in 2001. The French Open followed suit in 2006, in part because Frenchwoman Amelie Mauresmo topped the rankings.

In 2006, Venus wrote an essay for the *Times* of London that was instrumental in bringing the All England Club on board with the other Slams in offering equal prize money;[4] however, the ratings bonanza the sisters brought to sports broadcasting provided the economic evidence needed to justify equal pay. Finally, Wimbledon, the lone holdout, came around in 2007. That same year, Nike included Serena alongside Mia Hamm, Picabo Street, and volleyball great Gabrielle Reese in a campaign called "Athlete," which addressed inequality among young men and women in sports.[5]

Once Serena reached the status as one of the highest-profile athletes in the country, especially a black one operating in a predominantly white space, she transitioned from advocate to activist. She continued to be an ambassador for UNICEF and promote education; however, she began to take on more controversial issues. By the time she turned 30, Serena stood above Venus and other female athletes in terms of recognition, accolades, and activism.

In 2015, Serena penned an article for a *Wired* magazine edition on equality in the digital age, in which she wrote about why equality is just as important in Silicon Valley as it is on the football field:

> Equality is important. In the NFL, they have something called the Rooney Rule. It says that teams have to interview minority candidates for senior jobs. It's a rule that companies in Silicon Valley are starting to follow too, and that's great. But we need to see more women and people of different colors and nationalities in tech.[6]

Serena also advocated for using social media to support those harassed online. She mentioned J. K. Rowling's support during the body-shaming incident as an example and suggested that people send a picture of a puppy to victims of cyberbullying.

Her advocacy is clear, but her politics remain murky. Not that she is not paying attention. During the 2016 presidential campaign, Serena made it clear that she wouldn't vote for Trump, "or anyone else."[7] The *Washington Post* ran a story with the headline, "Serena Williams May Be Donald Trump's Neighbor, but She Won't Be Voting for Him." Of course, in the story, writer Cindy Boren goes on to point out that Serena is a Jehovah's Witness and won't be voting for anyone.[8]

At a time when sports stars like Colin Kaepernick, LeBron James, and Steph Curry were getting into Twitter wars with the president of the United States, Serena walked a fine line between weighing in and staying out of political debates. Yet, she couldn't ignore injustices that bled into the political realm. Instead of getting into public squabbles with Trump, Serena shed light on incidents.

On September 27, 2016, a month after Diamond Reynolds posted a video of her fiancée, Philando Castile, dying after police shot him during a traffic stop, Serena posted the following letter on her Facebook page:

Today I asked my 18-year-old nephew (to be clear he's black) to drive me to my meetings so I can work on my phone #safetyfirst. In the distance, I saw cop on the side of the road. I quickly checked to see if he was obliging by the speed limit. Then I remembered that horrible video of the woman in the car when a cop shot her boyfriend. All of this went through my mind in a matter of seconds. I even regretted not driving myself. I would never forgive myself if something happened to my nephew. He's so innocent. So were all "the others."

I am a total believer that not "everyone" is bad. It is just the ones that are ignorant, afraid, uneducated, and insensitive that is affecting millions and millions of lives.

Why did I have to think about this in 2016? Have we not gone through enough, opened so many doors, impacted billions of lives? But I realized we must stride on—for it's not how far we have come but how much further still we have to go.

I then wondered have I spoken up? I had to take a look at me. What about my nephews? What if I have a son, and what about my daughters? As Dr. Martin Luther King said, "There comes a time when silence is betrayal."

I

Won't

Be
Silent
Serena

The post went viral, and although she may have wanted to present a personal perspective on what she considered a social justice issue, she was now firmly entrenched in what had become a political debate. Being pro police and against police brutality need not be mutually exclusive; however, with heated rhetoric and boycotts from police unions and community activists, Americans were being asked to pick a side. Serena appeared to be on the Black Lives Matter side. Her friendship and association with Kaepernick did little to dispel that perception.

On July 31, 2017, Serena posted a message on social media that featured a picture of herself, pregnant, wearing a T-shirt with the words "phenomenal woman." Below the picture, she wrote, "Happy Black Women's Equal Pay Day." She coordinated the tweet with an essay she wrote for *Fortune* in which she pointed out the wage gap between black women and white females. She followed that up with interviews in which she addressed how poverty and economic disenfranchisement contribute to hardships for African American women.

"The cycles of poverty, discrimination, and sexism are much, much harder to break than the record for Grand Slam titles," she wrote. "For every black woman that rises through the ranks to a position of power, there are too many others who are still struggling."[9]

After revealing her near-death postpregnancy horror, Serena tweeted and posted about the disparities regarding mortality rates between black women and white women who give birth. The viral comments reinforced print, online, and television coverage of the issue. Doctors and health organizations have studied this issue for years—Serena helped make it a part of the morning news show conversation.

In January 2018, Serena donated $10,000 to help Colin Kaepernick's Los Angeles organization, Imagine L.A., which helps fight homelessness.[10] This was during a time when Kaepernick was suing the NFL for blackballing him because he started a movement in which he would kneel during the playing of the national anthem to bring attention to his stance against police brutality. Serena's decision to side with Kaepernick would reemerge after Nike chose the controversial quarterback to be the face of its campaign celebrating the 30th anniversary of the "Just Do It" slogan.

Nike's Kaepernick ad featured the Afro-wearing activist and the words "Believe in something. Even if it means sacrificing everything." A few days before the release of the ad, Kaepernick and former TV personality and activist Eric Reid cheered on Serena at the U.S. Open. Serena would also have a cameo in the television ad with Kaepernick. Trump supporters and others opposed to Kaepernick's stance on kneeling during the national anthem as a protest and vowed to boycott Nike and burn any gear emblazoned with the brand's signature swoosh.

During a press conference, a reporter asked Serena about the controversy. She told reporters that she stood with Kaepernick, saying, "He's done a lot for the African American community, and it's cost him a lot, and he continues to do the best he can to support."[11]

That same year, Serena skipped the 2018 Australian Open, but she made the news when she called out fellow American tennis player Tennys Sandgren for past racist tweets.[12] Sandgren, the Cinderella story of the 2018 Australian Open, came under fire for hundreds of "alt-right" tweets and likes on his Twitter page. After members of the media confronted him, he responded by saying, "Learning from mistakes was part of maturing." Serena didn't think his response went far enough. She demanded that he apologize and tweeted the following: "I don't need or want one. But there is an entire group of people that deserves an apology. I can't look at my daughter and tell her I sat back and was quiet. No! She will know how to stand up for herself and others—through my example."[13]

She punctuated that tweet with an emoji of a black power fist. Serena later went further and demanded an apology. The most accomplished American tennis player rarely enjoyed the type of knee-jerk patriotism showered on Sandgren, a man who was being exposed as sympathetic to white nationalists. With the power of her celebrity and one Twitter exchange, Serena snuffed out a white man's opportunity to rake in lucrative endorsements. She didn't reveal his troublesome past; however, she tipped the scale by rendering his response unacceptable.

Her activism would come under fire when she erupted at the 2018 U.S. Open. Serena raised the question about how women are perceived when they express anger. She also accused the chair umpire of racism. Serena used her postmatch press conference to blast what she believes is a double standard.

"I've seen other men call other umpires several things," she told reporters.

> I'm here fighting for women's rights and for women's equality, and for all kinds of stuff. For me to say "thief" and for him to take a game, it made me feel like it was a sexist remark. He's never taken a game from a man because they said "thief." For me, it blows my mind. But I'm going to continue to fight for women. [14]

She also complained about France's Alize Cornet receiving a code violation for changing her shirt (while wearing a sports bra) on the court. Men go shirtless on the court all the time without receiving a violation.

Motherhood seemed to fuel Serena's desire to affect change. While still pregnant, she told *Stellar* magazine,

> There are barriers I hope to break so my baby, whether boy or girl, won't have to live under those stipulations. . . . I definitely am a feminist. I like to stick up for women and women's rights. So many things happen and I just think, "Wow, why don't we have a chance? If that makes me a feminist, I am proud to be one." [15]

As tennis writers, political commentators, professional athletes, actors, and fans debated the merits of Serena's accusations of racism and sexism, she pressed on, unapologetic about her response to what she experienced on Ashe. It's the same venue where a chair umpire stole points from her in 2004, versus Jennifer Capriati. It's the place where a questionable foot-fault call ignited her anger and she was penalized a point against Sam Stosur. It was as if Serena was fed up with being toyed with on her home court, in her own country. Moreover, as she told reporters, she had a daughter who would someday look to her as an example.

In a postmatch press conference, reporters asked Serena what she'd tell her daughter about the outburst during the 2018 U.S. Open final. "I'll tell her, first of all, if she sees it, that, you know, I stood up for what I believed in. I stood up for what was right," she responded. "Sometimes things in life don't happen the way we want them but to always stay gracious and stay humble. I think that's the lesson we can all learn from this, just like I did." [16]

Earlier that year, Serena posted on her Facebook page, "Sexual harassment is about power. To combat it, we need more women in leadership, and that means more men stepping up to #MentorHer," in support of the Leaning.org initiative started by Facebook COO Sheryl Sandberg. The program is designed to close the gap between men and women in the boardroom.[17]

Serena continues in her efforts to empower women. Thanks in part to her, professional female tennis players now earn almost as much as their male counterparts. But even though female tennis players receive equal prize money at Grand Slams, they still make less money than men in other competitions. Despite playing fewer matches and winning 16 Grand Slam singles titles and no doubles titles, Novak Djokovic has earned more than $42 million more in career prize money than Serena. During a press conference at the 2019 Australian Open, Serena told reporters that the time had come for equal prize money for women at every event. She also encouraged her male counterparts to get behind the measure, despite rumblings coming from many of them on the subject. She commented, "Like I said the other day, in order for change to really be made, men and women have to work together, they have to have the same message, they have to support each other."[18]

Building schools for girls in Africa and supporting the Purple Purse campaign to fight financial abuse of women, the organization Black Girls Code, and the #MentorHer movement fall under Serena's vision for using education and economic empowerment as solutions to lifting women out of poverty and second-class citizenry.

In March 2018, Venus and Serena joined the advisory board of the Billie Jean King Leadership Initiative, an organization that promotes equality in the workplace.[19] King told a reporter that she is looking to Venus and Serena, as well as others in the younger generation, to continue the work she started, long after can continue the work. Serena also encourages men to join the fight for equal pay. "We need females supporting it and men advocating for it," she told CNBC during a 2018 interview on International Women's Day.[20]

In 2019, the U.S. national women's soccer team filed a lawsuit against the United States Soccer Federation for gender discrimination and violation of the Equal Pay Act and Title VII of the Civil Rights Act. Serena supported the female soccer players in the lawsuit.

"It's a battle. It's a fight. You know, we have had some incredible pioneers in our sport that stood up in the '70s and said, with this dollar, those 13 women said we're going to get paid what the men paid. They stood up way back then," Serena said. "I think at some point, in every sport, you have to have those pioneers, and maybe it's the time for soccer. Like, I'm playing because someone else stood up, and so what they are doing right now is hopefully for the future of women's soccer."[21]

A few months later, U.S. Soccer and the women's national team agreed to go into mediation to resolve the issue.

When she made the cover of *Forbes* magazine's richest self-made women, Serena used that opportunity to post messages about bolstering women through economic empowerment. She's consistent in her insistence that women gain financial freedom. Serena believes that whether trying to flee violence, poverty, or social isolation, women can improve their status through the power of the purse.

She has never had to endure the humiliation of being banished to segregated hotels, like Jackie Robinson. Serena hasn't had to round bases while facing death threats, like Hank Aaron, or face ostracism in the way of that track stars Tommie Smith and John Carlos did after hoisting black power signs at the 1968 Olympics; however, she remains a target of racial and sexist taunts. She's just managed to hit back online. She uses her digital platform to parlay personal insult and inequities into opportunities to alleviate social injustice, both virtually and in reality.

6

INTERNATIONAL FAME AND GLOBAL GIVING

Whether hosting a baby shower for a princess, competing in a dessert-making contest on an Australian cooking show, or addressing schoolgirls in Kenya, Serena is an international icon. Her celebrity is known throughout the world, and her charitable giving knows no borders.

WORLDWIDE CELEBRITY

Before she became a worldwide household name, Serena crossed over into the nonsports spotlight in the United States. In 2001, soon after she won her first Grand Slam, she started popping up in places foreign to most tennis players, for example, on the cover of magazines not related to sports and television dramas. Early on, Serena made her intentions clear: She planned on being more than just a tennis player.

During an interview in 2002, Serena told *Independent* writer Derrick Whyte that she started taking acting lessons in hopes of landing more roles. She joked about her busy tennis schedule conflicting with her desire to land a part in a feature film. "With my time schedule, I'd have to have a small role. . . . I'd like the movie to be all about me, so maybe I can get hurt in the beginning of the movie and I can stay in a coma until the end," she said. [1]

That same year, she played a small part in an episode of the ABC sitcom *My Wife and Kids*, starring Damon Wayans. Serena followed that up with another small part in the short-run Showtime crime drama *Street Time*. She also appeared on *Law & Order: Special Victims Unit*, and, in 2005, had a role in the hit drama *ER*. None of these roles were walk-on appearances in which she played herself, the type of rolls usually handed to professional athletes.

A famous athlete appearing on television and in movies was nothing new. Kareem Abdul-Jabbar was still playing professional basketball when he took a role in the 1978 Bruce Lee movie *Game of Death*. Yet, Serena's pursuits irked some people in the tennis community. Chris Evert even wrote a full-page open letter to Serena in *Tennis Magazine* in 2006, with the following opening paragraph:

> I've been thinking about your career, and something is troubling me. I appreciate that becoming a well-rounded person is important to you, as you've made that desire very clear. Still, a question lingers—do you ever consider your place in history? Is it something you care about? In the short term you may be happy with the various things going on in your life, but I wonder whether 20 years from now you might reflect on your career and regret not putting 100 percent of yourself into tennis. Because whether you want to admit it or not, these distractions are tarnishing your legacy.[2]

Serena ignored Evert and other naysayers, continuing to pursue her passions, regardless of how trivial or "distracting" they appeared to others. By the end of 2006, she had more acting credits than Grand Slam titles.

She seemed to enjoy being a celebrity. The more Grand Slam titles she won, the more her international celebrity grew. Her name was as recognizable in London and Paris as in the United States, where professional tennis takes a backseat to the NFL, NBA, MLB, and NHL, the four most popular sports leagues in the country.[3]

Although the sister act remained a huge draw on the WTA Tour, by 2010, Serena had shed her sidekick status. "Serena," had become its own entity.

In January 2010, Serena met Prince William at the Australian Open. After winning the tournament, she appeared as a guest on *Jimmy Kimmel Live* a few days later. Serena joked that when Prince William said Venus was his favorite, she told him that she preferred Harry. Laughing, Serena also told Kimmel that she did not curtsy to Prince William because she was an American. The nongesture seemed apropos considering Prince William was visiting the Australian Open, where Serena reigned as the queen of tennis and defending champion.

That summer, Queen Elizabeth II made her first visit to Wimbledon in 33 years.[4] Serena was among a handful of players selected to meet and shake hands with the queen. Dressed in an all-white ensemble, Serena curtsied to the queen. Always the perfectionist, she admitted to practicing her curtsy. Prior to meeting the queen, Serena told reporters, "I was going to curtsy today on the court afterward, but I think I flubbed it. So I am definitely going to work on it a little bit more. I'm trying to tone down my wrist action," she told reporters amid much laughter. She later said, "My curtsy is really fun. It's something that she'll [the queen] never forget."[5]

Serena had gained enough star power that other celebrities and professional athletes sought her appearance to bring more attention to their events. When tennis great Justine Henin could not participate in the BNP Paribas Fortis Best of Belgium exhibition, in Brussels, Serena stepped in at the last moment, right after she injured her foot celebrating her win in Wimbledon. The exhibition, a rematch of the 2009 U.S. Open semifinal, drew a record crowd of 35,681, breaking the record held by the "Battle of the Sexes" match between Billie Jean King and Bobby Riggs in 1973, in the Houston Astrodome.[6] Kim Clijsters defeated Serena in front of a world-record crowd. Initially billed as the "Best of Belgium," promoters rebranded the event as "Best of Belgium vs. Best of the World."[7]

Along with a tournament schedule that includes venues in Asia, Europe, North America, and Australia, Serena has participated in tennis exhibitions in Africa, the Caribbean, and South America, places that host few, if any, WTA Tour events. Serena and Venus played in exhibitions in Africa, New York, and Italy. In 2011, Serena and Venus made headlines while playing in an exhibition, the La Grande Sfida, an exhibition in Milan. During a doubles match with Italian stars Flavia Pennetta and Francesca Schiavone, the four players broke into a dance-off to Michael Jackson's "Beat It." Video of the dance went viral.[8]

"Serena! Serena! Serena!" fans yell whenever she competes at home or abroad. She's an unofficial ambassador of women's tennis. Whether it's little boys and girls in Paris or admiring adults in Istanbul, Serena's adoring fans believe in her as much as they do her tennis. Her name needs no translation. Even her nickname, Queen, is universal.

Like James Baldwin and Josephine Baker, black artists who got more love abroad than at home, Serena enjoys as much partisan support in Paris as she does in New York. She appears to feel at home throughout the world. She has owned homes in Paris and often rents the same space for her stays in London. She speaks fluent French and conversational Italian. Serena told *Fader* magazine, "One of the reasons I learned French was I wanted to win the French Open, and I wanted to speak French when I won. The second was because in most African countries, the main language outside of their local language is French or English. So I figured: I know English, maybe I can learn French."[9]

During the 2013 French Open, Serena spoke French in several on-court interviews. When she defeated Maria Sharapova in the final, Serena delivered her trophy ceremony speech in French.

Two weeks later, she suffered a painful three-set fourth-round loss at Wimbledon, ending a 34-match winning streak. Instead of returning home immediately to the United States for the hard-court season, Serena traveled to Bastad, Sweden, to play in the Collector Swedish Open, a lower-level clay-court tournament held after the clay-court season. It was her first trip to the seaside resort town, which she had heard was "like Cannes, but in Sweden." She said, "I definitely need to experience that."[10]

Upon her arrival, Swedish fans filled the streets of Bastad to greet Serena. The tournament's official YouTube channel posted a MTV-style video of Serena's grand entrance. The video featured Lady Gaga's "Paparazzi" as background music, as cameras followed Serena from her landing in a private jet to the tournament venue. Fans waved American flags and shouted, "We love you," as Serena made her way through the crowd. It was a rock star's welcome.

According to tennis writer Peter Bodo, tournament officials paid Serena a hefty appearance fee to show up for a tournament that featured no other top 20 players. "One of the main underlying themes for Williams these days has been to wring all the success and fun possible out of her career now that she's turned the corner into the home stretch," wrote Bodo. "So why not go to a nice, low-key event by a beach in a nation you never visited before and get in a little practice for the hard-court season in the U.S.?"[11]

It also gave fans a chance to see Serena up close. In 2014, Serena was among a handful of headliners paid as much as $1 million per match to play in the inaugural International Premier Tennis League (IPTL), a post-season team-tennis competition. The IPTL plays in Mumbai, New Delhi, Bangkok, and Manila, major cities without WTA Premier events.[12] Serena represented the Singapore Slammers the first season, which began in November 2014, and played her first match in Manila in front of screaming, adoring fans. The following IPTL season, Serena played for the Manila Mavericks.[13]

Serena enjoys worldwide notoriety partially because of tennis' international tentacles. International travel is mandatory for professional tennis players. The sport has expanded its global reach, with as many tournaments in China as in the United States. No longer a mainly European and North American sport, tennis' biggest matches outside of the Grand Slams are played in Madrid, Beijing, Doha, Dubai, Tokyo, and Wuhan, China. The WTA's year-end championship tournament has been held in Singapore and Istanbul.

Although the WTA's corporate headquarters are in St. Petersburg, Florida, it has a European headquarters in London, an Asia-Pacific office in Beijing, and a finals headquarters in Singapore.

With American football, the NBA, and even mixed martial arts eating up so much of the air time of sports coverage in the United States, it is easy to lose perspective on Serena's global reach. Serena is one of the biggest stars in a sport watched by more than 500 million people globally. According to a study conducted by SMG Insight, the WTA's global audience grew by 22.5 percent in 2015. That year, the WTA's magazine reached more than 530 million people.[14]

The New England Patriots' Tom Brady is arguably the best quarterback in the history of the NFL. The NFL is the most popular professional sports league in the United States and hosts the country's most-watched television event, the Super Bowl. Brady, however, came in at number 38 on ESPN's World Fame 100, which ranks athletes based on their worldwide popularity. Serena was number 12 and the top-ranked female.[15] According to ESPNW, Serena is the most recognizable sportswoman in the world.

Already known worldwide, Serena found herself at the center of one of the biggest international events of 2018, the wedding of Prince Harry to Meghan Markle. The wedding made history because the bride was American and biracial. Serena had entered into an interracial marriage less than a year before this royal wedding, reflecting her openness to different cultures and communities.

In the British tabloids, Serena was another one of Meghan's celebrity friends; however, Meghan and Serena are more than that—they are confidants. The two met in 2010, at a Super Bowl party in Miami. They became fast friends, texting and chatting often.

Still a newlywed herself, Serena walked in on the arm of her handsome husband, Alexis Ohanian. She sat near George and Amal Clooney, and across from the immediate members of the royal family. Serena scored an invite to the wedding and the exclusive private reception hosted by Prince Charles later that evening. Viewers in the United States needed commentators to point out who some of the guests were, especially British elites unfamiliar to American commoners. Serena needed no explanation. She's known throughout the world. Serena got a seat at the table with the House of Windsor, while seeking respect in her own country.

Although she is the among the most decorated American tennis players in Olympic history, Serena is one of the few active tennis icons never to have been the flag-bearer for her country. Such tennis greats as Rafael Nadal, Maria Sharapova, Caroline Wozniacki, and Roger Federer have been flag-bearers for their countries during the opening ceremonies at the Olympics.

Later that year, the Duchess of Sussex took a seat in the royal box, along with Kate Middleton, the Duchess of Cambridge, to watch the women's final at Wimbledon. Although Serena lost to Angelique Kerber, she won over a few hearts when she gave her runner-up speech. Through tears, Serena told the Centre Court crowd, "For all the moms out there, I was playing for you today." After her speech, Wimbledon's twitter account posted a video of Serena's comments with the caption, "Grace, poise, and emotion. A runner-up's interview given by a true champion."[16]

GLOBAL GIVER

Tennis opened the door to a world of possibilities, and Serena has used her international fame to become a global giver. After her sister's murder in 2003, and during a time of self-reflection, Serena stepped up her philanthropic game. Richard preached how important it was to never forget where you came from. He exposed his daughters to the less fortunate to keep them from slipping into "country club" complacency. Serena has never forgotten.

She made her first trip to Africa in November 2006, when she, her mom, Isha, and Lyn went to Ghana and Senegal. Serena said the trip helped her cope with the death of her sister. Almost three years had passed, and Serena still found it challenging to process Yetunde's murder. So she took time off from the tour to do some soul searching. "Africa lifted me from the doldrums and set me back down a positive path because since that trip I've been playing the best tennis of my career," Serena reflected. [17]

Cora Masters Barry, a close friend of Oracene's and founder of the Southeast Tennis and Learning Center in Washington, D.C., remembered accompanying the family on a trip to the slave castles in Senegal and seeing a side of Serena she believes gets ignored by the media. As they were touring the slave castles, Barry noticed Serena had some literature about the Jehovah's Witnesses. Before leaving, Serena went back into the slave castles one more time.

"Why are you going back in there, you just came out?" Barry asked. "Oh Ms. Barry," she said, "I want to take this [literature] inside, and maybe some other people can read it and benefit from it." Said Barry, "I thought that was the Serena a lot of people don't know, kind of gentle and interested and concerned about other people. I just thought that she showed a tremendous amount of sensitivity and compassion throughout the entire trip we traveled in Africa."

Barry said Serena and Venus have always been generous. "They are philanthropic and caring in terms of what they give back. They are good role models for that kind of a thing," she said. [18]

While visiting Ghana in 2006, Williams participated in a UNICEF health campaign that promoted immunizing children against deadly childhood diseases. Serena also worked with UNICEF volunteers to distribute free mosquito bed nets to help prevent malaria. [19]

In 2008, Serena returned to Africa. Instead of seeking solace, this time she was there to help. "For this trip, I was in a completely different frame of mind: I was going to give something back, not take something away," she wrote in her book *On the Line*. [20]

As guest editor for *Wired* magazine in October 2015, Serena wrote that she first put her plans to do charity work in Africa in a matchbook quote she wrote to herself during the 2008 U.S. Open. She wrote, "I will work in Africa and help kids and help people."[21]

On a trip to Africa that included looking at sites to open a possible school, Oracene told the *Daily Nation*, a newspaper in Kenya, "Serena loves anything education. . . . She hopes to help as many children go to school as she can."[22]

Serena focused on educating girls. "Now, sometimes in Africa, they send only the boys to school. So we had a strict rule that our schools had to be at least 40 percent of girls. It was impossible to get 50–50 boys to girls, and we really had to fight for 60–40. But we got it," she wrote in *Wired*.[23]

With the help of Hewlett-Packard and the nongovernmental organization Build African Schools, Serena opened the Serena Williams Secondary School in Matooni, Makueni, Kenya.[24] She was in Africa when she watched CNN declare Senator Barrack Obama the president-elect. She said she cried, a world away. On that same trip, Serena met Nelson Mandela, a hero of hers. She also contributed to the Schools for Africa program, started by Mandela.

The charities nearest to Serena's heart are those that address equity in access to education, economic empowerment, and antiviolence. She's part of a trend that has prominent young African Americans flexing their philanthropic muscle. LeBron James opened a school, and Chance the Rapper funded Chicago Public Schools. Hip hop artist Nicki Minaj paid tuition for black college students. The website Inside Philanthropy pointed out how Serena's past informs her philanthropy:

> Like her on-court persona, Serena is serving up strong philanthropic efforts (through her Serena Williams Fund, or "SWF") to address persistent problems like gun violence, educational inequity, and poverty, that have personally impacted her family. When it comes to gun violence, Williams has not been shy about her support for the Black Lives Matter movement and its push to stem the tide of police brutality against black Americans. She has also invested in the work of the Caliber Foundation, in support of families and victims affected by gun violence.[25]

In 2011, Serena became a UNICEF goodwill ambassador, with a focus on education.[26] A press release issued by UNICEF executive director Anthony Lake said Serena committed more than her name to the cause.

"We want not only their names, but their hearts, and talking with Serena a few months ago I was just so impressed by how big her heart is, and how devoted she is to the cause of children," Lake said.[27]

"This cause means a lot to me because I really want to be able to have an opportunity to help UNICEF make the world aware of challenges that children face," said Serena.[28]

In 2014, she held the first annual Serena Williams Ultimate RUN 5K through the South Beach section of Miami. The run supports charities to fight antiviolence.[29] The following year, Serena was among a host of celebrities who helped to promote UNICEF's World's Lesson campaign to educate children on sustainability efforts.[30] She was part of the 1 in 11 outreach project, designed to fund pilot programs to help educate marginalized children in Bangladesh, Indonesia, and Nepal. According to UNICEF, globally, 1 in 11 school-aged children are deprived of a quality education.[31]

In a statement issued by UNICEF in January 2015, Serena stated,

> In many countries we take it for granted that every child has the right to receive a quality education, but "1 in 11" children around the world do not enjoy that right—and without it, may never reach their full potential. . . . We need to kick-start global progress and get that number down to zero, so every child has the chance to learn.[32]

In 2017, Serena joined forces with All State Foundation Purple Purse, a program aimed at curbing domestic violence through economic empowerment of women facing financial abuse. The program provides funding to nonprofits that help victims of financial abuse escape the cycle of violence. "With social media, everyone has an opportunity to tell a story and make an impact," Serena said.

> I am proud to use my voice and influence to bring more awareness to financial abuse so people can get involved and make a positive change in their communities. As the public becomes more comfortable talking about domestic violence and financial abuse, it will also become easier to spot the signs, help a victim, or stand up to an abuser.[33]

Serena posted a purple purse she designed to her social media accounts and asked followers to donate to be entered in a chance to win the bag. She also appeared in a public service ad in which she described financial abuse as an "invisible weapon," used to hold women hostage in violent relationships.

Serena models world citizenship to her daughter. In Snapchat videos, you can hear Serena speaking to Olympia in French and sometimes in Spanish. Moreover, Olympia has inspired her mom to find new ways to contribute to society. Serena took designer clothing that belonged to Olympia and put it on an online retail resale account. Proceeds from the sale of the garments were donated to the Williams Sister Fund, which Serena set up with her sister Venus in 2016, to help fund the Yetunde Price Resource Center in Compton. [34]

Named in honor of her slain sister, the Yetunde Price Resource Center helps those affected by violence through emotional, mental, and financial support. The center opened in late 2017. Serena, along with Venus, took part in an event called "A Family Affair" at the Southeast Tennis and Learning Center's Williams Arena to raise funds for the resource center. Aside from playing tennis with inner-city kids, Serena spoke candidly about the impact her sister's murder had on her family and why it was so important to offer youth an emotional and psychological oasis from crime and poverty. One of the services the center offers is creative therapy.

"It's a way to express yourself, and to get whether it's anger or frustration or emotion out," Serena said.

> Even though I play tennis, I still have this creative outlet . . . in design to kind of put myself out there or just get all these emotions out on the court. And there's a lot of times where people are in the communities and they don't have a place or an area or somewhere they can go to put that energy—to get some of that negative energy out and be creative. [35]

Her transition into motherhood and marriage has allowed Serena to expand her celebrity and philanthropic causes championed by her husband, Alexis Ohanian, a tech entrepreneur and founder of Reddit. In February 2018, Ohanian and Williams rented out a movie theater to hold a private screening of the movie *Black Panther* for participants in Black Girls Code, a nonprofit organization with a mission to "increase the number of women of color in the digital technology space by the year 2040, by introducing girls ages seven to 17 to computer science." [36]

The girls attending the screening were unaware that they'd be watching the movie with Serena and her husband. When Serena walked into the darkened theater, the girls jumped up and down, screeched, and squealed as if Beyoncé had just taken the stage and they had front row seats.

7

FASHION FORWARD

Serena arrived on the tennis scene in the late 1990s with hair in beads and teeth in braces. Although many white commentators thought the beads edgy, in black communities beaded hair was a bit outdated, especially for anyone older than 12. The look, popularized by the female lead in the late 1970s R&B duo Peaches and Herb, crossed color lines in 1979, when white actress Bo Derek wore beads on her braids in the movie *10*. By the 1990s, short bobs and pixie cuts worn by Halle Berry, Toni Braxton, and Anita Baker dominated African American fashion magazines. So when Serena and Venus showed up with their hair full of white beads, the style was as perplexing to as many blacks as it was whites. To black women, the look was as outdated as Richard Williams's "Johnny Mac" short shorts.

Still, among professional tennis players, Serena and Venus looked different. Their braids, their skin, their style stood out. The braids represented an Americanized idea of Afrocentricity. An oddity on tour, those braids proved to be more than a fashion statement. They became a lightning rod, a symbol of the sisters' "otherness," and an easy target.

The beads made "click-clack" sounds as they played. During a match against Lindsay Davenport, Venus's beads fell from her hair and hit the court. The chair umpire ruled it a hindrance—an on-court violation if a player intentionally or unintentionally interferes with the opponent's ability to play the point. Chair umpires can order players to replay the point or award the point to the opponent. In this case, the umpire awarded Davenport the point. Venus, fuming about unfairness, became unglued and lost the match. Serena and Venus would soon shed the beads and opt for microbraids—long, thread-thin braids.

"I've always loved fashion. . . . I remember when I was a kid, my mom used to make all our outfits," Serena said in an interview with *Business of Fashion* magazine writer Imran Amed. "Back then, they had *Vogue* patterns. I would always see her pinning them and making all our clothes. And she taught us how to sew early on. So, I used to sew clothes for my dolls out of old socks, and I would cut them up and make little outfits out of them."[1]

Serena's first serious foray into the fashion industry began in 1998, when she signed a $12 million endorsement contract with German sneaker maker Puma. At the time, Puma was taking a chance on a player who had yet to crack the top 100 or win a WTA title. The collaboration with Puma would produce some of Serena's most memorable outfits and catapult her from fresh-faced teen to fashionista. Although short-lived, the Puma years helped Serena transition from ghetto princess to "glam slammer."

When Serena won the 1999 U.S. Open, she wore a basic yellow and white Puma dress. She was only 17 and still wore beads. Her earliest Puma outfits were bland and looked like any other tennis dresses. But after she turned 18, her kits became a bit more daring, like the tie-dyed lavender and purple skirt she wore in 2000, at the Summer Olympics and the U.S. Open.

However, it was in about 2002, the year Serena turned 21, that her on-court attire took a turn for the fierce. At the 2002 French Open, Serena wore a metallic pewter-colored dress with yellow trim. It looked more like something a 21-year-old might wear to a nightclub. Still, that outfit would soon be forgotten.

The 2002 U.S. Open marked the first time Serena entered a Grand Slam ranked number one. She had three Grand Slams titles under her belt and was establishing herself as a dominant force on the WTA Tour. She was also capitalizing on her growing fame at a time when reality television was creating overnight sensations. That year, *American Idol* debuted in the United States. While Kelly Clarkson sang her way to superstardom, Serena slayed her way into tennis and fashion history.

It was at the 2002 U.S. Open that Serena wore the "catsuit," a black faux-leather jumpsuit that hugged every curve on her body. Along with her blond braids in a ponytail, Serena's look was perfect for the New York nights at Flushing Meadows.

Puma allowed Serena to have substantial input into her designs. This included the infamous catsuit. "What most people didn't realize was it was so comfortable!" Serena wrote in *On the Line*. "Of course, that catsuit was so hot I would have worn it even if it was the most uncomfortable thing in the world, but it was designed with performance in mind."[2]

Outrageous but stylish, the catsuit remains one of the most-talked-about kits in tennis history. A replica of the catsuit was even on display at the Museum of Applied Arts and Sciences exhibit in 2003.[3]

Off the court, like many women in their early 20s, Serena wore edgy, racy, and fun outfits. She seemed to be embracing her role as a celebrity when she rocked the red carpet at the 2003 ESPN ESPYs wearing a severely low-cut, light magenta gown with a leg's-length slit up the front.

The Puma years expired in 2003, when Serena signed a reported $55 million deal with Nike. After she signed with Nike, she became a backhand swinging, walking billboard for sportswear. During Grand Slams, when Serena shed her warm-up jacket to reveal her latest look, it was like a New York fashion week preview.

Meanwhile, she capitalized on her newfound status as a fashionista. In 2003, she launched a clothing line called Aneres, Serena spelled backward. It was her first attempt at a career in fashion design. Serena premiered her Aneres clothing collection in December 2004. Despite publicity, the line flopped. Said Serena,

> Everyone that goes to fashion school wants to do eveningwear. . . . I stuck with that for years and years, and I loved it. But I was doing evening gowns, and we never actually sold anything—nothing that people could really actually buy in store. . . . So many times I would be at a meeting with Macy's or lots of other companies, and they would be like, "We love it. We love the presentation, but we're not going to get this collection." I've sat through so many of those meetings, more than I can count to be honest. And they're demoralizing.[4]

So, it was back to focusing on tennis and collaborating with Nike to express her fashion fixation. Topping the catsuit would not be easy, but Serena came close with a provocative urban cowgirl kit she wore at the 2004 U.S. Open. With studded details and footwear that looked like biker boots, that outfit is second only to the catsuit in terms of outrageousness.

Her style gained as much attention as her play, and sometimes the publicity was not all good. Some in the tennis world viewed her fashion pursuits as flighty, an unnecessary distraction. They saw her abundance in talent and athletic gifts as attributes that tethered her to tennis. Industry experts pressured Serena to pick one, fashion or tennis.

None of this mattered to Serena. She pursued her fashion passions both on and off the court despite the critics. When Serena wanted to showcase a new Nike outfit she helped design for her run at the 2005 Australian Open, some journalists were less than kind. Leading up to the tournament, the *Telegraph*'s Mark Hodgkinson blasted Serena for her "poor taste." He wrote,

> With a fashion show at a hotel in St Kilda, an edgy part of town that distrusts the mainstream, Williams showed off her lime-green-and-white Nike boots with her usual theatricality, ignoring the disparaging comments from the list's author that she has moved "from queen of tennis to female fashion menace." However, it is increasingly difficult to know where her priorities lie. As a tennis player? As a fashionista? [5]

Hodgkinson went on to hint that Serena's desire for a future in fashion could mean that 2005 would be the last year fans saw Serena in a tennis skirt. He even mocked Serena for being ranked number five on a worst-dressed list, one spot higher than her WTA ranking.

Hodgkinson's story ran under the headline, "Serena: From Queen of Tennis to Fashion Menace." Coincidently, the year Hodgkinson wrote the story criticizing Serena's fashion sense, she went on to win the Australian Open while wearing her lime-green boots. Serena continued to ignore critics. She appeared to relish her role as fashion ambassador. Similar to her aggressive nature on the court, she took risks and bucked the status quo. "She wears what she wears and embraces her body," said Dr. Delia Douglas. "With respect to her embodiment and comfort, she's like, 'I'm a black woman and this is what I look like. This is the body I have, and I'm living the life.'" [6]

Indeed, Serena wears what she likes when she wants to wear it. One notable example is the $40,000 pair of earrings with 13 carats worth of diamonds she wore to the 2005 U.S. Open. [7]

She said the following to *People* magazine about her fashion philosophy: "You need to have your staples, your classics. Something you can pick and have in your closet for two years and still wear it and still be really nice. And then have fun with a trend. Pair it up. So that way if you have great leggings you can still wear your staple."[8] Meanwhile, her partnership with Nike flourished. Between 2008 and 2011, she went through a formal jacket and cardigan phase for warm-ups. One of the more memorable ones was for Wimbledon in 2008. The dress was quite traditional, with a pleated skirt; however, the warm-up jacket was a white trench coat with belts, big buttons, and embellishments you would find on London Fog outerwear.

During the cardigan years, Serena revamped her fashion business. She no longer promoted the brand Aneres. Instead, she sold a private label Serena Collection through the Home Shopping Network (HSN). To help promote the affordable clothing, Serena made appearances on HSN and would even converse with fans who called in as excited to speak to her as they were to purchase the clothing.

One of Serena's earlier fashion influences was famed wedding dress designer Vera Wang. "Somewhere along the way, I developed this obsession with Vera Wang," she said. "I started to think if things didn't work out for me in tennis, I could always design."[9] She does, however, credit her father with offering the best advice on surviving the volatile world of fashion design. "Serena, you don't drown by falling into the water. You drown by letting yourself stay there," he told her.[10]

Serena believes that cloths can make a difference in the way she plays. In her autobiography, she devoted a chapter to "Fashion Statements," writing,

> I like to look my best on the court. I believe it's important. It goes to self-esteem. . . . I'm an athlete; I'm meant to draw strength from the weight room, from my iron will, from sheer force of my game; however, here I am, fussing over how I look, thinking that this, too, will make a difference.[11]

By 2012, Serena's look had matured from racy to regal. Between 2012 and 2017, Serena adopted an A-line-style dress that fell just below the hips. With a form-fitting, high-waist bodice, Serena's Nike Court outfits during this time looked similar to something drawn for video-game vixens. These were the warrior princess years. Serena wore black or red frizzy hair in a long ponytail with a headband. She looked like a superhero. Cartoonists often draw female superheroes with curvaceous hourglass figures, muscular arms, and a small waist that are a bit disproportionate to their larger hips and chest. These mythical, otherworldly women look quite like Serena.

Even her off-court attire looked statelier than that of other players. The elegant gold dress she wore at the 2012 Wimbledon Champions ball stood in stark contrast to the spaghetti-strapped, lingerie-like number she wore to that event in 2009.

As she accumulated titles and Grand Slams, Nike started creating more of a signature look for Serena, complete with fancy warm-up jackets and customized shoes with her name on them. She joined Roger Federer, Rafael Nadal, and Maria Sharapova as the ruling class in Nike Court's stable of tennis stars. Before the 2013 French Open, Nike held a "Kings of Lights" exhibition, in which the four stars played with the lights off, showcasing their outfits, which glowed in the dark.

The queen in Nike's royal court, Serena turned Grand Slams into fashion weeks. Fans anticipated her outfits almost as much as her play. Practice was just a preview, where Serena would wear Nike workout ensembles available to the public. Then on match days, the main events, came the big reveal, the moment after warm-ups when Serena would shed her jacket or sweater to show off her latest outfit. At the Australian and U.S. Opens, Grand Slams with late-night matches, Serena always had an evening version of her tournament kits.

What better way for Nike to sell its fashions than to have such a dominant player as a spokesmodel? Serena's movement, a blend of elegance and energy, brought life to her attire. After her wins, she worked the crowd with a wave, a twirl, and, finally, a pose. The more she won, the more exposure for Nike. Trophy ceremonies put her outfits onstage, with many photographers as focused on her as they would be any supermodel working a runway.

Renowned photographer Anita Aguilar told *Tennis* magazine's Steve Tignor that Serena was one of her favorite players to photograph. "Her intensity makes her constantly interesting," she said.

> She's really alive as a subject. Between points she walks with this kind of slow drag, but the second the point starts, she's fully alive. Even though she doesn't have perfect posture, she holds her head in a regal way. I like to get up close with her; you can really see the effort in her eyes. Moreover, I love the way she can fill the frame with her movement when she's in action. [12]

Serena's 2013 Wimbledon and U.S. Open dresses looked like something straight out of Wonder Woman with the V-neck bodice and flattering skirt.

In 2013, Marija Zivlak, editor of the Women's Tennis Blog, ran a story showcasing every outfit Serena wore during her record-breaking year. This included the tricolored color-blocking dress she wore when she came from behind to defeat Maria Sharapova at the Miami Open. Her 2013 French Open dress had a Greek goodness look.[13]

Serena is a fan favorite on the WTA's website and Facebook pages. She is often in the running for best dressed of the year. Serena is more than a spokesperson for Nike. In part of a statement that appeared in *Footwear News*, Serena mentioned her unique relationship with Nike. "I love my relationship with the [Nike] designers. . . . It isn't just, 'When I see you.' It's more like, 'Let's have a collaboration, 365 days a year.'"[14]

During the 2014 U.S. Open, Serena decided to go with an A-line with leopard print. The daytime pink print was such a hit that several fans wore it to Serena's matches.[15] She looked like a stylish Jane of the Jungle. She was wearing black leopard print when she tied Chris Evert and Martina Navratilova with 18 Grand Slam wins.

With her name linked to the greatest tennis players of all time, Serena's celebrity rose to a new level, and her choices both on and off the court gained even greater attention. At the 2015 Australian Open, she played in a neon yellow dress that exposed most of her back; however, for the most part, the dresses looked tame compared to some of the bare-midriff kits she sported in her early 20s.

During the 2015 season, Serena provided dresses from her HSN line to members of the Fed Cup team. Players wore Serena's HSN merchandise during the pretournament party held at each rubber. It was another way Serena managed to promote her fashion. "It's nice to combine my love for fashion with my love for tennis," Williams told Jacqueline Tsang in a 2015 edition of the *South China Morning Post*.[16]

Serena's 2015 Wimbledon dress was a near-replica of the Australian Open and French Open kits, which featured eye-catching geometric cut-outs at the waist. It seemed fitting to keep the same look while she chased a calendar-year Slam.

During the 2015 U.S. Open, Serena wore a red and black snake print dress for her night matches. It was one of edgiest outfits since her Puma years. Following her failed attempt to win a calendar-year Slam, a heartbroken Serena found solace in friends and the runway at Fashion Week in New York. Sitting front and center at Serena's fashion show was none other than *Vogue* editor in chief Anna Wintour, a fashion icon and one of Serena's biggest fans.

Reportedly the inspiration for the main character in the *Devil Wears Prada*, Wintour invites Serena to all the biggest see-and-be-seen parties and fashion shows. They sit next to one another near the runway, chatting like gal pals, despite their age difference of 30-plus years. [17]

Wintour was there to lend support to Serena by bringing out the fashion elite to see the tennis star show off her designs, in the same manner as such big names as Tommy Hilfiger, Dolce & Gabbana, and Ralph Lauren. After models pranced up and down the runway wearing Serena's designs, she came out to take a designer's bow. Flanked by friends, the runway was a place where Serena could be applauded and celebrated despite having just suffered one of the most crushing defeats of her career.

Serena's 2016 season began with her still trying to tie Steffi Graf's record of 22 Grand Slams. She opened the season with a two-piece yellow kit featuring a crop top that exposed much of her belly. Serena designed the outfit herself and told reporters that she wanted to pair the crop top with a classic skirt. "Hideous," is what an Australian Open fan reportedly called it. [18] She also ditched the long warrior princess ponytail for a short, sleek bob. She wore the same look at the French Open but in bright blue. She lost in the finals in both tournaments.

By Wimbledon 2016, Serena had gone back to her warrior princess look. She returned to her winning long ponytail and A-line dress. Her Wimbledon kit served as a testament to how Serena's fashion choices had evolved throughout the years. Among her more elegant offerings were the 2016 Wimbledon dress she wore when she clinched her record-tying 22nd Grand Slam title. The fluttery ruffled skirt, combined with a sporty fitted top, made her look majestic, like a queen of the court.

The dress was a hit but did cause some controversy after news outlets made a big stink about Serena's nipples. The British-based tabloid the *Sun* quoted one anonymous source as saying, "Producers have absolutely no say in what the players wear, which has made it difficult for them to avoid eye-popping shots on daytime telly." [19] Fans shot back, noting that Serena was wearing a bra and that she shouldn't be body shamed because some people were uncomfortable with two tiny body parts. [20]

At this point, Serena had eclipsed Billie Jean King, Martina Navratilova, and Chirs Evert in Grand Slams. She was on her way to tying Steffi Graf. Now an elder statesman of the sport, Serena appeared to be embracing her role as senior ambassador. Her fashion choices reflected that. She went for more tailored, stately dresses. Even the two-piece, abs-exposing ensembles she wore during the early part of 2016 featured longer, fuller skirts that covered her hips.

After matching Graf in most Slams won in the Open Era, Serena was now known as the greatest of all time. So it seemed natural that she'd dress like a real-life superhero. Her 2016 U.S. Open outfit ushered in a more tailored superheroine kit, complete with arms-length compression sleeves.

In 2017, *Sports Illustrated* released its "Fashionable 50," a list of the best-dressed athletes.[21] Serena came in at number three topping all tennis players, notably Federer, who came in at number four. In describing Serena's style, *InStyle* magazine's executive editor, Faye Penn, told *Sports Illustrated*, "Strong isn't just sexy, it's incredibly chic in Serena Williams's case. Power is her style statement, and everything flows from that."[22]

At the 2017 Australian Open, Serena's last match before giving birth to her daughter and getting married, Serena wore another A-line dress with her compression sleeves. She had tied Graf's record and seemed to be easing into a more mature, still stylish look.

"I miss the days when Serena's outfits were more outrageous, the beaded hair, denim ensemble, go-go boots, and tuxedo warm-up jacket," said Karin Burgess, editor of *Tennis Identity*, a tennis gear and fashion blog.[23]

A few months later, Serena announced her pregnancy via social media while sporting a yellow bathing suit, showing off an emerging baby bump. Pregnancy would not slow Serena down. She and fiancée Alexis Ohanian showed up at the 2017 Met Gala, with Serena looking aglow in an emerald gown with a plunging neckline.

At her 1950s-themed baby shower, Serena dressed in a poodle skirt and ankle socks, and posed next to a jukebox at a diner in West Palm Beach. Celebrity guests Eva Longoria, Ciara, and Kelly Rowland also dressed up, which made for fashionable photos on Instagram.

In early 2018, Serena launched another clothing line that featured a new S logo, which she rolled out during her return to Indian Wells. More upscale and pricier than her collaboration with the HSN, the new line is all Serena's. She's not collaborating or lending her name to someone else's venture. She owns it all. The look? Upscale casual with a hint of sexy. *Elle* called it a "win" for the iconic athlete-turned-fashion-designer.

Serena told *WWD* magazine that although she learned a great deal from her collaborations with HSN and Nike, those companies limited her creative control. With the new line, she has complete artistic freedom. "This is what I studied. So I was like, 'I really want to be able to start doing what I want, how I want it, and letting people see my vision in fashion, how I want it to be seen,'" she said.[24]

Vogue magazine's Steff Yotka noted Serena's input on these designs. "It's Williams's own fierce effortlessness that differentiates this collection from other celebrity-backed fashion lines. You can feel her hand in a varsity knit with the letter W emblazoned on the chest, just the right mix of sporty and curve-hugging sexy," Yotka wrote.[25]

Serena told Yotka,

> I got so tired of seeing only stretch jeans. . . . I wanted to bring structure back to jeans. You know, you don't see jeans that have structure that can fit skinny girls or curvy girls, but these do. They fit me so well, and, yes, they have a little give to them, so you can obviously get into them, but it brings it back to that classic jeans shape from the '80s.[26]

With Anna Wintour being a constant presence in Serena's players' box, a bad review was unlikely. Yet, Serena went all-in on this fashion endeavor. Instead of recreating a new web presence for her design, Serena transformed SerenaWilliams.com into her virtual fashion boutique. That domain name once pointed to pages about the athlete's upcoming tournaments, recent wins, and fun stories about her dog Chip. Now it was all about the new collection.

After the birth of her daughter, Serena carried a few extra pounds onto the court. The weight gain hindered her movement. She lost three matches in her return in 2018. She only lost four matches in all of 2013, the year she had her best record.

That did not stop her from grabbing headlines with a head-to-toe catsuit. She said the look was for all the moms—she even wore a safety pin in one ear. The suit was controversial for more than the way it accentuated Serena's bold curves. Some players wondered if the suit violated

WTA rules. Serena's first-round opponent at the French Open questioned if it was legal. Another player pointed out that she had been told she had to wear a skirt or shorts over leggings. Serena said the leggings were for health reasons, to help prevent blood clots.

French Open officials remained silent on the subject, and Serena wore the catsuit in three singles and three doubles matches. As if she were that wild and crazy 20-something woman, Serena basked in the buzz about her catsuit. Still, her fashion mishits seemed to be a thing of the past.

"They were just show pieces for what I call the court-walk style only Serena could get away with," Burgess said. "All were fashions that fit her age at the time as well as her awareness of her status as an athlete. Those kinds of looks went away as Serena matured and Nike pushed styles that recreational players could buy at retail."

In her first postpregnancy red carpet appearance, Serena wore a black Versace mini dress with gold embellishments on the sleeves and hemline to *Glamour* magazine's Women of Year Awards event in Brooklyn.

She often sports red on the red carpet, as she has worn to several *Vanity Fair* parties. At the Wimbledon Champions Ball, she has worn everything from a trendy black gown to a flowing gold dress with a train.

Serena has been on the cover of numerous sports magazines but also on the covers of *Vogue, Glamour, Essence, Shape, Self*, and *Vanity Fair*. Black women rarely grace the cover of these magazines. Black female athletes on the cover of *Vogue* and *Glamour* multiple times? Unheard-of.

Serena's fashion choices pushed tennis out of the sleepy country club world it had been steeped in. Even Serena's November 2017 wedding turned into a fashion event and wound up on the covers of *Vogue* and *Brides* magazines, as well as on several fashion and entertainment websites. Her wedding featured several looks, including two different reception dresses by Versace. Michelle Meneses needed 24 hours to bedazzle a pair of Nike sneakers with Swarovski crystals for Serena's wedding reception. Serena wore the sneakers during an after party that featured R&B group New Edition.[27] Photos of the sneakers wound up on *Vogue*, Yahoo!, *Women's Health*, People.com, and other news outlets. Meneses, an aspiring designer, received the publicity and thanked Serena for the honor of designing her shoes.

Serena told the British newspaper the *Telegraph*, "Fashion is hard; harder than tennis. . . . In tennis I make my own destiny, but in fashion, you have to rely on so many other people. You can't give up, even more so than in sport. I am still fighting to make the right choices . . . one step at a time."[28]

When it comes to marketing fashions, Serena is the Oprah of sports. If she's wearing it, it gets publicity and people buy it. During her 2018 Wimbledon comeback, her special edition "S" shirt sold out. Women who purchased it sent photos of themselves modeling the shirt, and Serena would post them on her Instagram and Twitter accounts.

When Serena took to the court at Wimbledon that year, she wore hosiery. While providing commentary for ESPN, Martina Navratilova seemed fixated on Serena's stockings. She could not stop talking about it. Serena said they were for circulation. No matter what Serena wears, she always makes a fashion statement.

Serena's 2018 U.S. Open tutu dress will forever be associated with her on-court tirade; however, even in the face of adversity and controversy, she wore just the right outfit to make a fashion statement. Usually, U.S. Open previews about Serena run in the sports pages. Yet, VanityFair.com gave fans a sneak peek at Serena's kit. The article focused on the collaboration with Louis Vuitton designer Virgil Abloh, a former creative director for Kanye West. The dress featured one long sleeve and a one-shoulder bodice with a tulle skirt. The nighttime kit was black, and the daytime came in baby blue.

In describing Serena's dress, Abloh told *Vanity Fair*,

> The dress is feminine but combines her aggression. It's partially revealing. It's asymmetrical. It has a sort of ballerina-esque silhouette to symbolize her grace. It's not about bells and whistles and tricks. It's just about it living on the body and expressing Serena's spirit with each swing of the racket.[29]

Serena's showdown with chair umpire Carlos Ramos sparked debate about the double standards women face when they express anger or outrage. How apropos that news accounts throughout the world featured a photograph of Serena wearing a ballerina-inspired dress, the essence of femininity, while pointing her finger at a man, demanding an apology.

While others continued to argue the merits of Serena's case, Serena was busy releasing new items for her fashion line. In October 2018, a long, plaid blazer she designed sold out when her pal Meghan, the Duchess of Sussex, wore it during a visit to Australia.[30]

At the 2019 Australian Open, her first Slam after the controversial U.S. Open, Serena chose to wear a metallic green shorts jumper. She had put 2018 behind her and marched fashion forward.

After the 2019 Australian Open, online fashion retailer Poshmark named Serena to its board of directors. Poshmark's CEO, Manish Chandra, told CNBC the company brought Serena on board because of her fashion sense instead of her celebrity. "What triggered my initial interest [in Williams] is there are very few people who have that focus on excellence," Chandra said. "What we are trying to build is a very diverse, independent board. . . . People who can guide us to the next level of growth. . . . Seeing she had the right experience . . . the passion for fashion . . . that's the way we looked at it."[31]

In an extensive interview with *Business of Fashion* magazine in May 2019, Serena talked about finding her niche in the fashion world and how she evolved from creating evening dresses no one wanted to designing casual wear for the masses. "We don't do athletic wear, and a part of me is really happy because I feel like every company out there is doing that. It's so oversaturated," she told the magazine.

By May 2019, Serena had appeared at more fashion events than tennis tournaments. While Naomi Osaka, Victoria Azarenka, Sloane Stephens, and other on-court adversaries competed in one of the WTA's premier events in Madrid, Serena laced up her sneakers for another event, the Met Gala in New York. The Met Gala is a celebrity costume party where A-listers parade around the Metropolitan Museum of Art in over-the-top fashions. In 2019, Serena hosted the event, along with Lady Gaga and Harry Styles. She wore a bright yellow dress with pink and yellow flowers, and butterflies, attached. She paired the look with neon yellow Nike Air Force 1 tennis shoes. Later that evening, Serena shed her gown to reveal a bodice, shorts, and thigh-high boots.

Celebrities dressed according to the theme for 2019: Camp: Notes on Fashion. Pairing casual sneakers with an ultra-glamourous evening gown reflected what *Vogue* magazine's Brooke Bobb wrote of Serena's style: "Williams's contribution to the subject might be a bit tougher to define, though one can argue that her disruptive, ultrafeminine style on the court—tutus, bodysuits, and loads of color—is a camp-ish reaction to the stiff, monochromatic, and traditionally conservative world of tennis."[32]

Within days of the Met Gala, Serena was in Paris for the French Open, where she included a message in her fashion statement. As a sort of clapback at her haters, she wore an Abloh-designed black-and-white-striped two-piece kit that featured the French words for mother, champion, queen, and goddess.

When Wimbledon rolled around, Serena posted herself and daughter Olympia dressed in matching Serena Collection shirts with the signature "S" in Wimbledon's purple and green colors. Meanwhile, her on-court apparel held special meaning. She wore an all-white Nike knit dress with cutouts in the back and a gold Nike logo brooch studded with 34 Swarovski crystals, representing her age the last time she won Wimbledon (2016). Nike dubbed the bedazzled swoosh the "broosh."[33]

8

BRAND SERENA

Serena transcends sports and cultures. She moves seamlessly through the worlds of philanthropy, business, and entertainment. She has managed to build bridges; make connections; and develop professional, personal, and financial portfolios as eclectic as her outfits.

A walking contradiction? No. Serena is so agile in her professional and personal pursuits that she blends in as easily as she stands out. The tennis player, activist, superhero, philanthropist, and fashion designer unites every aspect of her life under one entity: Brand Serena.

It has taken Serena a lifetime to construct Brand Serena, built to last beyond her playing days. It appeals across racial, geographical, political, gender, and socioeconomic lines. She somehow maintains her "Straight Out of Compton" cred while hobnobbing with royalty. One day she tweets about her love for Publix supermarket chicken wings. The next week she is touting the virtues of a raw vegan diet. Her followers trust in authenticity, even if contradictory.

Brand Serena includes endorsements, business ventures, strategic partnerships, and decades-long relationships with Wilson, Nike, and Pepsi-Co (Gatorade). She has been a spokesperson for Beats by Dre headphones since 2014. She has partnered with HSN to pitch her Serena Signature Fashion line, and she teamed up with Venus to buy a minority ownership stake in the Miami Dolphins.

According to *Forbes*, Serena is worth $225 million.[1] That does not include her husband's estimated net worth of $9 million. The primary source of her wealth comes from prize money earned. Serena has won more than $88 million in prize money, more than any woman in the history of sports. She first set the record for most prize money earned, $23 million, in 2009, when she topped famed golfer Annika Sorenstam.

Above all, Serena is a tennis player. Her winnings elevated the earnings of every female tennis player and increased the profile of the sport, therefore expanding branding opportunities. She and Venus are credited with helping to usher in an era of equal pay at Grand Slams and increased television exposure for female tennis players. [2]

Their success in prime time meant higher pay for even mid-level players. As of May 2019, Sara Errani, a 5-foot-5 player with no Grand Slam singles titles and only nine career WTA singles titles, and little-known outside of the tennis world and her native Italy, has earned more than $13 million. Errani, 32 and ranked number 284, pocketed $4 million more than Chris Evert, America's sweetheart and winner of more than 90 percent of her matches, 18 Grand Slams, and 134 singles titles.

Evert graced the covers of magazines and appeared on news shows. Serena and Venus, on the other hand, came to fame in the internet age and grew more famous at the advent of social media. Serena took the mass marketing tools available to her and developed a multidimensional, multi-platform mega brand. She is everywhere, all the time.

Before building her brand, Serena served as pitch person for others. Early on, she represented youthful exuberance. She put Puma in the conversation when it came to tennis fashion. By age 21, she had already signed multimillion-dollar endorsement deals. Mindful of stories of famous black athletes who go broke, Serena was determined not to be one of them. "I hear my Dad saying, 'Don't make money like other athletes and then go broke,'" she said in an interview with the *Telegraph*. [3]

At first, Serena's endorsements were tied to Venus. They came as a package deal, "The Williams Sisters." They appeared in "Got Milk" ads, on the covers of magazines, and in other commercials, together.

Bob Dorfman, a sports marketing expert and creative director at Baker Street Advertising in San Francisco, explained (via Fox Business) what made the Williams sisters such good pitch people. "Obviously winning comes first, and that's why I think Serena is ahead of Venus," he said.

> She's the best female tennis player out there and keeps on winning. But [in] addition to their athleticism and talent, they're smart. They sound intelligent on camera, they have charisma, they're very educat-

ed, and they're excellent role models for young girls. All of that works
together—they have performance, personality, and purity.[4]

They are also part of one of the greatest sports stories ever told. They've
been featured in documentaries, several books, and countless magazine
articles.

Cora Masters Barry cannot say enough about the Williams sisters'
approach to fame and fortune. "They're always looking to do better, both
in terms of knowledge, as well as business. They're not one dimensional.
They're multidimensional, Serena and Venus," said Barry. "Serena is
very multidimensional . . . and always being broad in her perspective in
terms of developing businesses. She's a great role model for that. She's
very enterprising."

Barry pointed out that Serena and Venus have never had financial
woes. "They have business money, and they have endorsement money.
And they have their money manager, Larry Bailey," she said.

> These girls can live 10 lifetimes, they won't go broke. They're not
> foolish. They don't have 15 cars in the garage and all that stuff that a
> lot of these athletes have. They don't do that. Serena has a few houses
> around the world, which is, I consider, a good investment, especially
> as opposed to spending a lot of money on hotels. They live a good life,
> but they don't live a lavish life. They don't spend unnecessarily.[5]

Serena also ventured into private-label deals, like her fashion line with
HSN. To promote the brand, Serena wore a ring from her HSN signature
collection during the 2009 season. The HSN collection sold out during its
debut.[6]

As Serena separated herself from Venus in terms of wins, she also
distanced herself in earnings and endorsements. In June 2009, Serena had
a Q score of 24, the highest among female athletes. Venus's score was
23.[7] The Q score is based on an annual survey conducted by a research
firm that measures the mass appeal of athletes and celebrities. In 2010,
Serena's Q score rose to 25, while Venus remained at 23.[8] By 2011,
Serena's Q score was about the same as Roger Federer's.

Henry Schafer, vice president of the Q Scores Company, said
Williams was tied with Roger Federer for the highest Q score among
tennis fans, and her recognition rate among general sports fans is 78
percent and among the general public, 70 percent. Schafer said the aver-

age sports personality had a 35 percent recognition rate in the general public.[9]

Pitching beauty and fashion products came naturally to the would-be fashion designer. In Serena's spare time, she became a nail technician. Her colorful fingernails landed her a sponsored deal with OPI nail lacquers in 2011. The company created a few nail colors in Serena's honor, called Glam Slam. Serena even painted Oprah Winfrey's toenails on an episode of Oprah's show.

Serena's name recognition, combined with her success on the court, made her a sought-after brand ambassador, especially among such blue-chip brands as IBM, Apple, and Chase Bank. Her appeal stretched worldwide. Serena had been wearing Berlei bras for a decade before signing a deal with the Australian-based lingerie company in 2014. The company featured Serena in an ad campaign that showed her bouncing two balls while wearing a bra and tights. She also appeared in commercials for Beats by Dre, Apple's iPhone 5, and Gatorade.

In 2015, *Forbes* magazine named Serena the most marketable athlete. That same year, luxury automaker Aston Martin named her its chief sporting officer, a lofty title for brand ambassador.

Whether driving an Aston Martin, bouncing balls in a Berlei bra, or talking to IBM's computer answering system, Watson, Serena enjoyed more commercial success in her 30s than in her 20s. In a 2015 interview with *Black Enterprise* magazine, Serena discussed balancing her business pursuits with her tennis career. "When I am competing and training, I am 100 percent focused," she said. "But I love being an entrepreneur and love working with other entrepreneurs on products and projects that are meaningful. Making time for that work is important and energizing. It is a balance but one that I enjoy."[10]

Despite falling short of the calendar-year Slam, Serena was named *Sports Illustrated*'s Sportsperson of the Year in 2015, solidifying her status among the greatest athletes of all time. In her acceptance speech for the award in December 2015, Serena told the New York City audience,

> I've had people look down on me. I've had people put me down because I didn't look like them—I look stronger. I've had people look past me because of the color of my skin. I've had people overlook me because I was a woman. I had critics say I will never win another Grand Slam when I was only at number seven, and now here I stand today with 21 Grand Slam titles and I'm still going.[11]

She stays in the spotlight, which keeps brands she endorses in the public eye. Whatever Audemars Piguet pays Serena to endorse its luxury watches, it's probably a bargain compared to the airtime given to close-ups of their products on her wrist at Grand Slams. She takes the court wearing Beats by Dre headphones and sports Nike shirts, shoes, and hats during press conferences at tournaments.

Another way Serena promotes brands is by being the "it girl" at the biggest events. She's become an A-list celebrity simply by being among the A-listers. A red-carpet staple, she's at the *Vanity Fair* Oscar parties, the ESPYs, and the Grammys. She counts Beyoncé, Anna Wintour, and other celebrities as close friends. Moguls, presidents, models, singers, rappers, authors, and ballers circulate in Serena's orbit. J. K. Rowling and Gladys Knight are huge fans. They are among the members of what might be considered Serena's celebrity groupies—stars who follow Serena's matches.

There's hardly ever a time when Serena does not make headlines. All the while, she shares her life with followers, a marketer's dream. According to *Forbes*, Serena and Novak Djokovic rank as tennis's biggest stars on social media.[12] With more than 11 million Twitter followers and millions more on Facebook, Instagram, and Snapchat, Serena is a social media butterfly who posts anything from the mundane—like getting her brows waxed—to the marvelous—a video of her boarding the bus to go to the evening wedding reception for Meghan Markle and Prince Harry. A former reality TV star, Serena has no problem appearing on camera with bushy eyebrows or exposing her darkened pregnant belly while undergoing an ultrasound. She and her husband post intimate moments with their daughter.

Forbes points out that although Maria Sharapova, Roger Federer, and Rafael Nadal can claim more followers on social media, Serena garners more interaction with her fans: "A video of Djokovic dancing with Williams at the 2015 Wimbledon Champions event had 300,000 interactions and was viewed nearly 7 million times."[13]

Contrary to how things usually work out for young female celebrities, the older Serena gets, it seems the more marketable she becomes. In 2017, Nielsen named Serena the "most marketable" athlete. The ranking is based on Nielsen's N-score talent tracker, which assesses the endorsement and casting potential of actors, athletes, musicians, and other celebrities in the United States. Nielsen's N-score accounts for awareness and likability, as well as 10 other attributes, for example, "influential," "role model," and "trendsetter." N-score values range from 1 to 100.[14]

Elizabeth Lindsey of the marketing agency Wasserman told CNNMoney that Serena benefits from being an older athlete who is still at the top. "Marketing is riskier than ever these days because everything moves so fast," she said. "The more you can take the risk out, the better, and older athletes are more proven. They've been called upon before, so they have experience, understand the responsibility of a deal and how to act."[15]

According to *Forbes*, Serena was the highest-paid female athlete in 2017, for the second year in a row, beating out Sharapova, who held that distinction for 11 consecutive years. The Russian's endorsement haul took a hit after she tested positive for a banned substance; however, Serena's accomplishments played a bigger role in her surge to the top in endorsement dollars. Serena was playing fewer matches and taking home less prize money, but she kept hauling in more endorsements.

Forbes' Kurt Badenhausen wrote,

> Her late-career tear has made Williams a compelling figure for marketers. She ranks second among active athletes, behind only LeBron James in the U.S., on Repucom's Celebrity DBI, which tracks consumer perceptions of celebrities based on awareness, as well as seven attributes. Her 89 percent awareness level ranks in the top 3 percent of the nearly 4,000 celebrities Repucom follows, and she scores highly on the aspiration and influence attributes in particular.[16]

Karina Oachis wrote in 2017, that Serena's personal branding practices go beyond tennis. The best-selling author suggested that Serena has credibility, consistency, strategic vision, the power of the mind, and empathy. Oachis believes Serena's credibility allowed her to weather controversial storms, for example, her 2009 outburst at the U.S. Open. "Because she built loyalty through a highly family-conscious image and a friendly reputation, her fans remained 'on her side,'" said Oachis.

Despite what sometimes looks like sporadic behavior, Serena's public persona is consistent. "An authentic personal brand—just like Serena's— cannot be self-created," wrote Oachis. "What you convey to your online public must be fully compatible with your real-life behavior. . . . Serena does follow a seamless pattern which is mainly based on values such as family, love, education, and equality."[17]

Those values are reflected in Serena's charitable giving, business relationships, and personal life. With a brand rooted in what's considered basic American values, Serena's been able to branch out into different business ventures rarely associated with black female sports stars. She entered the high-tech industry in May 2017, by accepting a seat on the board of directors for SurveyMonkey. This placed her among such high-tech heavyweights as Intuit CEO Brad Smith and Facebook COO Sherly Sandberg, who also served on the SurveyMonkey board.[18]

In July 2017, a still-pregnant Serena spoke to a gathering of technology-savvy women at the SheKnows Media #BlogHer17 conference in Orlando. She told ESPNW's Sarah Spain, "Silicon Valley is really, really, really not open yet to having a lot of women or anyone of color, male or female. Those two barriers alone are really things we have to break down in the fastest-growing part of the world in general in technology. . . . It's really important to me to not just be a seat warmer but to really be a voice."[19]

Her sponsors are as committed to her as she is to her fans. Three years after her first ad with Berlei, the company featured Serena in a new ad campaign to coincide with its 100-year anniversary. In the ad, a pregnant Serena talks about her hopes and dreams for her new child. "While the first Berlei 'Do It for Yourself' campaign shook the category up with an intimate insight into what Serena does just for herself—dance—this piece takes an even more intimate approach," said Lucielle Vardy, chief strategy officer at Emotive, the company that produced the ad for Berlei. "The emotional power of video, combined with Serena's very personal delivery, is exactly what we aimed for."[20]

There was a Gatorade "recovery bar" at her wedding, which featured Gatorade drinks, nutrition bars, and chews. Nike executives thought so highly of Serena's importance to the brand that the largest building on the company's Beaverton, Oregon, campus is named after her. The building is 1 million square feet and takes up three city blocks. This latest expansion of Nike headquarters stands as a symbol of Serena's impact on sports, business, and culture.

Serena expressed her excitement about the building in a post on Instagram, writing,

> What a year it has been. First a Grand Slam win followed by a [sic]
> awesome baby . . . then the most magical wedding. What next? How

about a building!! Nike announced yesterday that one of its new world headquarters buildings will be named after me. It will be the biggest on campus and is scheduled to open in 2019. I am honored and grateful![21]

She appeared on the cover of *Vogue* with her infant daughter, Alexis, who became the youngest person to ever grace the cover. Nielsen cited Serena's engagement, marriage, and birth of her daughter as selling points. With motherhood bringing in the mother lode in endorsements, Serena was finally being treated as the top tennis draw she is. She was also finally erasing the inequity of trailing Sharapova and Wozniacki in endorsement dollars.

Despite being a multimillionaire, Serena comes across as being down to earth. This resonates with consumers, making her seem approachable. She's quite the penny-pincher. During her pregnancy, she was spotted shopping at a dollar store.[22] Despite the glamorous trappings, Serena is downright frugal compared to many professional athletes. She remembers her first $1 million check and trying to deposit it through the drive thru. Early in her career she would let her business manager pick up her winnings. Although she enjoys her riches, she's thrifty and wants to avoid becoming another athlete-gone-bust story.

Firmly established as one of the greatest, Serena has reached Michael Jordan and Jack Nicholas status. These are athletes with brands so strong they can continue to endorse products long after retirement.

After the birth of daughter, HBO broadcast *Being Serena*, an original series that documented her journey through her engagement, wedding, and pregnancy. Her story seemed to be everywhere. Her wedding pictures made the rounds in *People*, on TMZ, and on every celebrity gossip blog. She made the cover of *Brides* magazine, wearing the second of three wedding dresses she wore at the big event. Soon after giving birth, she posted a video of her dancing in front of a private jet to Rihanna's hit "Lemon."[23]

The type of engagement Serena has with fans makes her an attractive brand ambassador. Her corporate sponsors can bypass the cost of traditional television or print ads and produce commercials for Serena to post to her followers. These digital marketing campaigns are cost effective and less intrusive than pop-up ads on YouTube or Facebook. It's Serena, sharing a video with her fans. Almost every month, sometimes weekly, Serena posts a commercial in which she is featured to her followers. She can be seen driving a Lincoln Navigator or talking about her new Nike shoes. When she shares something with followers, it may come across as more organic, less promotional.

Serena takes a compelling life story and turns it into a marketing opportunity. She had two postpartum surgeries. She used a postsurgery bandaging product by Neodyne Biosciences to aid healing. Within months, Neodyne Biosciences partnered with Serena to promote Embrace, a postsurgery scar defense system designed to reduce the visibility of scars. The campaign included a link to a website, SerenaEmbrace.com, and videos of Serena talking about how Embrace helped her heal. She also brought up the company while making a television appearance on ABC's *The View*.

Serena's postpregnancy nightmare became a hot topic. Media outlets picked up the story about the high mortality rate for black women giving birth. This got the postsurgery recovery adhesive mentioned on People.com, Essence.com, and Glamour.com, and in the *Huffington Post* and elsewhere.

When Serena made her appearance on *The View*, she wore a metallic trench coat dress with a Wakanda-like necklace. She wore a similar look on NBC's *Tonight Show with Jimmy Fallon*. But instead of the tailored trench, she wore a shimmery mini dress that looked more like a silky bronze bathrobe. What was she promoting that day? The postsurgery adhesive. Leave it to Serena to wear a glamourous outfit to promote something as unappealing as postsurgical scarring bandages. Brand Serena delivers.

She was featured in an ad campaign for the Lincoln Navigator sports utility vehicle. According to automotive culture website the Drive,

> This is the beginning of a new ad campaign with a clever message about the Navigator. Back in the '90s and 2000s, the folks who admired hulking American luxury SUVs might have liked them for their "balling" character. Now those same people have kids and might want a big SUV for functional purposes like hauling your family around. A perfect vehicle for that would be the new 2018 Lincoln Navigator Black Label that Williams is driving in the new promos.[24]

The ad aired during the Grammys, one of the biggest television advertising events outside of the Super Bowl.

"This [motherhood] just adds another dimension to Serena the person," said Jim Andrews, senior vice president with IEG, a WPP unit that tracks sponsorship spending. Her longtime sponsor Gatorade released a video as part of its "Sisters in Sweat" campaign, narrated by Serena. In the video, Serena is holding a baby, a double for her daughter, as she encourages her to play sports.[25]

Pampers featured Serena and Olympia in a "Wild Baby" ad campaign. Serena brought up the campaign on ABC's *Good Morning America*, which aired the commercial—a freebie for Procter & Gamble, Pampers's parent company. Serena also posted the commercial on YouTube, Instagram, and Twitter.

In March 2018, Serena brushed off the old Aneres brand name. *Allure* magazine reported that Serena had filed legal documents with the U.S. Patent and Trademark Office to launch a cosmetics line called Aneres.[26] Under her application, the line would allow Serena to use the Aneres brand on skincare, make-up, perfumes, lotions, soaps, and body wash, as well as hair products. It is another sign that Serena has big business plans for her postplaying days.

She launched Serena Ventures, a venture capital fund, in 2019. Serena had secretly provided funding for companies led by women or people of color since 2014. Serena Ventures made her endeavor more formal. She hired Alison Rapaport, a former accountant at J. P. Morgan, to oversee the fund. J. P. Morgan Chase is one of Serena's sponsors.[27]

The logo for Serena Ventures is the same S used for her clothing line. According to her site, Serena Ventures invests in start-up companies that "embrace diverse leadership, individual empowerment, creativity, and opportunity."[28]

It's unclear when Serena will retire from tennis; however, her entrepreneurial acumen is as reliable as her serve. As a brand ambassador, fashion designer, businessowner, and venture capitalist she has built an enduring brand.

In June 2019, Serena graced the cover of *Forbes* magazine. She was the only athlete to make *Forbes'* list of richest self-made women. The cover featured the following quote from Serena: "I want to be the brand instead of being the face."[29]

9

SECOND ACT

Iconic

Serena's career includes several hiccups, gaps, and reboots; however, her return to the court postpregnancy was nothing short of heroic. Serena was already in the record books, headed to the Hall of Fame and considered the greatest. After she reached the final in two Grand Slams within a year of having her first child, her stature soared.

Her pregnancy came as a surprise, and her announcement, via Instagram, was greeted with skepticism. She had just won the Australian Open and was one Grand Slam title shy of matching Margaret Court. No player on tour seemed capable of derailing Serena's route in the record books. She had also just regained the number-one ranking, having relinquished it in August 2016, after 186 consecutive weeks, a WTA record.

With her 23rd Slam, Serena sat alone atop the list of most Slam wins in the Open Era. She seemed unstoppable. Then came the cryptic Instagram post: A picture of Serena, dressed in a revealing yellow swimsuit, with the caption "20 weeks."

For a couple of days, speculation ran rampant. As soon as her spokesperson confirmed the revelation, the realization set it: Serena was about eight weeks pregnant when she won the Australian Open.

Questions arose: How did she do it? Would she or could she return after marriage and a baby?

At age 36, Serena had already defied father time. In 2013, she was the oldest woman to be ranked number one. She was 35 years and 125 days old when she won the 2017 Australian Open, which made her the oldest woman to win a Grand Slam in the Open Era.[1]

Chris Evert, who had texted Serena following the announcement, told the *New York Times*, "Getting married and having a child is a special journey. . . . She, to me, is more than ready for this lifestyle change. It's been 20 years on tour."[2]

Serena vowed to be back and assured her fans that this was just a detour on the path to more Grand Slam titles. She planned on returning in time to defend her title at the 2018 Australian Open.

She had an uncomplicated pregnancy; however, complications following her daughter's birth almost ended Serena's life. First, she had an emergency cesarean section. The next day, Serena grew short of breath while resting in the hospital. Afraid of alarming her mother, Serena got up out of bed and went to locate a nurse.

She told the nurse that she was having trouble breathing and needed a CT scan. Having dealt with dangerous blood clots, Serena told *Vogue*, the threat of the condition returning always loomed in the back of her head. The nurse assured her that it was probably just the medication; however, Serena persisted and insisted on doctors doing the CT Scan. They did and discovered small blood clots in her lungs.

Her postpartum nightmare would only get worse. Further complicating matters, coughing fits led to her C-section stitches popping open. According to *Vogue*, doctors then discovered that a "large hematoma had flooded her abdomen, the result of a medical catch-22 in which the potentially lifesaving blood thinner caused hemorrhaging at the site of her c-section."[3]

Doctors performed another procedure to prevent more clotting.

When news of Serena's ordeal went public, like so many events in her life, it became the focus of a national debate.

ProPublica used Serena's harrowing tale to bring attention to an article it ran in its "Lost Mothers" series, on how hospitals are failing black women. "It's been long-established that black women . . . fare worse in pregnancy and childbirth, dying at a rate more than triple that of white mothers," wrote Annie Waldman.[4]

After the blood clot ordeal, Serena laid on her back due to doctor-ordered postpregnancy bed rest.[5] She'd have to delay her return to practice and competition. She looked slower and a bit out of shape when she played an exhibition against Jelena Ostapenko in Abu Dubai in December 2017.

After the exhibition, Serena told reporters, "I don't think I am going to rate my performance. I have plenty of comebacks, from injuries, from surgeries, but I've never had a comeback after actually giving birth to a human being. So, in my eyes, I feel it was a wonderful, wonderful match for me."[6]

The superstar acknowledged that it was merely one step in what would be a long process back. But she was back. "Maybe this goes without saying," she said, "but it needs to be said in a powerful way: I absolutely want more Grand Slams."[7]

Still, there was no official word of withdrawal from the 2018 Australian Open.

On a chilly Sunday afternoon, with American flag-waving fans cheering, Lesley Kerkhove and Demi Schuurs of the Netherlands defeated Serena and Venus Williams, 6–2, 6–3, in a doubles match during a Fed Cup tie in Asheville, North Carolina. The match was almost meaningless. Behind two singles wins from Venus, the United States had already wrapped up the rubber and secured a spot in the semifinals of the WTA's equivalent to World Cup soccer; however, it would go down as an official loss and blemish Serena's otherwise stellar Fed Cup record—13–0 in singles and 3–2 in doubles.[8]

Losing to a couple of unknown players from the Netherlands was just one of the unusual occurrences Serena would experience in her first step toward a long-awaited return to tennis. It was the first time in a while she had appeared on a Fed Cup team and was not the number-one-ranked American. It was also her first trip for an official match with her husband and daughter in the players' box. Serena and her husband posted selfies of daughter Olympia watching while mommy supported her teammates courtside. Serena's Fed Cup run was more of a welcome-back party than an accurate measure of her tennis readiness. She still carried the extra weight from the pregnancy, and her decision to stick to doubles was a sign that Serena wasn't quite back in form.

"I do think she will be back, and I don't think she's coming back until she knows she can compete and win," said ESPN's tennis commentator, Chris McKendry, in January when everyone was still speculating if Serena would defend her title at the Australian Open. "Serena isn't out there just to compete."

McKendry, who played college tennis at Drexel, is a mother and re-members how her mind-set changed after having her first child. She recalled thinking about the baby during live broadcast. "It's just traveling with a baby and all of those things," said McKendry. "She's always had a wonderful team and family around her. Her husband seems fantastic. But traveling will never be quite the same. It takes a certain amount of tough-ness and determination for any sort of comeback. She's done it time and time again, and she'll do it again."[9]

Even getting back on the court just five months after two emergency surgeries could justify Serena slapping an "S" on her chest for Super-woman. But playing in a Grand Slam was different. Serena withdrew from the Australian Open because she doesn't like to just show up for participation trophies. She plays to win.

Just a week before the start of the Australian Open, then-president of the USTA, Katrina Adams, spoke about the prospect of Serena's return so soon after childbirth. "It's a big task for her to be able to come back and play the Australian Open," said Adams.

> It will be the most exciting thing if she does. If she doesn't feel that she's ready, that's understandable too. . . . Four months after giving birth is a tall task. I know she played last week in Abu Dubai in an exhibition, and she definitely didn't look like she was ready to play on the big stage for seven matches. I think it's just an accomplishment to see her back on the court playing competitive tennis.[10]

When Serena announced that she was withdrawing from the 2018 Australian Open, Patrick Mouratoglou was the first to hint that Serena's pregnancy might have been more difficult than anyone knew. "It's never an easy decision to skip a Grand Slam, I guess for any professional, and for sure for Serena," Mouratoglou told ESPN. "The thing is, when she gave birth, things didn't go as smooth as she expected. She had some complications—I mean, the baby was perfect, but she had some issues afterwards—and these medical issues delayed the moment that she could come back to practice."[11]

Within days, Serena revealed in the February issue of *Vogue* that she almost died after childbirth, due to complications associated with blood clots in her lungs.[12]

Mouratoglou told reporters that Serena would make her return at In-dian Wells in 2018. When asked if he was surprised about her coming back after such a scary child-birthing experience, Mouratoglou replied, "Nope. Because I feel like she hasn't ended her career."[13]

A few weeks after withdrawing from the Australian Open, Serena played in her first competitive match since giving birth in Asheville during the Fed Cup. Even though the Fed Cup does not count toward the WTA's ranking points, it was still real competition.

Serena was not the svelte player who'd crushed the competition in 2013. Even the baby-bump-playing Serena at the 2017 Australian Open looked at least 20 pounds lighter than postpregnancy Serena.

The Fed Cup match would serve as an indicator of how far Serena had come and how much work she still needed to do. Having already secured legendary status in the record books, Serena must now try to cement her status as the greatest of all time as a mother, wife, and survivor of a near-death postchildbirth scare.

After her loss, Serena acknowledged that an infant in the entourage added a new challenge. "I didn't manage my time well, but I was thinking about it in the future how to manage it better. . . . This is literally my first time traveling with the baby and everything. I'm going to try to do better. It was hard. It was the first time for me," she told the Associated Press.[14]

Considering her age and what she went through during her pregnancy, if Serena wanted to abandon her comeback efforts and retire, many would have been disappointed; however, most would have understood.

Yet, Serena told *Vogue*, "I've been playing tennis since before my memories started. . . . At my age, I see the finish line. And when you see the finish line, you don't slow down. You speed up."[15]

Serena decided to make her official return at the 2018 BNP Paribas Open in Indian Wells. She reached the third round before falling to Venus, 6–3, 6–4, the first loss to her older sister in almost four years.

Rising star Naomi Osaka defeated Serena soundly, 6–3, 6–2, at the Miami Open. After a first-round defeat at the Miami Open, Serena took time to work on her fitness and vowed to return in time for the clay-court season. When she withdrew from two clay-court premier events in Rome and Madrid, her status for the 2018 French Open looked in limbo.

Mouratoglou assured fans that Serena would be ready for Roland-Garros.

She would enter unseeded and ranked in the mid-400s. In true Serena style, the 23-time Grand Slam winner surprised fans with her form and fashion. Her full-length catsuit was among the most buzzworthy topics at the French. But it was her play that captured everyone's attention. Serena defeated two seeded players en route to what was supposed to be another showdown with Maria Sharapova.

Sharapova was playing solid tennis, and despite her three wins, Serena hadn't convinced anyone that she had returned to championship form. The morning of the scheduled match, Serena withdrew with a pec injury. She told reporters she couldn't even serve. Evidence of an injury surfaced in her third-round doubles match. In the third set, Serena was averaging service speeds of less than 75 miles per hour. Her top serves exceed 120 miles per hour. She had been averaging serves faster than 100 miles per hour in her previous matches.

Still, she had given fans a glimpse of how well she was progressing in her comeback. Wimbledon was around the corner. Although Serena was ranked number 183, the All England Club seeded her number 25 in a move that delighted some and angered others. When Serena went on maternity leave, she was ranked number one. French Open officials rejected the idea to seed Serena. Giving Serena a seed at Wimbledon meant one player would be bumped. It turned out to be number-32-ranked Dominika Cibulkova, who called the move unfair.

"Why should I not be seeded if I have the right to be?" Cibulkova told the *Telegraph*. "It's just not fair if there is a player [who misses out] and it's me now. I have the right, and I should be seeded, and if they put her in front of me then I will just lose my spot that I am supposed to have. I don't know if something like this ever happened before."[16]

A few days before her first match at Wimbledon, Serena posted a photo of her daughter Olympia, sitting on the grass court. During a pretournament press conference, a journalist asked Serena about whether her competitive spirit had waned with motherhood.

"You know, my competitive desire is definitely the same. . . . I don't think I ever actually lost that competitive side," she answered. "In fact, I feel like it's stronger because I've been through so much. I put so much on the back burner, I feel like even more so I'm even more competitive."[17]

At Wimbledon, Serena would be more comfortable on the grass. After all, she'd won the tournament seven times. A fourth-round showdown against 10th-seed Madison Keys loomed large; however, an unseeded qualifier, Evgeniya Rodina, also a mom, upset Keys, giving Serena an easier path to the quarterfinals.

Serena notched a straightforward 6–2, 6–2 win over Rodina, who appeared overwhelmed and overpowered. The most memorable part of the match may have been the handshake at the net when Serena warmly greeted Rodina. The media covered the rare showdown between two active players who are moms.

"It's really cool," Serena told reporters. "It shows that you can be a working mum and still be a Wimbledon quarterfinalist."[18]

After defeating Rodina, Serena faced a more challenging opponent in Italian Camila Giorgi. The always aggressive Giorgi plays in one gear, pedal to the metal. Her game can be as erratic as it is electrifying. When she's on target, she's a difficult player to beat. Relentless, Giorgi attacked Serena's serve and took the first set, 6–3. As it goes with Giorgi, she becomes predictably unpredictable. A master at adjusting her game plan, Serena began anticipating Giorgi's shots and swatting them away for winners. She also served seven aces in route to a 3–6, 6–3, 6–4 win.

Relieved to have survived the relentless Italian, Serena told reporters, "I knew I had to serve really well today because she was really aggressive on the returns." Despite being down a set, Serena told reporters she remained focused and never feared she'd lose the match, commenting, "It's weird. Sometimes I feel, 'Man, I'm in trouble.' Sometimes I feel, I can fight. For whatever reason, today I was so calm. Even when I was down the first set, I thought, 'Well, she's playing great. I'm doing a lot of the right things. It is what it is.'"[19]

One reporter asked if motherhood had mellowed her on-court demeanor. Serena responded, "No, just to be clear, that was just today. I mean, I'm hoping this is like a new thing. Honestly, I highly doubt it. It was just the way I felt today. I never felt it was out of my hands. It's weird. I can't describe it. I just felt calm. Hoping I can channel that all the time, but one day at a time."[20]

Serena indeed appeared more relaxed at Wimbledon; however, she arrived at the semifinals without having to face any seeded players. Most had already lost. Her semifinal opponent, number 13 Julia Georges, a big-hitting German who was having the best year of her career, was supposed to provide a challenge.

Georges was no match for Serena, who dispatched the Germain in one hour and 10 minutes. She advanced in search of her 30th Wimbledon final.

"It's crazy. I don't even know how to feel," Serena said in a postmatch interview. "I didn't expect to do so well in my fourth tournament back. I just feel when I don't have anything to lose, I can play so free. It's definitely not normal for me to be in a Wimbledon final. I'm just enjoying every moment."[21]

Now she faced Angelique Kerber in the finals. Kerber lost to Serena in the 2016 Wimbledon final. It was Serena's last appearance at the All England Club before going on maternity leave. But this was different. Kerber was in top form and exposed Serena's hindered movement. She went on to defeat Serena with ease.

Although Serena lost that match, merely making it to the final was a significant triumph. Serena insisted that the Wimbledon final was the beginning of her journey back.

Serena kept her summer schedule light. British number one Johanna Konta destroyed Serena, 6–1, 6–0, at the Silicon Valley Classic in San Jose, California. It was the worst defeat of Serena's career.[22]

After the match, Konta told the San Jose crowd that Serena "obviously wasn't playing anywhere near her best level," adding, "but I was just trying to play the match on my terms and do what I can out here and put aside the incredible champion she is and play the player on the day."[23]

Serena lost in the second round in Cincinnati. The uncharacteristic losses at Wimbledon and in San Jose made some wonder if age, motherhood, and marriage had worn Serena weary. With the U.S. Open a few weeks away, Serena looked ill-prepared.

Serena cruised through her opponents, dropping just one set on her way to the U.S. Open final, where Osaka awaited.[24] Osaka idolized Serena. A younger, healthier version of her idol, Osaka defeated Serena, 6–2, 6–4. The loss to Osaka and the drama surrounding Serena's rant against the chair umpire remained in the news for weeks.

Like she had done after tough losses at the U.S. Open, Serena ended her season at Flushing Meadows. She didn't return to the courts until 2019.

The 2019 season began in Perth, Australia, at the Hopman Cup. Along with compatriot Frances Tiafoe, Serena faced Switzerland's Federer and Belinda Bencic. The media covered the exhibition as if it were a showdown between Serena and Federer, considered the all-time greats.

Serena defeated Bencic in their singles contest and lost in the mixed doubles. The highlight of the match featured a short crosscourt rally between Serena and Federer that ended with a Tiafoe unforced error at the net. Following the match, Serena took an iconic selfie with a beaming Federer, who held the selfie stick to snap a shot of the game's two biggest stars.

Serena had more injuries in 2019, playing in fewer tournaments. Withdrawals after one or two matches were becoming more of a norm. Still, she managed to climb back into the top 10 despite completing fewer than nine matches. She was balancing her time as a mother and businesswoman with her goal to win more Grand Slams.

Going into the French Open, Serena had completed just one tournament without withdrawing or retiring. Just prior to the start of the tournament, Serena posted several pictures of her husband, her daughter, and her daughter's doll, Quai Quai, on Instagram, Twitter, and Snapchat. In fact, Serena posted as many photos at Disneyland Paris as she did of herself at practice.

She won her first two matches but lost in the third round to up-and-coming American Sofia Kenin, 2–6, 5–7. Serena decided to skip the Wimbledon tune-up tournaments and arrived at the All England Club with just a handful of tournaments under her belt.

Meanwhile, General Mills announced that Serena, pictured in her 2016 Wimbledon dress, would grace the cover of the Wheaties cereal box. She would become the second black female tennis player to make the cover. Althea Gibson was featured in 2001.[25]

"I have dreamt of this since I was a young woman, and it's an honor to join the ranks of some of America's most decorated athletes. I hope my image on this iconic orange box will inspire the next generation of girls and athletes to dream big," Serena stated in a press release issued by General Mills.[26]

With her iconic status cemented in paperboard, Serena continued her quest to tie and surpass Margaret Court's 24 Grand Slams. Regardless of the record, Serena had made the mother of all comebacks.

10

CONCLUSION

Serena continues to play, adding more records and accolades to an already stellar career. She's joked about playing as long as Roger Federer. She's talked about targeting the 2020 Summer Olympics. No matter how many Grand Slams Serena retires with, she can only solidify her legacy in sports, pop culture, and American and African American history.

Perhaps it's time to remove "arguably" from in front of "greatest of all time female tennis player" when talking about Serena. What's the argument for the others—Steffi Graf, Martina Navratilova, and Margaret Court? Every match or tournament Serena wins diminishes their claim to the title and bolsters hers.

John McEnroe started calling Serena the greatest of all time before she even tied Evert and Navratilova at 18 Grand Slams. In making his case for Serena during an interview with CNN, McEnroe said,

> I've seen them all. What Billie Jean King has done for the game and the way she played was more like how I played, and Martina Navratilova, Chris Evert won a billion tournaments, Steffi Graf . . . but to me overall, when Serena's on, she's the best I've ever seen play, the whole package as far as what she can bring to the table. [1]

The case for the greatest has always been about more than numbers. Jim Brown is ranked number 10 among the NFL's all-time leading rushers; however, few football experts consider Brown the 10th best. In most arguments, he's ranked ahead of Emmitt Smith, who holds the NFL record for most rushing yards. Brown gets credit for his dominance in his era.

Similarly, Smith holds the records but gets less credit because he played with All-Pros and is considered the beneficiary of a system stacked in his favor. Former Houston Oilers running back Earl Campbell is ranked outside the top 30 among all-time rushers. He's in the greatest of all-time conversation based on the eyeball test—he looked more dominant. He ran through and over defenders, and anyone who watched him play marveled at the way he destroyed defenses.

Serena dominated contemporaries, amassed records, and passed the eyeball test. There will always be skeptics and naysayers. But the consensus is that Serena is the greatest female tennis player of all time. She has the most Slam titles in the Open Era. She is tied with Graf for most consecutive weeks at number one. She has a higher winning percentage in Grand Slam finals than Graf, Navratilova, King, or Evert. Surprisingly, Serena also has the highest winning percentage on grass (89.1), besting Navratilova, a nine-time Wimbledon champion, and Federer, winner of eight Wimbledon titles.

The only debate is whether she might be considered the greatest tennis player, male or female. Federer weighed in. When asked to name the greatest player of all time, male or female, Federer told the *Wall Street Journal*'s Jason Gay that Williams is the greatest tennis player of all time, man or woman.

"It's been fascinating to watch. . . . She had a totally different upbringing—I came up through Switzerland with the federation, she did it with her dad and her sister. It's an amazing story unto itself—and then she became one of the greatest, if not the greatest, tennis players of all time," said Federer.[2]

Serena has a multifaceted game that she enhanced as she aged.

"Anyone who believes there's been a player with as many all-around tennis attributes as Serena is either wrong or a liar," wrote Chris Chase for Fox Sports.[3]

Sometimes she's deservedly included in discussions about the greatest overall female athlete, best American athlete, or best sportsperson of all time. In the case of best female athlete of all time, Serena's career outshines such track legends as Jackie Joyner-Kersee and Wilma Rudolph. Serena has won more Olympic gold medals (four) than Joyner-Kersee and Rudolph.

Some have argued that she's the greatest American athlete period, better than Muhammad Ali, Michael Jordan, LeBron James, and Michael Phelps. Elevating Serena to the status of greatest American athlete gained traction in 2015, as she made a run at Graf's record for most Slams.

There are no official "greatest of all time" awards. These debates take place in bar rooms, at watercoolers, in Twitter threads, and on sports talk radio. Still, as an athlete consistently considered in these debates, Serena has already reached legendary status.

It's difficult to compare athletes from different eras and different sports, but for a good "GOAT" (greatest of all time) argument, longevity, dominance, performance, and titles must be considered. In terms of longevity, Phelps's reign in the pool is the closest thing to Serena's tenure in tennis. Serena will never amass as many Olympic gold medals as Phelps. Swimming gives out medals for every event. Tennis players must win several matches to compete for one medal. But like Phelps, Serena holds records in an international sport. Unlike with Phelps, racism and sexism are intertwined in most of the discussions about Serena's greatness.

This notion of Serena as the greatest didn't sit well with many fans or sports columnists. Her place in history is often marginalized simply because plenty of people don't like her. In an article entitled "Serena Williams Isn't 'America's Sweetheart,' but She Is America's Greatest Champion," Douglas Perry, a sports columnist for the *(Portland) Oregonian*, wrote,

> It's true that the average American sports fan hasn't embraced Williams. Racism certainly has played a role in some of the antipathies she's faced over the years—we remain a long way from a colorblind society; however, it's not the whole story. For one thing, you also have to consider sexism. Strong, independent women still can be scary to many of us, whether we even recognize it or not. Put her race and her gender together, then add in a sport that fell from top-tier status in the U.S. when John McEnroe and Jimmy Connors retired 20 years ago, and her relatively small-time place on the American sports landscape becomes an unmovable reality. She could have 30 Wimbledon trophies on her mantle and she still wouldn't be as beloved in her native land as Derek Jeter—or even Danica Patrick.[4]

Perry included a quote from Mark Reason, a journalist from New Zealand who seemed perplexed by Serena's lack of support in the United

States. Reason wrote, "The greatest female tennis player of all time, America's only current athlete who dominates a major sport, might be beloved in old age when the color has faded a bit, but right now, she's just too black."[5]

Serena's reign stretches from old-school players like Navratilova, who was still playing when Serena turned pro, to the open-stance hitters of today. She was one of the last players to switch from natural gut (made from animal intestines) strings to monofilament, a durable synthetic racket string that emerged in the 1990s and became popular with younger players. Serena and Federer were two of the last top players to use all-natural gut, made from cows and sheep. The natural gut helped produce more power but was more susceptible to changing weather and far less durable. Serena started using a hybrid mix of gut and monofilament in 2012, the year she teamed up with Mouratoglou.[6]

Serena was in her 30s when she made the switch. She had to become familiar with the new toys the kids were playing with, and she managed to adjust. Many all-time greats stuck around to add longevity to their resumes. But how many hung around and stayed on top? Ali didn't. His final fights ended in defeat and humiliation. Hank Aaron captured the home run crown while sporting a pot belly and with little game left. Serena won her 23rd Slam while pregnant and reclaimed the number-one ranking. She reached two Grand Slam finals less than a year after giving birth to her first child.

"Serena's burning desire to prove to the world that she is the greatest athlete in history makes her such a dominant tennis player," said Vijay Freeman, editor at *Black Tennis Magazine*. "She has a perfectionist ethic and sets big goals in that she plays every point to win and plays every match/tournament to win it all. She outworks her opponents on-court and off-court (cross-training) with sufficient warm-up tournaments prior to she hates to lose."[7]

In fact, Serena often says she hates losing more than she enjoys winning. She can become down-right petulant after she loses a match. Having been raised to feel invincible, Serena dreads defeat because deep down, she believes she's in control of the outcome. So often, commentators say, the match rests on Serena's racket as if her opponent has little sway in the results. If Serena is at 100 percent and focused, it's her match to lose.

Having secured the Open Era record for most Grand Slams, marriage and motherhood provided her with an easy exit. But no, Serena insists she has much to prove and accomplish. After winning her semifinal match at the 2018 U.S. Open, Serena told fans she felt like she had already won. During her postmatch interview, she spoke as if she planned to play many more years. "I just feel like not only is my future bright, even though I'm not a spring chicken, but I still have a very, very bright future. That is super exciting for me," she said.[8]

Freeman believes Serena will go down in history as one of the greatest athletes for her perseverance as much as for her dominance.

> Serena's mental toughness accounts for over 70 percent of her wins because she had to recover from adverse conditions and setbacks on several occasions in her career. The most notable was during her illness and foot injury in 2010, where she could not play competitively for six-plus months. Rather than sit and nurse herself, she went out on court using a scooter to hit balls to maintain her strokes during recovery. All of this determination comes out during match play, as her opponents are intimidated from the start. Plus, Serena believes in her ability so much that she never stops fighting in a match. Even when she is not at her best, she will grind out matches doing whatever it takes to win.[9]

Serena's passionate play, the fist pumps, the roars, and her signature "c'mon" contribute to her legacy and lifts fans from their seats whether they are in the stadium or watching from a couch at home.

The phrases "competitive spirit" and "mental toughness" get thrown around. Her run at the 2017 Australian Open was made all the more astounding by the fact that she was pregnant. She learned just weeks before the tournament that she was expecting.

"Serena did not lose a set during the entire tournament while she was pregnant knowing the complications that it could bring later during childbirth," Freeman said. "Serena knew that her time to win a major was running out, and she made it. The determination was so great that she was able to push past the barriers to make history in dominant fashion."[10]

Dominance, brilliance, and resilience are part of Serena's legacy as an athlete. Her impact on African Americans may be even greater. In that regard, Serena is more trailblazer than a pioneer. Althea Gibson, Arthur

Ashe, and Zina Garrison came before her; however, she's paved the way for so many who have followed her career path.

More than 40 years passed between Gibson's last Grand Slam title win (1958) and Serena's first. When Osaka hoisted the U.S. Open trophy, she became the fourth active black female player with a Grand Slam title. Serena, Venus, Naomi Osaka, and Sloane Stephens have a combined 32 Grand Slam singles titles. Four black women, playing at the same time, have four times as many Grand Slam titles as Ashe and Gibson combined.

At the 2018 U.S. Open, Osaka, Keys, and Serena reached the semifinals. That meant there were three black women in the final four for the second consecutive year. In 2017, Venus, Keys, and Stephens reached the semifinals.

That this was not big news is a testament to Serena's and Venus's legacies. All those matches between Serena and Venus meant tennis fans had grown accustomed to watching two black women vying for the sport's most prestigious trophies.

While Serena and Osaka battled on Ashe, Hailey Baptiste and Dalayna Hewitt, two black girls, were winning their semifinals match in the U.S. Open junior competition. Cori "Coco," Gauff, also black, was seeded number one in girls' singles. These three black girls would make up all but one of the players in the girls' doubles finals. Gauff's partner, Catherine "Caty" McNally, is white

Going into the 2018 U.S. Open, there were four black women in the top 20, and Serena wasn't among them. In 2018, there were more black women in the top 100 in tennis than triple the amount of African Americans in the World Series that year.

How "America's favorite pastime" ended up with so few African Americans is another story. The story here is that Serena helped render tennis' lack of diversity a moot point. The head of the USTA is black. The director of player development at the USTA is a black man. At the 2016 Olympics, three of the four singles players representing the United States were black women.

The younger players point to Venus and Serena as the reason they go into the sport. When Serena turned pro, there were other African American women on tour. Katrina Adams, Lori McNeil, and Chanda Rubin were nearing the end of their careers. Serena broke ground in terms of leveraging her wins for financial gains outside of prize money for women of color.

Stephens was able to land a contract to represent Under Armour long before she won a Grand Slam. Her win against Serena put her on the map, and Serena and Venus no doubt made it easier to market Stephens. After just one win against Serena, sportswriters were already asking, "Is Sloane Stephens the New Serena?"[11]

Upon first meeting Sloane, Serena recalled her thoughts. "I saw her in the locker room. She was another black girl," Serena says, joking about the first time they met. "I was like, 'Hey!' That's when I first noticed her. 'What up, girl?'"

When asked if she saw herself as a mentor to Sloane, Serena replied, "I don't know." She continued, "I would need a better definition of the word 'mentor.' I just feel like being the older one. Maybe some of the younger players look up to me. It's interesting. It's hard to be a real mentor when you're still in competition, so I think it's a little bit of everything."[12]

Naomi Osaka of Japan, who is half Haitian and half Japanese, defeated Serena in the first round of the Miami Open. Osaka had just won her first WTA title, Indian Wells. Serena was still out of shape and not quite ready for someone of Osaka's fitness and power in the first round. After winning the match in straight sets, Osaka told the crowd how nervous she was walking onto the court to face her idol.

"I don't know if anybody knows this, but Serena's my favorite player," said Osaka. "Just playing against her is kind of like a dream for me, so I'm very grateful that I was able to play her, and it's even better that I was able to win. . . . I just kind of wanted to impress her, and I just wanted to make her say, 'Come on!' one time, and I think she did, so I'm really happy about that."[13]

Anytime Serena faces a young player for the first time, it's a surreal moment for them; however, the significance of seeing all these young black women following in her footsteps is not lost on the legend.

The 2017 U.S. Open final played out like a living testament to the Williams sisters. Stephens faced Madison Keys, whose father is black, in the final. They were both representing the United States. There on Arthur Ashe Stadium, a venue named after an African American tennis pioneer, stood two young black tennis players, representing the country and following in the footsteps of Venus and Serena. It would be the first time in 10 years that an American not named Serena would win a Grand Slam title.

During the U.S. Open, *Guardian* writer Bryan Armen Graham wrote about the impact of African American women in tennis. Under a headline that included a play on Trump's 2016 campaign slogan, "The U.S. Open Showed Black Women Have Made American Tennis Great Again," Graham wrote,

> And for the first time, the demographics women reflect America as it truly is. That it was Stephens, who is black, defeated Keys, whose mother is white and whose father is black, is not insignificant in a sport predominantly owned, played, and watched by affluent white people.
>
> It's not hyperbolic to say American tennis is in the suddenly vibrant state it's in because of black women, who have been among the most oppressed and marginalized people in the country's history. . . .
>
> It's been said a legacy is planting seeds in a garden you never get to see, but it's taken only one generation to behold the #BlackGirlMagic first teased in the 1950s and sown by a pair of sisters from Compton come into full blossom. Those fruits were on further display on Sunday as Cori "Coco" Gauff, a 13-year-old from Florida, became the youngest girl to play in the U.S. Open girls' finals since the event began in 1974. Her favorite player? Serena.[14]

Gauff won the junior French Open title in 2018. That the top players in America are black and the top junior, the future of American tennis, is also black, has Serena's fingerprints all over it. Of course, Venus helped pave the way; however, Serena occupies a place atop the record books, alone.

She took the baton from Garrison and blew past the competition, even Venus. Her continued dominance and popularity gave more young women hope. They could see themselves holding a tennis racket, hoisting trophies, and walking red carpets. Playing professional tennis was no longer some long-shot dream. With Serena showing how to do it, playing professional tennis seemed like a wise choice. Even the top WNBA players make less in salary than some mid-level tennis players.

Taylor Townsend, an African American player whose career high was number 71, had never won a WTA title or even reached the quarterfinals of a Grand Slam. Yet, at age 22, she had earned more than $1.2 million in prize money. In the WNBA, a sport that is majority black female, the top players earn about $100,000 per year. Going into Wimbledon in 2018, Serena had played in only three tournaments and failed to reach the quarterfinals in any of them. Still, she had earned more than $348,000 in prize money.

As a role model for professional excellence and financial gain, why wouldn't young black girls want to follow Serena into tennis? Moreover, it's not just African American girls who consider Serena their inspiration for going into tennis. Japan's Osaka, Canada's Francoise Abanda, and Great Britain's Heather Watson are women of color who call Serena their idol.

She'll get an arena, schools, and possibly even streets named after her. Nike has already named its largest building at its new corporate headquarters after her. Players will study her game. Historians will measure where she fits into the record books. Serena is already legendary, having left her mark in sports, business, and pop culture. She's in hip-hop videos and mentioned in rap lyrics. In Kanye West's hit song "Gold Digger," the rapper laments, "But I'm lookin' for the one, have you seen her? My psychic told me she'll have an ass like Serena."

She's on posters and in murals, and her name is etched on trophies and engraved on walls. But perhaps more than anything, Serena changed the face of tennis. She brought a black woman's perspective to the forefront of conversations regarding equal pay, body image, work–life balance, domestic abuse, and economic empowerment.

Serena could finish her career with or without the most Grand Slam titles in tennis history. "In our minds, she's the greatest of all time," Chris Evert said via ESPN broadcast after Serena lost to Simona Halep, 6–2, 6–2, in the 2019 Wimbledon final.

After the loss, Serena met with reporters in a postmatch press conference. She appeared more reflective than saddened. She answered questions about her future, her opponent, and her chances of winning that elusive 24th Slam.

The last question came from a female reporter who asked Serena about comments attributed to Billie Jean King. According to the reporter, King thought Serena focused on too many activities outside tennis and should consider scaling back her celebrity and activism, specifically fighting for equality. With her chin up and her eyes focused on the reporter, Serena responded, "The day I stop fighting for equality and for people that look like you and me will be the day I'm in my grave."[15]

A month later, Serena reached the final of the 2019 U.S. Open, another opportunity to win her 24th Grand Slam title. After defeating Sharapova in the opening round of the tournament, Serena took an almost routine route to the finals, dropping just one set in six matches. The opponent and obstacles awaiting her were eerily similar to what she faced against Osaka the previous year. Like Osaka, Bianca Andreescu, 19, hit hard, idolized Serena and had already beaten her that year.

In the first game of the match, Serena struggled with her serve and nerves. Andreescu pounced and took the first set 6–3. She raced out to a 5–1 lead in the second set before Serena roared back to level things at 5–5. The pro-Serena crowd in Arthur Ashe erupted. Jubilant fans hoped they were witnessing an epic comeback. However, Andreescu steadied herself. Serena faltered, her serve vanished. Andreescu won the title, 6–3, 7–5.

Once a dominant closer, Serena was 21–4 in Grand Slam finals from 1999 to 2015. She was now 0–4 since returning from maternity leave.

During the press conference, a reflective Serena pondered what could have been and why she keeps coming up short. "I believe I could have done more today. I believe I could have just been more Serena today," she told reporters. "I honestly don't think Serena showed up. I have to kind of figure out how to get her to show up in Grand Slam finals."[16]

Meanwhile, ESPN aired a commercial from Chase Bank that featured footage of Serena's journey through her pregnancy. The ad begins with sonogram images of Olympia in the womb. Other images included Serena in the hospital the day she gave birth, her later fiddling with a breast pump and playing with her daughter. In the background, a teenage Serena's voice describes how it felt to win her first Grand Slam title, the 1999 U.S. Open. A clip of the then 17-year-old Serena beaming at that first Slam trophy as if it were her baby fades to video of a glowing 37-year-old kissing her toddler. Then these words appear on the screen: "Since 1999, this mama keeps going." The ad captures the essence of Serena's legacy. Even when her play falls short, her influence endures.[17]

Appendix

ALL-TIME RECORDS

OPEN ERA GRAND SLAM SINGLES TITLES LEADERS

Player (NAT)	Australian Open	French Open	Wimbledon	U.S. Open	Total
Serena Williams (USA)	7	3	7	6	23
Steffi Graf (GER)	4	6	7	5	22
Chris Evert (USA)	2	7	3	6	18
Martina Navratilova (USA)	3	2	9	4	18
Margaret Court (AUS)	4	3	1	3	11
Monica Seles (USA)	4	3		2	9
Billie Jean King (USA)		1	4	3	8
Evonne Goolagong Cawley (AUS)	4	1	2		7
Justine Henin (BEL)	1	4		2	7

Player (NAT)	Australian Open	French Open	Wimbledon	U.S. Open	Total
Venus Williams (USA)			5	2	7

ALL-TIME GRAND SLAM SINGLES TITLES LEADERS

Player (NAT)	Australian Open	French Open	Wimbledon	U.S. Open	Total
Margaret Court (AUS)	11	5	3	5	24
Serena Williams (USA)	7	3	7	6	23
Steffi Graf (GER)	4	6	7	7	22
Helen Willis Moody (USA)		4	8	7	19
Chris Evert (USA)	2	7	3	6	18
Martina Navratilova (USA)	3	2	9	4	18
Billie Jean King (USA)	1	1	6	4	12
Maureen Connolly (USA)	1	2	6	4	9
Monica Seles (USA)	4	3		2	9
Suzanne Lenglen (FRA)		2	6		8
Molly Bjurstedt Mallory (USA)				8	8

OPEN ERA MOST GRAND SLAM MATCH WINS

Player (NAT)	W	L
Serena Williams (USA)	343	48
Martina Navratilova (TCH/ USA)	306	49
Chris Evert (USA)	299	37
Steffi Graf (USA)	278	32
Venus Williams (USA)	268	75
Arantxa Sanchez Vicario (ESP)	210	54
Lindsay Davenport (USA)	198	51
Maria Sharapova (RUS)	197	51
Monica Seles (YUG/USA)	180	31
Conchita Martinez (ESP)	174	63

TOP 10 CAREER PRIZE MONEY LEADERS

Player (NAT)	Career Prize Money*
Serena Williams (USA)	$90,382,096
Venus Williams (USA)	$41,505,102
Maria Sharapova (RUS)	$38,621,964
Caroline Wozniacki (DEN)	$34,052,445
Simona Halep (ROU)	$33,228,806
Petra Kvitova (CZE)	$30,137,342
Victoria Azarenka (BLR)	$30,042,918
Angelique Kerber (GER)	$28,514,052
Agnieszka Radwanska (POL)	$27,683,807
Martina Hingis (SUI)	$24,749,074

*as of July 19, 2019

MOST CONSECUTIVE WEEKS AT NUMBER ONE

Player	Number of Weeks	Dates
Steffi Graf	186	August 17, 1987–March 10, 1991

Player	Number of Weeks	Dates
Serena Williams	186	February 18, 2013–September 12, 2016
Martina Navratilova	156	June 14, 1982–June 9, 1985
Chris Evert	113	May 10, 1976–June 6, 1993

MOST YEARS FINISHING IN THE TOP 10

Player	Number of Years
Martina Navratilova	20
Chris Evert	19
Serena Williams	15
Steffi Graf	13
Monica Seles	13
Venus Williams	13
Billie Jean King	12
Virginia Wade	12
Kerry Melville Reid	11
Arantxa Sanchez Vicario	11

MOST OLYMPIC MEDALS

Player	Gold	Silver	Bronze	Total
Venus Williams	4	1		5
Kathleen McKane Godfree*	1	2	2	5
Serena Williams	4			4
Arantxa Sanchez Vicario		2	2	4

*before Open Era

Olympic Medal count from the International Tennis Federation. All other stats from the Women's Tennis Association.

NOTES

I. SERENA'S COUNTRY CLUB UPBRINGING

1. Richard Williams, with Bart Davis, *Black and White: The Way I See It* (New York: Atria Books, 2014), 158.

2. Williams, *Black and White*.

3. Williams, *Black and White*, 163.

4. Williams, *Black and White*, 190.

5. Williams, *Black and White*.

6. Jay Busbee, "Compton Country Club: The Birthplace of Serena Williams's Rise to Stardom," *Yahoo Sports*, September 17, 2015. Retrieved December 27, 2017, from https://sports.yahoo.com/news/compton-country-club--the-birthplace-of-serena-williams-rise-to-stardom-201223323.html.

7. Clay Fowler, "Campaign Builds to Name Compton-Area Tennis Court after Venus and Serena Williams," *San Gabriel Valley Tribune* (via *Los Angeles Daily News*), September 17 2015. Retrieved December 27, 2017, from https://www.dailynews.com/2015/09/17/campaign-builds-to-name-compton-area-tennis-courts-for-serena-and-venus-williams/.

8. Williams, *Black and White*, 215.

9. Shirelle Phelps, *Contemporary Black Biography*, vol. 20 (Farmington Hills, MI: Gale Research, 1999).

10. Williams, *Black and White*, 272.

11. Rick Macci, *Tennis Pro*, July 29, 2017 (M. L. Corbett, interviewer). Unless otherwise noted subsequent quotes from Rick Macci were taken from this interview.

12. Serena Williams, with Daniel Paisner, *On the Line* (New York: Grand Central Publishing, 2009), 91.

13. Williams, *Black and White*, 278.

14. Williams, *On the Line*.

15. Polk County Public Schools records.

16. Polk County Sheriff Department citation, issued December 1992, to Rita Doles, DARE and school resource officer.

17. Williams, *On the Line*, 100.

18. Williams, *On the Line*, 100.

19. Williams, *On the Line*, 101.

20. Ben Rothenberg, "Returning to the Top but with a New View," *New York Times*, October 26, 2012. Retrieved December 27, 2017, from https://www.nytimes.com/2012/10/27/sports/tennis/serena-williams-back-on-the-rise-with-newfound-appreciation.html?_r=0.

21. Lulu Ramadan, "What Were They Like? Coach Recalls Venus, Serena's Youth in Delray," *Palm Beach Post*, July 21, 2017. Retrieved December 27, 2017, from https://www.palmbeachpost.com/news/what-were-they-like-coach-recalls-venus-serena-youth-delray/rRyl6bQmy2xLnoI9hYn5UJ/.

22. Ramadan, "What Were They Like?"

23. Ramadan, "What Were They Like?"

24. Williams, *On the Line*, 103.

25. Robin Finn, "Time to Rock the Boat on Robbing the Cradle," *New York Times*, January 2, 1994. Retrieved December 27, 2017, from https://www.nytimes.com/1994/01/02/sports/on-tennis-time-to-rock-the-boat-on-robbing-the-cradle.html.

26. Robin Finn, "Teenager Fighting to Turn Pro at 14 Puts Off Lawsuit for Now," *New York Times*, October 6, 1995. Retrieved December 27, 2017, from https://www.nytimes.com/1995/10/06/sports/tennis-teen-ager-fighting-to-turn-pro-at-14-puts-off-lawsuit-for-now.html.

2. QUEEN OF THE COURT

1. Robin Finn, "Tennis: A Family Tradition at Age 14," *New York Times*, October 31, 1995. Retrieved December 15, 2017, from https://www.nytimes.com/1995/10/31/sports/tennis-a-family-tradition-at-age-14.html.

2. Serena Williams, with Daniel Paisner, *On the Line* (New York: Grand Central Publishing, 2009), 115.

3. Williams, *On the Line*, 116.

4. Williams, *On the Line*, 116.

5. Lisa Olson, "Spirlea Stays on Bumpy Road No Apology for Venus," *New York Daily News*, November 14, 1997. Retrieved December 15, 2017, from http:/

/www.nydailynews.com/archives/sports/spirlea-stays-bumpy-road-no-apology-venus-article-1.772890.

6. "Major Matches between Venus and Serena Williams," *ESPNW*, January 2017. Retrieved December 15, 2017, from http://www.espn.com/espnw/news-commentary/slideshow/13206202/2/1998-australian-open-second-round-venus-wins-7-6-4-6-1.

7. Williams, *On the Line*, 118.

8. "Venus Beats Sister at Lipton," *CBS News*, March 28, 1999. Retrieved December 15, 2017, from https://www.cbsnews.com/news/venus-beats-sister-at-lipton/.

9. "The 1999 Lipton Championships," *ASAP Sports*, March 28, 1999. Retrieved December 15, 2017, from http://www.asapsports.com/show_interview.php?id=22315.

10. "Hingis, Williams Feud Is Over," *CBS News*, September 4, 1999. Retrieved December 15, 2017, from https://www.cbsnews.com/news/hingis-williams-feud-is-over/.

11. S. L. Price, "Father Knew Best," *Sports Illustrated*, September 20, 1999. Retrieved December 15, 2017, from https://www.si.com/vault/1999/09/20/8110667/father-knew-best-with-her-galvanizing-win-at-the-us-open-serena-williams-proved-dad-righthe-predicted-that-she-not-older-sister-venus-would-be-the-better-playerbut-may-have-created-family-tension.

12. Mike Lupica, "Serena Williams's First U.S. Open Title," *New York Daily News*, September 9, 2016. Retrieved December 15, 2017, from http://www.nydailynews.com/sports/more-sports/great-day-tennis-long-time-coming-article-1.2014993.

13. Selena Roberts, "Serena Wins Match, Then Takes Shot at Hingis," *New York Times*, September 2, 1999. Retrieved December 15, 2017, from http://www.nytimes.com/1999/09/03/sports/u-s-open-serena-williams-wins-match-then-takes-a-shot-at-hingis.html.

14. "The 2000 Ericsson Open," *ASAP Sports*, March 27, 2000. Retrieved December 15, 2017, from http://www.asapsports.com/show_interview.php?id=22196.

15. Selena Roberts, "Serena Williams Wins as Boos Pour Down," *New York Times*, March 18, 2001. Retrieved December 15, 2017, from http://www.nytimes.com/2001/03/18/sports/tennis-serena-williams-wins-as-the-boos-pour-down.html.

16. "Indian Wells, Women," *ASAP Sports*, March 21, 2001. Retrieved December 15, 2017, from http://www.asapsports.com/show_interview.php?id=22089.

17. Mike Puma, "Venus Defeats Serena in 2001 U.S Open Final," *ESPN Classic*, September 8, 2004. Retrieved December 15, 2017, from http://www. espn.com/classic/s/add_williams_venus_and_serena.html.

18. Stephen Bierley, "Final Accolade for the Williamses," *Guardian*, June 6, 2002. Retrieved January 31, 2018, from https://www.theguardian.com/sport/ 2002/jun/07/tennis.frenchopen2002.

19. L. Jon Wertheim, "The Two and Only the French Open Removed All Doubt: Serena and Venus Williams Are in a Class by Themselves," *Sports Illustrated*, June 17, 2002. Retrieved January 31, 2018, from https://www.si.com/ vault/2002/06/17/325325/the-two-and-only-the-french-open-removed-all-doubt-serena-and-venus-williams-are-in-a-class-by-themselves.

20. Wertheim, "The Two and Only the French Open Removed All Doubt."

21. Wertheim, "The Two and Only the French Open Removed All Doubt."

22. "The 2003 Australian Open," *ASAP Sports*, January 23, 2003. Retrieved January 31, 2018, from http://www.asapsports.com/show_interview.php?id= 11643.

23. Christopher Clarey, "Comeback Keeps Final in the Family," *New York Times*, January 23, 2003. Retrieved January 31, 2018, from http://www.nytimes. com/2003/01/24/sports/tennis-comeback-keeps-final-in-family.html.

24. "Williams Hurt by Jeers," *BBC Sports*, June 3, 2003. Retrieved January 31, 2018, from http://news.bbc.co.uk/sport2/hi/tennis/french_open_2003/ 2967190.stml.

25. Jon Henderson, "Sensational Sharapova Is a Russian Revelation," *Guardian*, July 3, 2004. Retrieved January 30, 2018, from https://www.theguardian. com/sport/2004/jul/04/wimbledon2004.wimbledon4.

26. Chris Broussard, "Williams Receives an Apology and Umpires' Open Is Over," *New York Times*, September 9, 2004. Retrieved January 31, 2018, from http://www.nytimes.com/2004/09/09/sports/tennis/williams-receives-apology-and-umpires-open-is-over.html.

27. Alix Ramsey, "Williams Sisters Fear Umpiring Conspiracy," *Telegraph*, September 9, 2004. Retrieved January 31, 2018, from http://www.telegraph.co .uk/sport/tennis/usopen/2386415/Williams-sisters-fear-umpiring-conspiracy.html.

28. Steve Tignor, "Mariana Alves's Missed Call Ushers in Hawk-Eye," *Tennis.com*, November 19, 2015. Retrieved January 31, 2018, from http:// www.tennis.com/pro-game/2015/11/2004-mariana-alves-missed-call-ushers-hawk-eye/56853/.

29. "Williams Comeback Stuns Sharapova," *BBC Sports*, January 27, 2005. Retrieved January 30, 2018, from http://news.bbc.co.uk/sport2/hi/tennis/ 4207687.stm.

30. Pat Cash, "Williams Is Lost Cause," *Times* (London), January 14, 2007. Retrieved January 31, 2018, from https://www.thetimes.co.uk/article/williams-is-lost-cause-pvnphxvp2x6.

31. Christopher Clarey, "Williams Shocks Sharapova to Win Australian Open," *New York Times*, January 27, 2007. Retrieved January 31, 2018, from http://www.nytimes.com/2007/01/27/sports/27iht-web.0127tennis.4368100.html.

32. Associated Press, "Serena Survives Slugfest vs. Venus; Safina Cruises into Semis," *ESPN*, September 3, 2008. Retrieved January 31, 2018, from http://www.espn.com/sports/tennis/usopen08/news/story?id=3567251.

33. Caroline Cheese, "Venus and Serena Through to Final," *BBC Sports*, July 5, 2009. Retrieved January 30, 2018, from http://news.bbc.co.uk/sport2/hi/tennis/8129629.stm.

34. Mark Sappenfield, "Serena Williams Foot Fault: What Did She Say and Why Did She Say It?" *Christian Science Monitor*, September 13, 2009. Retrieved January 30, 2018, from https://www.csmonitor.com/USA/2009/0913/p02s01-usgn.html.

35. "Williams Apologizes for Abusing Line Judge," *Guardian*, September 14, 2009. Retrieved January 30, 2018, from https://www.theguardian.com/sport/2009/sep/14/serena-williams-us-open-kim-clijsters.

36. "Serena Williams in Tears after Triumph," *Evening Standard*, June 21, 2011. Retrieved February 1, 2018, from https://www.standard.co.uk/sport/tennis/serena-williams-in-tears-after-triumph-6413685.html.

37. Associated Press, "Djokovic New No.1; Serena drops to 175th," *Newsday*, July 4, 2011. Retrieved February 1, 2018, from https://www.newsday.com/sports/tennis/djokovic-new-no-1-serena-williams-drops-to-175th-1.3003090.

38. Simon Briggs, "U.S. Open 2011: Sam Stosur Lifts Crown after Serena Williams Rants at Umpire in Women's Final," *Telegraph*, September 12, 2011. Retrieved February 1, 2018, from https://www.telegraph.co.uk/sport/tennis/usopen/8756549/US-Open-2011-Sam-Stosur-lifts-crown-after-Serena-Williams-rants-at-umpire-in-womens-final.html.

39. "Serena Williams Fined $2,000 for Umpire Rant," *BBC Sports*, September 11, 2011. Retrieved February 1, 2018, from https://www.bbc.com/sport/tennis/14876919.

40. Douglas Robson, "Mouratoglou: The Man behind Serena's Latest Surge," *USA Today*, September 2, 2013. Retrieved January 30, 2018, from https://www.usatoday.com/story/sports/tennis/2013/09/02/us-open-2013-serena-williams-patrick-mouratoglou-partnership/2755659/.

41. "2012 Wimbledon," *ASAP Sports*, July 7, 2012. Retrieved January 31, 2018, from http://www.asapsports.com/show_interview.php?id=81404.

42. "Kuznetsova 10 Years at Sanchez-Casal Academy in Barcelona," *Sanchez-Casal Academy*. Retrieved January 31, 2018, from https://www.sanchez-casal.com/public/assets/pdf/playersAtp/c8bcddc1-2959-43eb-a453-15d753a4a9a9.pdf.

43. Associated Press, "Serena Survives Quarterfinals Scare," *ESPN*, June 4, 2013. Retrieved January 31, 2018, from http://www.espn.com/tennis/french13/story/_/id/9340833/2013-french-open-serena-williams-fends-svetlana-kuznetsova.

44. "French Open 2013: Serena Williams Forced to Fight Back against Svetlana Kuznetsova to Claim Place in Semifinals," *Telegraph*, June 4, 2013. Retrieved January 31, 2018, from https://www.telegraph.co.uk/sport/tennis/frenchopen/10098983/French-Open-2013-Serena-Williams-forced-to-fight-back-against-Svetlana-Kuznetsova-to-claim-place-in-semi-finals.html.

45. "Serena Wins 18th Slam," *ESPN*, September 8, 2014. Retrieved February 1, 2018, from http://www.espn.com/tennis/usopen14/story/_/id/11484243/2014-us-open-serena-williams-beats-caroline-wozniacki-win-3rd-straight.

46. "Serena Wins 18th Slam."

47. Jon Wertheim, "Serena Williams Wins Australian Open, 19th Major Title, in Championship Form," *Sports Illustrated*, January 31, 2015. Retrieved February 1, 2018, from https://www.si.com/tennis/2015/01/31/serena-williams-beats-sharapova-wins-australian-open-title.

48. Jessie Lawrence, "U.S. Open Ticket Prices Climbing with Serena Williams Looking to Win a Grand Slam," *Forbes*, July 13, 2015. Retrieved February 1, 2018, from https://www.forbes.com/sites/jesselawrence/2015/07/13/2015-u-s-open-ticket-prices-climbing-with-serena-williams-looking-to-win-grand-slam/#3d710dd72b2a.

49. "Ticket Prices for U.S. Open Women's Final Plunge after Serena's Loss," *Reuters*, September 11, 2015. Retrieved February 1, 2018, from https://www.reuters.com/article/us-tennis-open-tickets/ticket-prices-for-u-s-open-womens-final-plunge-after-serenas-loss-idUSKCN0RB2MI20150911.

50. "Australian Open 2017: Serena Williams Beats Venus Williams to Set Grand Slam Record," *BBC Sports*, January 28, 2017. Retrieved February 1, 2018, from https://www.bbc.com/sport/tennis/38781553.

51. Lisa Respers France, "Serena Williams Is Pregnant, Will Return to Tennis in 2018," *CNN*, May 22, 2017. Retrieved February 1, 2018, from https://www.cnn.com/2017/04/19/sport/serena-williams-baby/index.html.

52. Susannah Cullinane, "Serena Williams Sends a Message to Mothers after Wimbledon Loss," *CNN.com*, July 15, 2018. Retrieved February 1, 2018, from https://www.cnn.com/2018/07/15/tennis/serena-williams-wimbledon-mothers/index.html.

53. Ravi Ubha, "End of an Era for Serena Williams," *CNN.com*, March 6, 2015. Retrieved February 1, 2018, from https://www.cnn.com/2015/03/06/tennis/serena-williams-bajin-tennis/index.html.

54. Jon Healy, "Serena Williams U.S. Open Breakdown Blow-by-Blow," *Australian Broadcasting Company*, September 9, 2018. Retrieved February 1, 2018, from https://www.abc.net.au/news/2018-09-09/serena-williams-us-open-breakdown-blow-by-blow/10218962?section=sport.

55. David Waldstein and Ben Rothenberg, "Serena Williams Accuses Official of Sexism in U.S. Open Loss to Naomi Osaka," *New York Times*, September 8, 2018. Retrieved February 1, 2018, from https://www.nytimes.com/2018/09/08/sports/serena-williams-vs-naomi-osaka-us-open.html.

56. Jon Wertheim, "Four Days Later, Reassessing the Serena–Ramos Controversy," *Sports Illustrated*, September 12, 2018. Retrieved February 1, 2018, from https://www.si.com/tennis/2018/09/12/serena-williams-carlos-ramos-us-open-controversy-umpire-penalty.

57. Alyssa Roenigk, "Serena Williams Hasn't Lost Focus—She's Gained Perspective," *ESPN*, July 15, 2019. Retrieved February 1, 2018, from https://www.espn.com/tennis/story/_/id/27191585/serena-williams-lost-focus-gained-perspective.

3. SISTERLY LOVE

1. "Patrick McEnroe," *ATP World Tour*. Retrieved January 31, 2018, from http://www.atpworldtour.com/en/players/patrick-mcenroe/m048/titles-and-finals.

2. Hiroko Okudaira, Yusuke Kinari, Noriko Mizutani, Fumio Ohtake, and Akira Kawaguchi, "Older Sisters and Younger Brothers: The Impact of Siblings Preference for Competition," *Personality and Individual Differences* 82 (August 2015): 81–89.

3. Jon Wertheim, *Venus Envy: A Sensational Season inside the Women's Tennis Tour* (New York: Harper, 2001).

4. Sylvia Rimm, "The Effects of Sibling Competition," an excerpt from *See Jane Win*, *Family Achievement Clinic*. Retrieved January 31, 2018, from http://www.sylviarimm.com/article_sibcomp.html.

5. Serena Williams, with Daniel Paisner, *On the Line* (New York: Grand Central Publishing, 2009), 49.

6. Williams, *On the Line*, 50.

7. Williams, *On the Line*, 92.

8. Nick Callow, "Venus? You Should See Her Sister," *Independent*, June 22, 1997. Retrieved January 31, 2018, from http://www.independent.co.uk/sport/ wimbledon-1997-venus-you-should-see-her-sister-1257346.html.

9. Callow, "Venus? You Should See Her Sister."

10. Dave Rineberg, *Venus and Serena: My Seven Years as Hitting Coach for the Williams Sisters* (Hollywood, FL: Frederick Fell, 2003), 147.

11. "Oprah Talks to Venus and Serena Williams," *Oprah.com*, March 2003. Retrieved January 31, 2018, from http://www.oprah.com/omagazine/oprahs-interview-with-venus-and-serena-williams/2.

12. "Oprah Talks to Venus and Serena Williams."

13. "The 1999 Lipton Championships," *ASAP Sports*, March 28, 1999. Retrieved December 15, 2017, from http://www.asapsports.com/ show_interview.php?id=22315.

14. Williams, *On the Line*, 43.

15. Williams, *On the Line*, 45.

16. Rineberg, *Venus and Serena*, 140.

17. Rineberg, *Venus and Serena*, 142.

18. Rineberg, *Venus and Serena*, 160.

19. John Roberts, "Williams Sisters' Rare Bond Produces Problems," *Independent*, June 24, 2002. Retrieved December 15, 2017, from https://www. independent.co.uk/sport/tennis/williams-sisters-rare-bond-produces-problem-181338.html.

20. Mark Kreidler, "There's No Evidence to Prove Sisters Tanked," *ESPN*, March 20, 2002. Retrieved January 29, 2018, from http://www.espn.com/ columns/kreidler/1158786.html.

21. Andy Cotton, "Pat Cash Tried to Impugn the Williams Sisters' Wimbledon Accomplishment, but They're Bigger Than Him and That Simpering Chris Evert Put Together," *Austin Chronicle*, July 14, 2000. Retrieved January 29, 2018, from https://www.austinchronicle.com/columns/2000-07-14/77897/.

22. Robert Philip, "Sister Act 'Sad for Women's Tennis,' Says Mauresmo," *Telegraph*, July 5, 2002. Retrieved January 29, 2018, from https://www. telegraph.co.uk/sport/tennis/wimbledon/3030608/Sister-act-sad-for-womens-tennis-says-Mauresmo.html.

23. Bruce Jenkins, "Williams Sisters Let Tennis Do the Talking," *San Francisco Chronicle*, July, 3 2002, https://www.sfgate.com/sports/jenkins/article/ Williams-sisters-let-tennis-do-the-talking-3314407.php.

24. Rineberg, *Venus and Serena*, 160.

25. "2002 U.S. Open," *ASAP Sports*, September 7, 2002. Retrieved January 23, 2018, from http://www.asapsports.com/show_interview.php?id=11673.

26. Paul Newman, "Mad, Dad, and Dangerous to Know: The Strange World of Tennis Parents from Hell," *Independent*, March 11, 2006. Retrieved May 2,

2018, from https://www.independent.co.uk/sport/tennis/mad-dad-and-dangerous-to-know-the-strange-world-of-tennis-parents-from-hell-6106941.html.

27. Robin Finn, "Teenager Says Dad Physically Abused Her," *New York Times*, August 28, 1998. Retrieved May 2, 2018, from https://www.nytimes.com/1998/08/28/sports/tennis-teen-ager-says-father-physically-abused-her.html.

28. Newman, "Mad, Dad, and Dangerous to Know."

29. Finn, "Teenager Says Father Physically Abused Her."

30. "Williams Sisters to Star in Reality Show," *Guardian*, March 29, 2005. Retrieved May 2, 2018, from https://www.theguardian.com/media/2005/mar/29/broadcasting.realitytv.

31. Bill Hewitt, "Fatal Volley," *People.com*, September 19, 2003. Retrieved January 23, 2018, from http://people.com/archive/fatal-volley-vol-60-no-13/.

32. Williams, *On the Line*, 149.

33. Williams, *On the Line*, 158.

34. Williams, *On the Line*, 162.

35. David K. Li, "Williams Sisters Funeral Too Tragic for Dad," *New York Post*, September 20, 2003. Retrieved January 23, 2018, from https://nypost.com/2003/09/20/williams-sis-funeral-too-tragic-for-dad/.

36. Mark Hodgkinson, "Custody Battle for Williams Family," *Telegraph*, January 23, 2004. Retrieved January 23, 2018, from http://www.telegraph.co.uk/sport/tennis/australianopen/2371726/Custody-battle-for-Williams-family.html.

37. William Dodd, "Williams Sisters' Off-Court Troubles," *Independent*, June 20, 2004. Retrieved January 23, 2018, from https://www.independent.ie/world-news/americas/williams-sisters-offcourt-troubles-26221653.html.

38. "Selling the Sisters," *Guardian*, January 9, 2005. Retrieved January 23, 2018, from https://www.theguardian.com/sport/2005/jan/09/tennis.features.

39. Rob Haskell, "Serena Williams on Motherhood, Marriage, and Making Her Comeback," *Vogue.com*, January 10, 2018. Retrieved January 23, 2018, from https://www.vogue.com/article/serena-williams-vogue-cover-interview-february-2018?verso=true.

40. George Bellshaw, "Serena Williams Reveals How She Shook Off Sisterly Love to Develop Tactic to Beat Venus," *Metro*, January 10, 2018. Retrieved February 1, 2018, from http://metro.co.uk/2018/01/10/serena-williams-reveals-shook-off-sisterly-love-develop-tactic-beat-venus-7219688/.

41. V. Freeman, January, 28, 2018 (M. L. Corbett, interviewer).

42. V. Freeman, January, 28, 2018 (M. L. Corbett, interviewer).

43. Bellshaw, "Serena Williams Reveals How She Shook Off Sisterly Love to Develop Tactic to Beat Venus."

44. Juan Jose Vallego, "Serena and Venus: Sisters in Arms," *Rolling Stone*, September 9, 2015. Retrieved February 1, 2018, from https://www.rollingstone. com/sports/features/serena-and-venus-williams-sisters-in-arms-20150909.

45. Sandra Hardwitt, "Serena Beats Sister Venus to Win Australian Open," *USA Today*, January 18 2017. Retrieved January 31, 2018, from https://www. usatoday.com/story/sports/tennis/aus/2017/01/28/serena-williams-beats-siser-venus-win-australian-open/97180312/.

46. Embry Roberts, "Serena Williams Posts Loving Tribute to Sister Venus," *Today.com*, January 29, 2017. Retrieved January 31, 2018, from https://www. today.com/news/serena-williams-posts-tribute-sister-venus-after-australian-open-win-t107526.

47. Wertheim, *Venus Envy*, 4.

4. GALVANIZING GIRL POWER AND
BLACK GIRL MAGIC

1. Alex Tresniowski, "Serena, Serene," *People.com*, March 19, 2007. Retrieved July 17, 2017, from https://people.com/archive/serena-serene-vol-67-no-11/.

2. A. J. Daulerio, "Oh Jason You've Really Gone and Done It Now," *Deadspin*, July 7, 2009. Retrieved July 17, 2017, https://deadspin.com/oh-jason-youve-really-gone-and-done-it-now-5309173.

3. Delia Douglas, January 14, 2018 (M. L. Corbett, interviewer). Unless otherwise noted subsequent quotes from Delia Douglas were taken from this interview.

4. Kim Golombisky, September 27, 2017 (M. L. Corbett, interviewer). Unless otherwise noted subsequent quotes from Kim Golombisky were taken from this interview.

5. Ben Rothenberg, "Tennis's Top Women Balance Body Image with Ambition," *New York Times*, July 10, 2015. Retrieved July 17, 2017, from https:// www.nytimes.com/2015/07/11/sports/tennis/tenniss-top-women-balance-body-image-with-quest-for-success.html.

6. Noelle Devoe, "Why This Article Body Shaming Serena Williams Has Twitter Raging," *Seventeen*, July 14, 2015. Retrieved July 17, 2017, from https:// www.seventeen.com/health/fitness/news/a32346/article-body-shaming-serena-williams-in-a-major-publication-has-twitter-raging/.

7. Margaret Sullivan, "Double Fault in Article on Serena Williams and Body Image," *New York Times*, July, 13, 2015. Retrieved July 17, 2017, from https:// publiceditor.blogs.nytimes.com/2015/07/13/double-fault-in-article-on-serena-williams-and-body-image/.

8. Chris Chase, "Serena Williams Losing to Ronda Rousey for ESPYs Female Athlete of the Year Is a Complete Joke," *USA Today*, July 16, 2015. Retrieved July 17, 2017, from http://ftw.usatoday.com/2015/07/ronda-rousey-serena-williams-espys-best-female-athlete-joke-worthless.

9. Ariana Bacle, "J. K. Rowling Shuts Down a Serena Williams Hater with One Perfect Tweet," July 11, 2015. Retrieved July 17, 2017, from http://ew.com/article/2015/07/11/serena-williams-jk-rowling-tweet/.

10. Claudia Rankine, "The Meaning of Serena Williams," *New York Times Magazine*, August 25, 2015. Retrieved July 17, 2017, from https://www.nytimes.com/2015/08/30/magazine/the-meaning-of-serena-williams.html.

11. Melissa Harris-Perry, *Sister Citizen: Shame Stereotypes, and Black Women in America* (New Haven, CT: Yale University Press, 2013), 210.

12. Dexter Thomas, "Why Everyone Is Saying 'Black Girls Are Magic,'" *Los Angeles Times*, September 9, 2015. Retrieved July 17, 2017, from https://www.latimes.com/nation/nationnow/la-na-nn-everyones-saying-black-girls-are-magic-20150909-htmlstory.html.

13. Nicole Monique, January 28, 2018 (M. L. Corbett, interviewer).

14. Nicole Monique, January 28, 2018 (M. L. Corbett, interviewer).

15. Melissa Harris-Perry, "Serena Williams Is Unstoppable: 'Am I the Greatest? I Don't Know. I'm the Greatest That *I* Can Be,'" *Glamour*, June 7, 2016. Retrieved July 17, 2017, from https://superselected.com/serena-williams-covers-glamour-magazine-with-interview-by-melissa-harris-perry/.

16. Donald Hunt, "Traci Green Leads Harvard Tennis Program to Ivy League Title," *Philadelphia Tribune*, May 16, 2017. Retrieved February 3, 2017, from http://www.phillytrib.com/ap/sports/traci-green-leads-harvard-tennis-program-to-ivy-league-title/article_ff1447d1-cc5e-528e-a2a1-0777d0f06377.html.

17. Errin Whack, "Why Serena Williams Is the Definition of #BlackGirlMagic," *ESPN*, September 11, 2015. Retrieved December 27, 2017, from http://www.espn.com/espnw/athletes-life/article/13625369/why-serena-williams-definition-blackgirlmagic.

18. Nicole Monique, January 28, 2018 (M. L. Corbett, interviewer).

19. Nicole Monique, January 28, 2018 (M. L. Corbett, interviewer).

20. Ricardo Hazell, "Maria Sharapova's Book Reveals Her Fear of a Serena-Led Tennis Planet," *Shadow League*, September 11, 2017. Retrieved December 27, 2017, from https://www.theshadowleague.com/story/maria-sharapova-s-book-reveals-her-fear-of-a-black-tennis-planet.

21. Bim Adewunmi, "Maria Sharapova's Rivalry with Serena Williams Is All in Her Head," *BuzzFeed*, September 9, 2017. Retrieved December 27, 2017, from https://www.buzzfeednews.com/article/bimadewunmi/maria-sharapovas-rivalry-with-serena-williams-is-in-her-head.

22. Whack, "Why Serena Williams Is the Definition of #BlackGirlMagic."

23. Traci L. Green, January 27, 2018 (M. L. Corbett, interviewer).

24. Rebecah Jacobs, "Nike Names World Headquarters Building after Serena Williams," *Black America Web*, December 7, 2017. Retrieved December 27, 2017, from https://blackamericaweb.com/2017/12/07/blackgirlmagic-nike-names-its-biggest-and-newest-building-after-serena-williams/.

25. "Fifteen-Year-Old from Atlanta Is the Youngest Player to Win French Open Qualifier," *AJC Sports*, May 24, 2019. Retrieved December 27, 2017, from https://www.ajc.com/sports/year-old-from-atlanta-the-youngest-player-win-french-open-qualifier/rJOYJTfyHrImYGTCoJjTaI/.

26. Cindy Boren, "Serena Williams Will Deliver Message about Women's Power—during the Super Bowl," *Washington Post*, January 16, 2019. Retrieved December 27, 2017, from https://www.washingtonpost.com/sports/2019/01/16/serena-williams-will-deliver-message-about-womens-power-during-super-bowl/?utm_term=.bb53df67368c.

5. DIGITAL AGE ACTIVIST

1. John Parsons, "Williams Bows Out to Boos," *Telegraph*, June 6, 2003. Retrieved July 17, 2017, from https://www.telegraph.co.uk/sport/tennis/frenchopen/2405480/Williams-bows-out-to-boos.html.

2. Martin Jacques, "Tennis Is Racist—It's Time We Do Something about It," *Guardian*, June 25, 2003. Retrieved July 17, 2017, from https://www.theguardian.com/sport/2003/jun/25/wimbledon2003.tennis11.

3. Ravi Ubha, "Pageantry of the 2001 U.S. Open Final Will Not Be Forgotten," ESPN, June 18, 2008, https://www.espn.com/sports/tennis/wimbledon08/columns/story?columnist=ubha_ravi&id=3472391.

4. Venus Williams, "Wimbledon Has Sent Me a Message: I'm Only a Second-Class Champion," *Times*, June 26, 2006. Retrieved July 17, 2017, from https://www.thetimes.co.uk/article/wimbledon-has-sent-me-a-message-im-only-a-second-class-champion-f056h05hmzq.

5. "Nike Assembles All-Star Cast for Equality in Women's Sports," *Nike.com*, August 24, 2007. Retrieved July 17, 2017, from https://news.nike.com/news/nike-assembles-all-star-cast-calling-for-equality-in-womens-sports.

6. Serena Williams, "The Ball Is in Your Court," *Wired*, October 2015. Retrieved July 17, 2017, from https://www.wired.com/2015/10/serena-williams-guest-editor-race-gender-equality/.

7. Jacob Leibenluft, "Why Don't Jehovah's Witness Vote?" *Slate*, June 26, 2008. Retrieved July 17, 2017, from http://www.slate.com/articles/news_and_politics/explainer/2008/06/why_dont_jehovahs_witnesses_vote.html.

8. Cindy Boren, "Serena Williams May Be Donald Trump's Neighbor, but She Won't Be Voting for Him," *Washington Post*, June 1, 2016. Retrieved July 17, 2017, from https://www.washingtonpost.com/news/early-lead/wp/2016/06/01/serena-williams-may-be-donald-trumps-neighbor-but-she-wont-be-voting-for-him/?utm_term=.86ad203d6cdf.

9. Serena Williams, "Serena Williams: How Black Women Can Close the Pay Gap," *Fortune*, July 31, 2017. Retrieved July 17, 2017, from http://fortune.com/2017/07/31/serena-williams-black-women-equal-pay/.

10. Dan Gartland, "Serena Williams Matches Colin Kaepernick's Donation to Los Angeles Homelessness Charity," *Sports Illustrated*, January 23, 2018. Retrieved February 1, 2018, from https://www.si.com/tennis/2018/01/23/colin-kaepernick-charity-serena-williams-donation.

11. Adam Reed, "Serena Williams Backs Nike's Powerful Statement," *CNBC*, September 5, 2018. Retrieved February 1, 2018, from https://www.cnbc.com/2018/09/05/serena-williams-on-nike-colin-kaepernick-advertising-campaign.html.

12. Eli Rosenberg and Cindy Boren, "'You're Hastening the Hell You Wish to Avoid'; Controversial American Delivers a Shot and Is Called Out by Serena Williams," *Washington Post*, January 22, 2018. Retrieved February 1, 2018, from https://www.washingtonpost.com/news/early-lead/wp/2018/01/22/meet-americas-new-tennis-sensation-tennys-sandgren-he-should-never-have-tweeted/?utm_term=.abca0d391d5e.

13. Laura Wagner, "Serena Williams Calls on Tennys Sandgren to Apologize," *Deadspin*, January 24, 2018. Retrieved January 31, 2018, from https://deadspin.com/serena-williams-calls-on-tennys-sandgren-to-apologize-1822373452.

14. ASAPSports Transcript, Serena Williams press conference, U.S. Open, September 8, 2018, http://www.asapsports.com/show_interview.php?id=143461.

15. Liz Connor, "Serena Williams on Feminism and Motherhood: There Are Barriers I Hope to Break for My Child," *Evening Standard*, August 7, 2017. Retrieved April 28, 2018, from https://www.standard.co.uk/lifestyle/london-life/serena-williams-on-feminism-and-motherhood-there-are-barriers-i-hope-to-break-a3605476.html.

16. ASAPSports Transcript, Serena Williams press conference, U.S. Open, September 8, 2018, http://www.asapsports.com/show_interview.php?id=143461.

17. Andrew Das, "U.S. Women's Soccer Team Sues U.S. Soccer for Gender Discrimination," *New York Times*, March 8, 2019. Retrieved March 10, 2018, from https://www.nytimes.com/2019/03/08/sports/womens-soccer-team-lawsuit-gender-discrimination.html .

18. "2019 Australian Open," *ASAP Sports*, January 19, 2019. Retrieved January 12, 2019, from http://www.asapsports.com/show_interview.php?id=146763.

19. "Serena and Venus Williams Join Advisory Board of the Billie Jean King Leadership Initiative, Nonprofit Focused on Promoting Equality and Inclusion in the Workplace," *PRNewswire*, April 10, 2018. Retrieved January 12, 2019, from https://www.prnewswire.com/news-releases/serena-and-venus-williams-join-advisory-board-of-the-billie-jean-king-leadership-initiative-bjkli-non-profit-focused-on-promoting-equality-and-inclusion-in-the-workplace-300626837.html.

20. Jessica Golden, "Venus and Serena Williams: Men Need to Be Advocates for Pay Equality, Too," *CNBC*, March 8, 2018. Retrieved March 10, 2018, from h ttps://www.cnbc.com/2018/03/08/venus-and-serena-williams-men-need-to-be-advocates-for-pay-equality.html.

21. "2019 BNP Paribas Open," *ASAP Sports*, March 8, 2019. Retrieved March 10, 2018, from http://www.asapsports.com/show_interview.php?id= 147546.

6. INTERNATIONAL FAME AND GLOBAL GIVING

1. Derrick Whyte, "Serena Prepares for Acting Career," *Independent*, August 10, 2002. Retrieved August 12, 2019, from https://www.independent.co.uk/sport/tennis/serena-prepares-for-acting-career-172763.html.

2. "Chris Evert Takes on Serena Williams," *Pro Tennis Fan*, March 29, 2006. Retrieved August 12, 2019, from https://www.protennisfan.com/2006/03/chris_evert_tak.html.

3. Jim Norman, "Football Still Americans' Favorite Sport to Watch," *Gallup.com*, January 4, 2018. Retrieved February 1, 2018, from http://news.gallup.com/poll/224864/football-americans-favorite-sport-watch.aspx.

4. Sylvia Hui, "Queen Elizabeth II Makes First Visit to Wimbledon in 33 Years," *Christian Science Monitor*, June 24, 2010. Retrieved February 1, 2018, from https://www.csmonitor.com/From-the-news-wires/2010/0624/Queen-Elizabeth-II-makes-first-visit-to-Wimbledon-in-33-years.

5. Paul Majendie, "Serena Williams Promises Curtsy Queen Will Never Forget," *Reuters*, June 22, 2010. Retrieved February 1, 2018, from https://www.reuters.com/article/us-tennis-wimbledon-serena-queen-idUSTRE65L43D20100622.

6. "Record Crowd Sees Clijsters Beat Serena Williams," *BBC Sports*, July 9, 2010. Retrieved February 1, 2018, from http://news.bbc.co.uk/sport2/hi/tennis/8803116.stm.

7. Marija Zivlak, "World-Record Crowd Watches Kim Clijsters Beat Serena Williams," *Women's Tennis Blog*, July 9, 2010. Retrieved February 1, 2018,

from http://www.womenstennisblog.com/2010/07/09/world-record-tennis-crowd-watches-kim-clijsters-beat-serena-williams/.

8. "Francesca Schiavone Wins Exhibition," *ESPN*, December 6, 2011. Retrieved February 1, 2018, from https://www.espn.com/tennis/story/_/id/7310474/francesca-schiavone-defeats-venus-williams-serena-williams-exhibition.

9. Elena Bergeron, "How Serena Williams Became the GOAT," *Fader*, October 4, 2016, Retrieved February 1, 2018, from https://www.thefader.com/2016/10/04/serena-williams-interview-cover-story.

10. "Serena Goes for Another First in Bastad," *Women's Tennis Association*, July 2013. Retrieved February 1, 2018, from https://www.wtatennis.com/news/serena-goes-another-first-bastad.

11. Peter Bodo, "Birds of a Feather," *Tennis.com*, July 16, 2013. Retrieved February 1, 2018, from http://www.tennis.com/pro-game/2013/07/birds-feather/48397/.

12. Kamakshi Tandon, "IPTL Spends Nearly $24 Million on Inaugural Teams," *Tennis.com*, March 3, 2014. Retrieved February 1, 2018, from http://www.tennis.com/pro-game/2014/03/itpl-spends-nearly-24-million-inaugural-teams/50789/.

13. "IPTL Draft: Serena Williams Goes to Manila Mavericks," *ABS/CBN Sports*, April 12, 2015. Retrieved February 1, 2018, from https://sports.abs-cbn.com/tennis/news/2015/04/12/iptl-draft-serena-williams-goes-manila-mavericks-1745.

14. "WTA's Digital-TV Audience Keeps Rising," *Women's Tennis Association*, July 2013. Retrieved February 1, 2018, from http://www.wtatennis.com/news/wtas-tv-digital-audiences-keep-rising.

15. "ESPN World Fame 100 2018," *ESPN.com*. Retrieved February 1, 2018, from http://www.espn.com/espn/feature/story/_/id/23519390/espn-world-fame-100-2018#.

16. Cody Fitzpatrick, "World Congratulates Kerber, Serena on Wimbledon Success," *Baseline*, July 14, 2018. Retrieved February 1, 2019, from http://baseline.tennis.com/article/75327/world-reacts-comeback-tastic-wimbledon-final.

17. Serena Williams, with Daniel Paisner, *On the Line* (New York: Grand Central Publishing, 2009), 178.

18. Cora Masters Barry, July 27, 2017 (M. L. Corbett, interviewer).

19. "Tennis Ace Serena Williams Appointed UNICEF's Newest Goodwill Ambassador," *UNICEF USA*, September 2011. Retrieved February 1, 2019, from https://www.unicefusa.org/press/releases/tennis-ace-serena-williams-appointed-unicef%E2%80%99s-newest-goodwill-ambassador/8071.

20. Williams, *On the Line*, 185.

21. Serena Williams, "The Ball Is in Your Court," *Wired*, October 2015. Retrieved July 17, 2017, from https://www.wired.com/2015/10/serena-williams-guest-editor-race-gender-equality/.

22. "The Mother behind the Williams Sisters," *Daily Nation*, November 25, 2008. Retrieved July 17, 2017, from https://www.nation.co.ke/lifestyle/living/1218-494902-p4mbdbz/index.html.

23. Williams, "The Ball Is in Your Court."

24. Philip Sambu, "Serena to Visit Kenya," *Capital FM*, November 10, 2008. Retrieved July 17, 2017, from https://www.capitalfm.co.ke/sports/2008/11/10/serena-to-visit-kenya/.

25. Paul Perry, "Past as Prologue: Where Serena Williams's Philanthropy Comes From," *Inside Philanthropy*, September 2016. Retrieved January 30, 2018, from https://www.insidephilanthropy.com/home/2016/9/15/past-as-prologue-where-serena-williamss-philanthropy-comes-f.html.

26. "Tennis Star Serena Williams Becomes UNICEF's Latest Goodwill Ambassador, with a Focus on Education," *UNICEF*, September 2011. Retrieved July 25, 2017, from https://www.unicef.org/people/people_59874.html.

27. "Tennis Star Serena Williams Becomes UNICEF's Latest Goodwill Ambassador."

28. "Tennis Star Serena Williams Becomes UNICEF's Latest Goodwill Ambassador."

29. "Serena Williams Completes Her First 5K Run," *South Florida Times*, December 18, 2014. Retrieved July 25, 2017, from http://www.sfltimes.com/sports/florida-sports/serena-williams-completes-her-first-5k-run.

30. "Neymar, Serena Williams, and Kolo Touré Join UNICEF and the Global Goals Campaign to Launch the World's Largest Lesson," *UNICEF*, November 2015. Retrieved July 25, 2017, from https://www.unicef.org/media/media_83097.html.

31. "FC Barcelona Foundation, Reach Out to Asia, and UNICEF Launch '1 in 11' Campaign," *UNICEF*, January 2015. Retrieved February 1, 2018, from https://www.unicef.org/media/media_78451.html.

32. "FC Barcelona Foundation, Reach Out to Asia, and UNICEF Launch '1 in 11' Campaign."

33. "Allstate Foundation Purple Purse and Serena Williams Launch National Street Art Campaign to Make Domestic Violence and Financial Abuse Visible," *PRNewswire*, June 21, 2018. Retrieved February 1, 2018, from https://www.prnewswire.com/news-releases/allstate-foundation-purple-purse-and-serena-williams-launch-national-street-art-campaign-to-make-domestic-violence-and-financial-abuse-visible-300670207.html.

34. "The Unique Way Serena Williams Is Giving to Charity," *Rolling Out*, March 8, 2019. Retrieved February 1, 2018, from https://rollingout.com/2019/03/08/the-unique-way-serena-williams-is-giving-to-charity/.

35. Kelly L. Carter, "Venus and Serena Talk Violence and Its Effect on Them and Others," *Undefeated*, December 3, 2017. Retrieved December 1, 2017, from https://theundefeated.com/features/venus-and-serena-williams-talk-violence-at-a-family-affair-presented-by-oath-washington-dc/.

36. Black Girls Code, http://www.blackgirlscode.com/.

7. FASHION FORWARD

1. Imran Amed, "Serena Williams: The Champion's Mindset," *Business of Fashion*, April 23, 2019. Retrieved February 4, 2018, from https://www.businessoffashion.com/articles/people/serena-williams-the-champions-mindset.

2. Serena Williams, with Daniel Paisner, *On the Line* (New York: Grand Central Publishing, 2009), 130.

3. "'Catsuit' Tennis Outfit Designed and Made by Puma," *Museum of Applied Arts and Sciences*, 2002. Retrieved February 4, 2018, from https://collection.maas.museum/object/347001.

4. Amed, "Serena Williams."

5. Mark Hodgkinson, "Serena: From Queen of Tennis to Fashion Menace," *Telegraph*, January 14, 2005. Retrieved February 4, 2018, from https://www.telegraph.co.uk/sport/tennis/australianopen/2353735/Serena-from-queen-of-tennis-to-fashion-menace.html.

6. Delia Douglas, January 14, 2018 (M. L. Corbett, interviewer). Unless otherwise noted subsequent quotes from Delia Douglas were taken from this interview.

7. Associated Press, "Serena Williams Breaks Out Another Pair $40K Earrings," *ESPN.com*, August 31, 2005. Retrieved February 4, 2018, from https://www.espn.com/sports/tennis/usopen05/news/story?id=2148225.

8. Brittany Talarico, "Serena Williams on Designing Her Line in between Tennis Tournaments: 'It Was a Lot,'" *People*, September 17, 2015. Retrieved February 4, 2018, from http://people.com/style/serena-williams-on-designing-her-line-in-between-tennis-tournaments-it-was-a-lot/.

9. Williams, *On the Line*, 132.

10. Williams, *On the Line*, 133.

11. Williams, *On the Line*, 123.

12. Steve Tignor, "Tennis through the Lens," *Tennis.com*, September 11, 2013. Retrieved February 4, 2018, from http://www.tennis.com/photos-video/2013/09/tennis-through-lens/49128/.

13. Marija Zivlak, "All Nike Dresses Serena Wore during Her 78 Match Wins and 11 Trophy Lifts in 2013," *Women's Tennis Blog*, November 27, 2013. Retrieved February 4, 2018, from http://www.womenstennisblog.com/2013/11/27/all-nike-dresses-serena-wore-during-her-78-match-wins-and-11-trophy-lifts-in-2013/.

14. *Footwear News*, January 29, 2018, https://footwearnews.com/2015/fn-spy/athletic-outdoor/serena-williams-us-open-nike-mark-parker-55349/.

15. Bobby Chintapalli, "Serena Williams's Leopard Dress Draws Attention," *USA Today*, September 3, 2014. Retrieved February 4, 2018, from https://www.usatoday.com/story/sports/tennis/2014/09/03/serena-williams-nike-leopard-print-dress/15020023/.

16. Jacqueline Tsang, "Serena Williams Rules in Women's Tennis while Also Making Her Mark in Fashion," *South China Morning Post*, July 2, 2015. Retrieved February 2, 2018, from http://www.scmp.com/magazines/style/article/1826481/serena-williams-rules-womens-tennis-while-also-making-her-mark.

17. Dan Can, "Fashion BFF's Serena Williams and Anna Wintour Buddy Up again at Fendi's MFW Show," *Daily Mail*, September 22, 2016. Retrieved February 2, 2018, from http://www.dailymail.co.uk/tvshowbiz/article-3802150/Fashion-BFFs-Serena-Williams-Anna-Wintour-buddy-Fendi-catwalk-Milan.html.

18. "Serena Williams Reveals She Designed the Garish Yellow Tennis Ensemble Slammed as 'Hideous' by Australian Open Spectators—to Bring 'Pop Culture and Fun' to the Courts," *Daily Mail*, January 22, 2016. Retrieved February 2, 2018, from https://www.dailymail.co.uk/femail/article-3411920/Serena-says-new-outfit-pops-Australian-Open.html.

19. Lucy Jones, "Shocked Wimbledon Fans Slam BBC after It Shows Serena Williams's 'Distracting' Nipples," *Sun*, July 7, 2016. Retrieved February 18, 2018, from https://www.thesun.co.uk/news/1402901/angry-viewers-slam-bbc-as-serena-williams-flashes-her-nipples-during-wimbo-quarter-final/.

20. Jenna Lemoncelli, "Serena Williams Body Shamed for Nipples at Wimbledon: Fans Come to Her Defense," *Hollywood Life*, July 7, 2016. Retrieved February 18, 2018, from http://hollywoodlife.com/2016/07/07/serena-williams-body-shamed-wimbledon-2016-nipples-fans-defense/.

21. "Fashionable 50," *Sports Illustrated*, July 24, 2017. Retrieved April 10, 2018, from https://www.si.com/vault/2017/07/19/fashionable-50#.

22. "Fashionable 50."

23. Katherine Burgess, January 26, 2018 (M. L. Corbett, interviewer). Unless otherwise noted subsequent quotes from Katherine Burgess were taken from this interview.

24. Leigh Nordstrom, "Serena Williams Hopes 'S' Means Success," *WWD*, May 30, 2018. Retrieved April 10, 2018, from http://wwd.com/eye/people/exclusive-serena-williams-launches-serena-line-1202683280/.

25. Steff Yotka, "Serena Williams Is Launching Her Own Direct-to-Consumer Fashion Collection—and It's Really Good," *Vogue*, May 30, 2018. Retrieved June 10, 2018, from https://www.vogue.com/article/serena-williams-launches-serena-fashion-collection?verso=true.

26. Yotka, "Serena Williams Is Launching Her Own Direct-to-Consumer Fashion Collection."

27. Liana Satenstein, "It Took Serena Williams's Professional Bedazzler 24 Hours to Customize Her Wedding Sneakers," *Vogue*, November 22, 2017. Retrieved June 10, 2018, from https://www.vogue.com/article/serena-williams-bedazzled-wedding-nike-sneakers.

28. Sarah Royce-Greensill, "Serena Williams on Exercising While Pregnant and Why Fashion Is Harder Than Tennis," *Telegraph*, August 21, 2017. Retrieved January 28, 2018, from http://www.telegraph.co.uk/luxury/jewellery/serena-williams-exercising-pregnant-fashion-harder-tennis/.

29. Erika Harwood, "Serena Williams Will Wear Virgil Abloh at the U.S. Open," *Vanity Fair*, August 13, 2018. Retrieved January 28, 2018, from https://www.vanityfair.com/style/2018/08/serena-williams-will-wear-virgil-abloh-at-the-us-open.

30. Rachel Epstein, "Meghan Markle Twinned with Serena Williams and Wore a Blazer from Her Collection," *Marie Claire*, October 17, 2018. Retrieved January 28, 2018, from https://www.marieclaire.com/fashion/a23852722/meghan-markle-serena-williams-matching-blazer/.

31. Lauren Thomas, "Serena Williams Joins Online Retailer Poshmark's Board of Directors," *CNBC*, February 20, 2019. Retrieved January 28, 2018, from https://www.cnbc.com/2019/02/20/serena-williams-joins-online-retailer-poshmarks-board-of-directors.html.

32. Brooke Bobb, "A Met Gala Is Born! Lady Gaga, Harry Styles, and Serena Williams Will Cochair Fashion's Biggest Night in 2019—Here's What It Means," *Vogue*, October 12, 2018. Retrieved January 28, 2018, from https://www.vogue.com/article/met-gala-2019-lady-gaga-harry-styles-serena-williams?verso=true.

33. Abby Gardner, "The Hidden Meaning behind Serena Williams's Wimbledon 2019 Outfit," *Glamour*, July 3, 2019. Retrieved January 28, 2018, from https://www.glamour.com/story/serena-williamss-wimbledon-2019-outfit-broosh-meaning.

8. BRAND SERENA

1. "America's Richest Self-Made Women," *Forbes*, June 4, 2019. Retrieved October 1, 2019, from https://www.forbes.com/self-made-women/list/2/ #tab:overall.

2. Lynn Zinser, "Titan of Tennis vs. the Next Big Thing," *New York Times*, September 10, 2011. Retrieved February 1, 2018, from https://www.nytimes. com/2011/09/10/sports/tennis/serena-williams-to-face-wozniacki-who-wants-to-be-next-big-thing.html.

3. Elizabeth Grice, "I Didn't Do That Drug Thing Because of Venus," *Telegraph*, November 11, 2009. Retrieved January 30, 2018, from http://www. telegraph.co.uk/sport/tennis/williamssisters/6539057/Serena-Williams-I-didnt-do-that-drugs-thing-because-of-Venus.html.

4. Associated Press, "Serena Sets Career Prize Money Mark," *ESPN*, January 29, 2009. Retrieved January 30, 2018, from http://www.espn.com/sports/ tennis/aus09/news/story?id=3870020.

5. Cora Masters Barry, July 27, 2017 (M. L. Corbett, interviewer).

6. "Tennis Legend Serena Williams Aces with Sell Out of Exclusive New Collection on HSN," *Home Shopping Network*, May 5, 2009. Retrieved January 30, 2018, from https://corporate.hsn.com/newsroom/pressrelease/tennis-legend-serena-williams-aces-with-sell-out-of-exclusive-new-collection-on-hsn/.

7. Terry Lefton, "Some of the Interest in New Sports Scores Isn't at the Top," *Sports Business Daily*, June 29, 2009. Retrieved January 30, 2018, from https://www.sportsbusinessdaily.com/Journal/Issues/2009/06/29/ Marketingsponsorship/Some-Of-The-Interest-In-New-Sports-Q-Scores-Isnt-At-The-Top.aspx.

8. Terry Lefton, "Penalty Drop: Tiger Woods Plummets on Sports Q Scores List," *Sports Business Daily*, June 7, 2010. Retrieved January 30, 2018, from https://www.sportsbusinessdaily.com/Journal/Issues/2010/06/07/ Marketingsponsorship/Penalty-Drop-Tiger-Woods-Plummets-On-Sports-Q-Scores-List.aspx.

9. Lynn Zinser, "Serena Williams to Face Wozniacki, Who Wants to Be Next Big Thing," *New York Times*, September 9, 2011. Retrieved January 30, 2018, from https://www.nytimes.com/2011/09/10/sports/tennis/serena-williams-to-face-wozniacki-who-wants-to-be-next-big-thing.html.

10. Roz A. Gee, "Serena Williams Talks Business, Branding, and Sports Performance," *Black Enterprise*, October 6, 2015. Retrieved January 30, 2018, from http://www.blackenterprise.com/serena-williams-talks-business-branding-and-sports-performance/.

11. Megan McCluskey, "Serena Williams's Inspiring Sportsperson of the Year Acceptance Speech," *Time*, December 16, 2015. Retrieved January 30,

2018, from http://time.com/4152274/serena-williams-sportsperson-of-the-year-acceptance-speech/.

12. Kurt Badenhausen, "Novak Djokovic and Serena Williams Are Tennis' Biggest Stars on Social Media," *Forbes*, September 9, 2016. Retrieved January 30, 2018, from https://www.forbes.com/sites/kurtbadenhausen/2016/09/09/novak-djokovic-and-serena-williams-are-tennis-biggest-social-media-stars/#59e8eab4101a.

13. Badenhausen, "Novak Djokovic and Serena Williams Are Tennis' Biggest Stars on Social Media."

14. "Tops of 2017: Pro Athlete Marketability," *Nielsen*, December 21. 2017. Retrieved January 30, 2018, from http://www.nielsen.com/us/en/insights/news/2017/tops-of-2017-pro-athlete-marketability.html.

15. Ahiza Garcia, "Older Athletes Are Killing It on the Field and in Endorsements," *CNNMoney*, January 31, 2018. Retrieved January 30, 2018, from http://money.cnn.com/2018/01/31/news/companies/tom-brady-roger-federer-sponsorship/index.html.

16. Kurt Badenhausen, "Serena Williams Tops Sharapova as the World's Highest-Paid Female Athlete," *Forbes*, June 6, 2016. Retrieved January 30, 2018, from https://www.forbes.com/sites/kurtbadenhausen/2016/06/06/serena-tops-sharapova-as-the-worlds-highest-paid-female-athlete/#51d0b9901fda.

17. Karina Oachis, "Key Concepts to Learn from the Personal Brand of Serena Williams," May 2017, https://www.karinaochis.com/key-concepts-to-learn-from-the-personal-brand-of-serena-williams/.

18. Sara Swisher, "Serena Williams Is Joining SurveyMonkey Board," *Vox*, May 24, 2017. Retrieved January 30, 2018, from https://www.vox.com/2017/5/24/15683476/serena-williams-joins-survey-monkey-board.

19. Sarah Spain, "Serena Williams Focusing on Business, Charity, Family While Away from Tennis," *ESPN.com*, June 23, 2017. Retrieved January 30, 2018, from http://www.espn.com/espnw/voices/espnw-columnists/article/19719611/serena-williams-focusing-business-charity-family-away-tennis.

20. "Berlei Celebrates 100 Years with Second Chapter of Serena Williams 'Do It for Yourself' Campaign," *Marketing*, August 4, 2017. Retrieved January 30, 2018, from https://www.marketingmag.com.au/news-c/berlei-williams/.

21. Melissa Minton, "Nike Headquarters Names Building after Serena Williams," *Architectural Digest*, December 7, 2017. Retrieved January 30, 2018, from https://www.architecturaldigest.com/story/nike-headquarters-names-building-after-serena-williams.

22. "Serena Williams Flaunts Million-Dollar Bump . . . at Dollar Tree!" *TMZ*, May 4, 2017. Retrieved February 4, 2018, from http://www.tmz.com/2017/05/04/serena-williams-dollar-store-baby-bump/.

23. "Serena Williams Ass Shakin' and Servin' Aces . . . in Front of Private Jet," *TMZ*, January 10, 2018. Retrieved February 1, 2018, from http://www.tmz.com/2018/01/10/serena-williams-dancing-private-jet-lemon/.

24. Eric Brandt, "Serena Williams Is the Newest Lincoln Brand Ambassador," *Drive*, February 15, 2018. Retrieved February 1, 2018, from https://www.thedrive.com/news/18497/serena-williams-is-the-newest-lincoln-brand-ambassador.

25. E. J. Shultz, "Serena Williams's New Gatorade Spot Includes Her Baby's Double," *Ad Age*, November 20, 2017. Retrieved January 31, 2018, from http://adage.com/article/cmo-strategy/serena-williams-gatorade-spot-includes-baby-s-body-double/311356/.

26. Marci Robin, "Serena Williams Is Reportedly Launching a Beauty Brand," *Allure*, March 12, 2018. Retrieved January 31, 2018, from https://www.allure.com/story/serena-williams-beauty-brand.

27. Simon Ogus, "Serena Williams Announces Her VC Firm on Instagram after Five Years Investing in Diverse Companies," *Forbes*, April 19, 2019. Retrieved May 20, 2019, from https://www.forbes.com/sites/simonogus/2019/04/19/serena-williams-announces-her-vc-firm-on-instagram-after-five-years-investing-in-diverse-companies/#2d7ceadf7bac.

28. Serena Ventures, https://www.serenaventures.com/.

29. Kurt Badenhausen, "America's Richest Self-Made Women: Inside Serena Williams's Plan to Ace Venture Investing," *Forbes*, June 3, 2019. Retrieved June 20, 2019, from https://www.forbes.com/sites/kurtbadenhausen/2019/06/03/inside-serena-williams-plan-to-ace-venture-investing/#6f7a289a7787.

9. SECOND ACT

1. John Berkok, "At 37, Venus Williams Can Become the Oldest Player to Win a Major," *Tennis.com*, January 2, 2018. Retrieved February 1, 2018, http://www.tennis.com/pro-game/2018/01/37-venus-williams-can-become-oldest-player-win-major/71015/.

2. Christopher Clarey, "Serena Williams Confirms She's Pregnant after Day of Speculation," *New York Times*, April 19, 2017, https://www.nytimes.com/2017/04/19/sports/tennis/serena-williams-pregnant-snapchat.html.

3. Rob Haskell, "Serena Williams on Motherhood, Marriage, and Making Her Comeback," *Vogue.com*, January 10, 2018. Retrieved January 23, 2018, from https://www.vogue.com/article/serena-williams-vogue-cover-interview-february-2018?verso=true.

4. Annie Waldman, "How Hospitals Are Failing Black Mothers," *ProPublica*, December 27, 2017. Retrieved February 17, 2018, from https://www.propublica.org/article/how-hospitals-are-failing-black-mothers.

5. Haskell, "Serena Williams on Motherhood, Marriage, and Making Her Comeback."

6. Associated Press, "Serena Williams Returns with Exhibition Loss to Jelena Ostapenko," *ESPN*, December 30, 2017. Retrieved January 23, 2018, from http://www.espn.com/tennis/story/_/id/21916440/serena-williams-returns-exhibition-loss-jelena-ostapenko.

7. Haskell, "Serena Williams on Motherhood, Marriage, and Making Her Comeback."

8. "Serena Williams," *FedCup.com*. Retrieved February 17, 2018, from https://www.fedcup.com/en/players/player.aspx?id=800205424.

9. Chris McKendry, January 4, 2018 (M. L. Corbett, interviewer).

10. Katrina Adams, January 4, 2018 (M. L. Corbett, interviewer).

11. Simon Chambers, "Serena's Coach Backs Decision to Skip Australian Open," *ESPN*, January 5, 2018. Retrieved January 30, 2018, from http://www.espn.com/tennis/story/_/id/21970713/serena-coach-patrick-mouratoglou-backs-decision-withdraw-australian-open.

12. Rob Haskell, "Love All," *Vogue*, February 1, 2018. Retrieved February 26, 2018, from https://archive.vogue.com/article/2018/2/1/love-all.

13. Gatto Luigi, "Patrick Mouratoglou: 'Serena Williams Plans to Come Back in Indian Wells,'" *TennisWorld*, January 21, 2018. Retrieved January 31, 2018, from http://www.tennisworldusa.org/tennis/news/Serena_Williams/51124/patrick-mouratoglou-serena-williams-plans-to-come-back-in-indian-wells-/.

14. Steve Megargee, "Serena Williams Loses in Doubles, US Advances in Fed Cup," February 11, 2018, Associated Press, https://www.apnews.com/046313260b434a92a2fd4d95c4ecb484.

15. Haskell, "Love All."

16. Simon Briggs, "Serena Williams Named 25th Seed for Wimbledon 2018," *Telegraph*, June 27, 2018. Retrieved July 7, 2018, from https://www.telegraph.co.uk/tennis/2018/06/27/serena-williams-named-25th-seed-wimbledon-2018/.

17. "The Championships Wimbledon," *ASAP Sports*, July 1, 2018. Retrieved July 7, 2018, from http://www.asapsports.com/show_interview.php?id=141996.

18. Charlie Eccleshare and Mick Cleary, "Serena Williams Wins Battle of the Working Mothers to See Off Evgeniya Rodina and Reach Wimbledon 2018 Quarter-Final," *Telegraph*, July 9, 2018, https://www.telegraph.co.uk/tennis/2018/07/09/serena-williams-vs-evgeniya-rodina-wimbledon-2018-live-score/.

19. "The Championships," *ASAP Sports*, July 10, 2018. Retrieved July 17, 2018, from http://www.asapsports.com/show_interview.php?id=141846.

20. "The Championships."

21. "Serena Williams through to Wimbledon 2018 Final after Victory over Julia Georges," *Mirror*, July 12, 2018. Retrieved July 17, 2018, from https://www.mirror.co.uk/sport/tennis/serena-williams-through-wimbledon-2018-12906380.

22. "Serena Williams Suffers the Worst Defeat of Her Career," *CNN*, August 1, 2018. Retrieved August 8, 2018, from https://www.cnn.com/2018/08/01/tennis/serena-williams-johanna-konta-silicon-valley-classic-spt-intl/index.html.

23. Charlie Eccleshare, "Johanna Konta Thumps Serena Williams to Inflict Most One-Sided Defeat of Her Career," *Telegraph*, August 1, 2018, https://www.telegraph.co.uk/tennis/2018/08/01/johanna-konta-thumps-serena-williams-inflict-one-sided-defeat/.

24. "Famed Hitting Partner Sascha Bajin Joins Forces with Naomi Osaka," *Women's Tennis Association*, December 6, 2017. Retrieved February 1, 2018, from http://www.wtatennis.com/news/sascha-bajin-join-forces-naomi-osaka.

25. Hannah Chubb, "Serena Williams Finally Gets Her Own Wheaties Box: 'I Have Dreamt of This,'" *People*, June 26, 2019. Retrieved July 7, 2019, from https://people.com/food/serena-williams-first-wheaties-box-cover/.

26. "Wheaties Scores an Ace with Serena Williams Wheaties Box," *General Mills*, June 25, 2019. Retrieved July 7, 2019, from https://www.generalmills.com/en/News/NewsReleases/Library/2019/June/Wheaties-scores-an-ace-with-Serena-Williams-Wheaties-box.

10. CONCLUSION

1. Don Riddell, "John McEnroe: 'Attlia the Hun' of Tennis," *CNN*, February 21, 2013. Retrieved February 3, 2018, from https://edition.cnn.com/2013/02/20/sport/tennis/john-mcenroe-tennis/index.html.

2. Jason Gay, "Roger Federer Can't Be Stopped," *Wall Street Journal*, May 23, 2018. Retrieved June 3, 2018, from https://www.wsj.com/articles/roger-federer-cant-be-stopped-1527080506.

3. Chris Chase, "Serena Williams Is the Best Tennis Player Ever. So Why Is Her Career the Greatest?" *Fox Sports*, January 28, 2017. Retrieved February 3, 2018, from https://www.foxsports.com/tennis/story/serena-williams-greatest-tennis-player-ever-wins-australian-open-2017-venus-martina-steffi-012817.

4. Douglas Perry, "Serena Williams Isn't 'America's Sweetheart,' but She Is America's Greatest Champion," *Oregon Live*, February 23, 2015. Retrieved February 3, 2018, from https://www.oregonlive.com/the-spin-of-the-ball/index.ssf/2015/02/serena_williams_isnt_americas.html.

5. Mark Reason, "Serena Williams Just a Little Too Black to Be Accepted in the United States," *Stuff*, February 4, 2015. Retrieved February 3, 2018, from

https://www.stuff.co.nz/sport/opinion/65740611/reason-serena-williams-just-a-little-too-black-to-be-accepted-in-united-states.

6. Kamakshi Tandon, "Conventional Ways of Serena," *ESPN*, September 4, 2012. Retrieved February 3, 2018, from http://www.espn.com/tennis/usopen12/story/_/id/8333931/us-open-conventional-serena.

7. V. Freeman, January, 28, 2018 (M. L. Corbett, interviewer).

8. Scott Stump, "Serena Williams on Motherhood, Return to Tennis: 'I Feel Like I've Already Won,'" *Today*, September 7, 2018. Retrieved September 17, 2018, from https://www.today.com/parents/serena-williams-motherhood-i-feel-i-ve-already-won-t137064.

9. V. Freeman, January, 28, 2018 (M. L. Corbett, interviewer).

10. V. Freeman, January, 28, 2018 (M. L. Corbett, interviewer).

11. Nicholas McCarvel, "Is Sloane Stephens the New Serena of American Tennis?" *Daily Beast*, January 22, 2013. Retrieved February 3, 2018, from https://www.thedailybeast.com/is-sloane-stephens-the-new-serena-of-american-tennis.

12. Paul Newman, "Sloane Stephens Sets Up Test for Serena Williams's Mentoring," *Independent*, January 22, 2013. Retrieved February 3, 2018, from https://www.independent.co.uk/sport/tennis/sloane-stephens-sets-up-test-of-serena-williams-mentoring-8460940.html.

13. Alysha Tsuji, "Naomi Osaka Had the Greatest Reaction to Beating Serena Williams at Miami Open," *USA Today*, March, 21, 2018. Retrieved September 17, 2018, from https://www.usatoday.com/story/sports/ftw/2018/03/21/naomi-osaka-had-the-greatest-reaction-to-beating-serena-williams-at-miami-open-omg/111141426/.

14. Bryan Armen Graham, "The U.S. Open Showed Black Women Have Made American Tennis Great Again," *Guardian*, September 11, 2017. Retrieved September 17, 2018, from https://www.theguardian.com/sport/2017/sep/11/sloane-stephens-us-open-tennis-venus-williams.

15. "Serena Williams Vows to Never Stop Fighting for Equality," Wimbledon Press Conference, *ESPN*, July 13, 2019. Retrieved July 28, 2019, from http://www.espn.com/videohub/video/clip/_/id/27181898.

16. Steve Tignor, "A Unified Theory of Why Serena Williams Is Struggling in Slam Finals," *Tennis.com*, September 8, 2019. Retrieved September 10, 2019, from http://www.tennis.com/pro-game/2019/09/serena-williams-grand-slam-final-losses-bianca-andreescu-us-open/84832/.

17. Scott Stump, NBC Today Show, "New Serena Williams Commercial Reminds Us That All Moms Are Champions," September 5, 2019, https://www.today.com/parents/new-serena-williams-commercial-reminds-us-all-moms-are-champions-t161964.

BIBLIOGRAPHY

"2002 U.S. Open." *ASAP Sports*, September 7, 2002. Retrieved January 23, 2018, from http://www.asapsports.com/show_interview.php?id=11673.

"The 2003 Australian Open." *ASAP Sports*, January 23, 2003. Retrieved January 31, 2018, from http://www.asapsports.com/show_interview.php?id=11643.

"2012 Wimbledon." *ASAP Sports*, July 7, 2012. Retrieved January 31, 2018, from http://www.asapsports.com/show_interview.php?id=81404.

"2019 Australian Open." *ASAP Sports*, January 19, 2019. Retrieved January 12, 2019, from http://www.asapsports.com/show_interview.php?id=146763.

"2019 BNP Paribas Open." *ASAP Sports*, March 8, 2019. Retrieved March 10, 2018, from http://www.asapsports.com/show_interview.php?id=147546.

Adewunmi, B. "Maria Sharapova's Rivalry with Serena Williams Is All in Her Head." *Buzz-Feed*, September 9, 2017. Retrieved December 27, 2017, from https://www.buzzfeednews.com/article/bimadewunmi/maria-sharapovas-rivalry-with-serena-williams-is-in-her-head.

"Allstate Foundation Purple Purse and Serena Williams Launch National Street Art Campaign to Make Domestic Violence and Financial Abuse Visible." *PRNewswire*, June 21, 2018. Retrieved February 1, 2018, from https://www.prnewswire.com/news-releases/allstate-foundation-purple-purse-and-serena-williams-launch-national-street-art-campaign-to-make-domestic-violence-and-financial-abuse-visible-300670207.html.

Amed, I. "Serena Williams: The Champion's Mindset." *Business of Fashion*, April 23, 2019. Retrieved February 4, 2018, from https://www.businessoffashion.com/articles/people/serena-williams-the-champions-mindset.

Associated Press. "Djokovic New No.1; Serena drops to 175th." *Newsday*, July 4, 2011. Retrieved February 1, 2018, from https://www.newsday.com/sports/tennis/djokovic-new-no-1-serena-williams-drops-to-175th-1.3003090.

———. "Serena Sets Career Prize Money Mark." *ESPN*, January 29, 2009. Retrieved January 30, 2018, from http://www.espn.com/sports/tennis/aus09/news/story?id=3870020.

———. "Serena Survives Quarterfinals Scare." *ESPN*, June 4, 2013. Retrieved January 31, 2018, from http://www.espn.com/tennis/french13/story/_/id/9340833/2013-french-open-serena-williams-fends-svetlana-kuznetsova.

———. "Serena Survives Slugfest vs. Venus; Safina Cruises into Semis." *ESPN*, September 3, 2008. Retrieved January 31, 2018, from http://www.espn.com/sports/tennis/usopen08/news/story?id=3567251.

———. "Serena Williams Breaks Out Another Pair $40K Earrings." *ESPN*, August 31, 2005. Retrieved February 4, 2018, from https://www.espn.com/sports/tennis/usopen05/news/story?id=2148225.

————. "Serena Williams Returns with Exhibition Loss to Jelena Ostapenko." *ESPN*, December 30, 2017. Retrieved January 23, 2018, from http://www.espn.com/tennis/story/_/id/21916440/serena-williams-returns-exhibition-loss-jelena-ostapenko.

"Australian Open 2017: Serena Williams Beats Venus Williams to Set Grand Slam Record." *BBC Sports*, January 28, 2017. Retrieved February 1, 2018, from https://www.bbc.com/sport/tennis/38781553.

Bacle, A. "J. K. Rowling Shuts Down a Serena Williams Hater with One Perfect Tweet." July 11, 2015. Retrieved July 17, 2017, from http://ew.com/article/2015/07/11/serena-williams-jk-rowling-tweet/.

Badenhausen, K. "America's Richest Self-Made Women: Inside Serena Williams's Plan to Ace Venture Investing." *Forbes*, June 3, 2019. Retrieved June 20, 2019, from https://www.forbes.com/sites/kurtbadenhausen/2019/06/03/inside-serena-williams-plan-to-ace-venture-investing/#6f7a289a7787.

————. "Novak Djokovic and Serena Williams Are Tennis' Biggest Stars on Social Media." *Forbes*, September 9, 2016. Retrieved January 30, 2018, from https://www.forbes.com/sites/kurtbadenhausen/2016/09/09/novak-djokovic-and-serena-williams-are-tennis-biggest-social-media-stars/#59e8eab4101a.

————. "Serena Williams Tops Sharapova as the World's Highest-Paid Female Athlete." *Forbes*, June 6, 2016. Retrieved January 30, 2018, from https://www.forbes.com/sites/kurtbadenhausen/2016/06/06/serena-tops-sharapova-as-the-worlds-highest-paid-female-athlete/#51d0b9901fda.

Bellshaw, G. "Serena Williams Reveals How She Shook Off Sisterly Love to Develop Tactic to Beat Venus." *Metro*, January 10, 2018. Retrieved February 1, 2018, from http://metro.co.uk/2018/01/10/serena-williams-reveals-shook-off-sisterly-love-develop-tactic-beat-venus-7219688/.

Bergeron, E. "How Serena Williams Became the GOAT." *Fader*, October 4, 2016, Retrieved February 1, 2018, from https://www.thefader.com/2016/10/04/serena-williams-interview-cover-story.

Berkok, J. "At 37, Venus Williams Can Become the Oldest Player to Win a Major." *Tennis.com*, January 2, 2018. Retrieved February 1, 2018, from http://www.tennis.com/pro-game/2018/01/37-venus-williams-can-become-oldest-player-win-major/71015/.

"Berlei Celebrates 100 Years with Second Chapter of Serena Williams 'Do It for Yourself' Campaign." *Marketing*, August 4, 2017. Retrieved January 30, 2018, from https://www.marketingmag.com.au/news-c/berlei-williams/.

Bierley, S. "Final Accolade for the Williamses." *Guardian*, June 6, 2002. Retrieved January 31, 2018, from https://www.theguardian.com/sport/2002/jun/07/tennis.frenchopen2002.

Bobb, B. "A Met Gala Is Born! Lady Gaga, Harry Styles, and Serena Williams Will Cochair Fashion's Biggest Night in 2019—Here's What It Means." *Vogue*, October 12, 2018. Retrieved January 28, 2018, from https://www.vogue.com/article/met-gala-2019-lady-gaga-harry-styles-serena-williams?verso=true.

Bodo, P. "Birds of a Feather." *Tennis.com*, July 16, 2013. Retrieved February 1, 2018, from http://www.tennis.com/pro-game/2013/07/birds-feather/48397/.

Boren, C. "Serena Williams May Be Donald Trump's Neighbor, but She Won't Be Voting for Him." *Washington Post*, June 1, 2016. Retrieved July 17, 2017, from https://www.washingtonpost.com/news/early-lead/wp/2016/06/01/serena-williams-may-be-donald-trumps-neighbor-but-she-wont-be-voting-for-him/?utm_term=.86ad203d6cdf.

————. "Serena Williams Will Deliver Message about Women's Power—during the Super Bowl." *Washington Post*, January 16, 2019. Retrieved December 27, 2017, from https://www.washingtonpost.com/sports/2019/01/16/serena-williams-will-deliver-message-about-womens-power-during-super-bowl/?utm_term=.bb53df67368c.

Brandt, E. "Serena Williams Is the Newest Lincoln Brand Ambassador." *Drive*, February 15, 2018. Retrieved February 1, 2018, from https://www.thedrive.com/news/18497/serena-williams-is-the-newest-lincoln-brand-ambassador.

Briggs, S. "Serena Williams Named 25th Seed for Wimbledon 2018." *Telegraph*, June 27, 2018. Retrieved July 7, 2018, from https://www.telegraph.co.uk/tennis/2018/06/27/serena-williams-named-25th-seed-wimbledon-2018/.

————. "U.S. Open 2011: Sam Stosur Lifts Crown after Serena Williams Rants at Umpire in Women's Final." *Telegraph*, September 12, 2011. Retrieved February 1, 2018, from https://www.telegraph.co.uk/sport/tennis/usopen/8756549/US-Open-2011-Sam-Stosur-lifts-crown-after-Serena-Williams-rants-at-umpire-in-womens-final.html.

Broussard, C. "Williams Receives an Apology and Umpires' Open Is Over." *New York Times*, September 9, 2004. Retrieved January 31, 2018, from http://www.nytimes.com/2004/09/09/sports/tennis/williams-receives-apology-and-umpires-open-is-over.html.

Busbee, J. "Compton Country Club: The Birthplace of Serena Williams's Rise to Stardom." *Yahoo Sports*, September 17, 2015. Retrieved December 27, 2017, from https://sports.yahoo.com/news/compton-country-club--the-birthplace-of-serena-williams-rise-to-stardom-201223323.html.

Callow, N. "Wimbledon 1997: Venus? You Should See Her Sister." *Independent*, June 22, 1997. Retrieved January 31, 2018, from http://www.independent.co.uk/sport/wimbledon-1997-venus-you-should-see-her-sister-1257346.html.

Can, D. "Fashion BFF's Serena Williams and Anna Wintour Buddy Up again at Fendi's MFW Show." *Daily Mail*, September 22, 2016. Retrieved February 2, 2018, from http://www.dailymail.co.uk/tvshowbiz/article-3802150/Fashion-BFFs-Serena-Williams-Anna-Wintour-buddy-Fendi-catwalk-Milan.html.

Carter, K. L. "Venus and Serena Talk Violence and Its Effect on Them and Others." *Undefeated*, December 3, 2017. Retrieved December 1, 2017, from https://theundefeated.com/features/venus-and-serena-williams-talk-violence-at-a-family-affair-presented-by-oath-washington-dc/.

Cash, P. "Williams Is Lost Cause." *Times* (London), January 14, 2007. Retrieved January 31, 2018, from https://www.thetimes.co.uk/article/williams-is-lost-cause-pvnphxvp2x6.

"'Catsuit' Tennis Outfit Designed and Made by Puma." *Museum of Applied Arts and Sciences*, 2002. Retrieved February 4, 2018, from https://collection.maas.museum/object/347001.

Chambers, S. "Serena's Coach Backs Decision to Skip Australian Open." *ESPN*, January 5, 2018. Retrieved January 30, 2018, from http://www.espn.com/tennis/story/_/id/21970713/serena-coach-patrick-mouratoglou-backs-decision-withdraw-australian-open.

"The Championships." *ASAP Sports*, July 10, 2018. Retrieved July 17, 2018, from http://www.asapsports.com/show_interview.php?id=141846.

"The Championships Wimbledon." *ASAP Sports*, July 1, 2018. Retrieved July 7, 2018, from http://www.asapsports.com/show_interview.php?id=141996.

Chase, C. "Serena Williams Is the Best Tennis Player Ever. So Why Is Her Career the Greatest?" *Fox Sports*, January 28, 2017. Retrieved February 3, 2018, from https://www.foxsports.com/tennis/story/serena-williams-greatest-tennis-player-ever-wins-australian-open-2017-venus-martina-steffi-012817.

————. "Serena Williams Losing to Ronda Rousey for ESPYs Female Athlete of the Year Is a Complete Joke." *USA Today*, July 16, 2015. Retrieved July 17, 2017, from http://ftw.usatoday.com/2015/07/ronda-rousey-serena-williams-espys-best-female-athlete-joke-worthless.

Cheese, C. "Venus and Serena Through to Final." *BBC Sports*, July 5, 2009. Retrieved January 30, 2018, from http://news.bbc.co.uk/sport2/hi/tennis/8129629.stm.

Chintapalli, B. "Serena Williams's Leopard Dress Draws Attention." *USA Today*, September 3, 2014. Retrieved February 4, 2018, from https://www.usatoday.com/story/sports/tennis/2014/09/03/serena-williams-nike-leopard-print-dress/15020023/.

"Chris Evert Takes on Serena Williams." *Pro Tennis Fan*, March 29, 2006. Retrieved August 12, 2019, from https://www.protennisfan.com/2006/03/chris_evert_tak.html.

Chubb, H. "Serena Williams Finally Gets Her Own Wheaties Box: 'I Have Dreamt of This.'" *People*, June 26, 2019. Retrieved July 7, 2018, from https://people.com/food/serena-williams-first-wheaties-box-cover/.

Clarey, C. "Comeback Keeps Final in the Family." *New York Times*, January 23, 2003. Retrieved January 31, 2018, from http://www.nytimes.com/2003/01/24/sports/tennis-comeback-keeps-final-in-family.html.

————. "Williams Shocks Sharapova to Win Australian Open." *New York Times*, January 27, 2007. Retrieved January 31, 2018, from http://www.nytimes.com/2007/01/27/sports/27iht-web.0127tennis.4368100.html.

Connor, L. "Serena Williams on Feminism and Motherhood: There Are Barriers I Hope to Break for My Child." *Evening Standard*, August 7, 2017. Retrieved April 28, 2018, from https://www.standard.co.uk/lifestyle/london-life/serena-williams-on-feminism-and-motherhood-there-are-barriers-i-hope-to-break-a3605476.html.

Conyers, J. J. *Race in American Sports*. Jefferson, NC: McFarland, 2014.

Cotton, A. "Pat Cash Tried to Impugn the Williams Sisters' Wimbledon Accomplishment, but They're Bigger Than Him and That Simpering Chris Evert Put Together." *Austin Chronicle*, July 14, 2000. Retrieved January 29, 2018, from https://www.austinchronicle.com/columns/2000-07-14/77897/.

Cullinane, S. "Serena Williams Sends a Message to Mothers after Wimbledon Loss." *CNN.com*, July 15, 2018. Retrieved February 1, 2018, from https://www.cnn.com/2018/07/15/tennis/serena-williams-wimbledon-mothers/index.html.

Das, A. "U.S. Women's Soccer Team Sues U.S. Soccer for Gender Discrimination." *New York Times*, March 8, 2019. Retrieved March 10, 2018, from https://www.nytimes.com/2019/03/08/sports/womens-soccer-team-lawsuit-gender-discrimination.html.

Daulerio, A. J. "Oh Jason You've Really Gone and Done It Now." *Deadspin*, July 7, 2009. Retrieved July 17, 2017, from https://deadspin.com/oh-jason-youve-really-gone-and-done-it-now-5309173.

Devoe, N. "Why This Article Body Shaming Serena Williams Has Twitter Raging." *Seventeen*, July 14, 2015. Retrieved July 17, 2017, from https://www.seventeen.com/health/fitness/news/a32346/article-body-shaming-serena-williams-in-a-major-publication-has-twitter-raging/.

Djata, S. *Blacks at the Net: Black Achievement in the History of Tennis*. Syracuse, NY: Syracuse University Press, 2008.

Dodd, W. "Venus, Serena, and the Inconspicuous Consumption of Blackness: A Commentary on Surveillance, Race Talk, and New Racism(s)." *Journal of Black Studies* 43, no. 2 (2012): 127–45.

————. "Venus, Serena, and the Women's Tennis Association: When and Where 'Race' Enters." *Sociology of Sport Journal* 22, no. 3 (2005): 263–76.

————. "Williams Sisters' Off-Court Troubles." *Independent*, June 20, 2004. Retrieved January 23, 2018, from https://www.independent.ie/world-news/americas/williams-sisters-off-court-troubles-26221653.html.

Eboda, M. "Why Serena Is the Greatest Sportsperson Ever." *Guardian*, September 7, 2016. Retrieved March 20, 2017, from https://www.theguardian.com/commentisfree/2016/sep/07/serena-williams-greatest-sportsperson-ever.

Epstein, R. "Meghan Markle Twinned with Serena Williams and Wore a Blazer from Her Collection." *Marie Claire*, October 17, 2018. Retrieved January 28, 2018, from https://www.marieclaire.com/fashion/a23852722/meghan-markle-serena-williams-matching-blazer/.

"ESPN World Fame 100 2018." *ESPN.com*. Retrieved February 1, 2018, from http://www.espn.com/espn/feature/story/_/id/23519390/espn-world-fame-100-2018#.

"Famed Hitting Partner Sascha Bajin Joins Forces with Naomi Osaka." *Women's Tennis Association*, December 6, 2017. Retrieved February 1, 2018, from http://www.wtatennis.com/news/sascha-bajin-join-forces-naomi-osaka.

"Fashionable 50." *Sports Illustrated*, July 24, 2017. Retrieved April 10, 2018, from https://www.si.com/vault/2017/07/19/fashionable-50#.

"FC Barcelona Foundation, Reach Out to Asia, and UNICEF Launch 1 in 11 Campaign." *UNICEF*, January 2015. Retrieved February 1, 2018, from https://www.unicef.org/media/media_78451.html.

Finn, R. "On Tennis; Time to Rock the Boat on Robbing the Cradle." *New York Times*, January 2, 1994. Retrieved December 27, 2017, from https://www.nytimes.com/1994/01/02/sports/on-tennis-time-to-rock-the-boat-on-robbing-the-cradle.html.

————. "Teenager Fighting to Turn Pro at 14 Puts Off Lawsuit for Now." *New York Times*, October 6, 1995. Retrieved December 27, 2017, from https://www.nytimes.com/1995/10/06/sports/tennis-teen-ager-fighting-to-turn-pro-at-14-puts-off-lawsuit-for-now.html.

————. "Teenager Says Dad Physically Abused Her." *New York Times*, August 28, 1998. Retrieved May 2, 2018, from https://www.nytimes.com/1998/08/28/sports/tennis-teen-ager-says-father-physically-abused-her.html.

————. "Tennis: A Family Tradition at Age 14." *New York Times*, October 31, 1995. Retrieved December 15, 2017, from https://www.nytimes.com/1995/10/31/sports/tennis-a-family-tradition-at-age-14.html.

Fitzpatrick, C. "World Congratulates Kerber, Serena, on Wimbledon Success." *Baseline*, July 14, 2018. Retrieved February 1, 2019, from http://baseline.tennis.com/article/75327/world-reacts-comeback-tastic-wimbledon-final.

Fowler, C. "Campaign Builds to Name Compton-Area Tennis Court after Venus and Serena Williams." *San Gabriel Valley Tribune* (via *Los Angeles Daily News*), September 17 2015. Retrieved December 27, 2017, from https://www.dailynews.com/2015/09/17/campaign-builds-to-name-compton-area-tennis-courts-for-serena-and-venus-williams/.

France, L. R. "Serena Williams Is Pregnant, Will Return to Tennis in 2018." *CNN*, May 22, 2017. Retrieved February 1, 2018, from https://www.cnn.com/2017/04/19/sport/serena-williams-baby/index.html.

"Francesca Schiavone Wins Exhibition." *ESPN*, December 6, 2011. Retrieved February 1, 2018, from https://www.espn.com/tennis/story/_/id/7310474/francesca-schiavone-defeats-venus-williams-serena-williams-exhibition.

"French Open 2013: Serena Williams Forced to Fight Back against Svetlana Kuznetsova to Claim Place in Semifinals." *Telegraph*, June 4, 2013. Retrieved January 31, 2018, from https://www.telegraph.co.uk/sport/tennis/frenchopen/10098983/French-Open-2013-Serena-Williams-forced-to-fight-back-against-Svetlana-Kuznetsova-to-claim-place-in-semi-finals.html.

Garcia, A. "Older Athletes Are Killing It on the Field and in Endorsements." *CNNMoney*, January 31, 2018. Retrieved January 30, 2018, from http://money.cnn.com/2018/01/31/news/companies/tom-brady-roger-federer-sponsorship/index.html.

Gardner, A. "The Hidden Meaning behind Serena Williams's Wimbledon 2019 Outfit." *Glamour*, July 3, 2019. Retrieved January 28, 2018, from https://www.glamour.com/story/serena-williamss-wimbledon-2019-outfit-broosh-meaning.

Gartland, D. "Serena Williams Matches Colin Kaepernick's Donation to Los Angeles Homelessness Charity." *Sports Illustrated*, January 23, 2018. Retrieved February 1, 2018, from https://www.si.com/tennis/2018/01/23/colin-kaepernick-charity-serena-williams-donation.

Gay, J. "Roger Federer Can't Be Stopped." *Wall Street Journal*, May 23, 2018. Retrieved June 3, 2018, from https://www.wsj.com/articles/roger-federer-cant-be-stopped-1527080506.

Gee, R. A. "Serena Williams Talks Business, Branding, and Sports Performance." *Black Enterprise*, October 6, 2015. Retrieved January 30, 2018, from http://www.blackenterprise.com/serena-williams-talks-business-branding-and-sports-performance/.

Golden, J. "Venus and Serena Williams: Men Need to Be Advocates for Pay Equality, Too." *CNBC*, March 8, 2018. Retrieved March 10, 2018, from https://www.cnbc.com/2018/03/08/venus-and-serena-williams-men-need-to-be-advocates-for-pay-equality.html.

Graham, B. A. "The U.S. Open Showed Black Women Have Made American Tennis Great Again." *Guardian*, September 11, 2017. Retrieved September 17, 2018, from https://www.theguardian.com/sport/2017/sep/11/sloane-stephens-us-open-tennis-venus-williams.

Gray, F. C., and Y. Rice Lamb. *Born to Win: The Authorized Biography of Althea Gibson*. Hoboken, NJ: John Wiley & Sons, 2004.

Grice, E. "I Didn't Do That Drug Thing Because of Venus." *Telegraph*, November 11, 2009. Retrieved January 30, 2018, from http://www.telegraph.co.uk/sport/tennis/williamssisters/6539057/Serena-Williams-I-didnt-do-that-drugs-thing-because-of-Venus.html.

Hardwitt, S. "Serena Beats Sister Venus to Win Australian Open." *USA Today*, January 18 2017. Retrieved January 31, 2018, from https://www.usatoday.com/story/sports/tennis/aus/2017/01/28/serena-williams-beats-siser-venus-win-australian-open/97180312/.

Harris-Perry, M. "Serena Williams Is Unstoppable: 'Am I the Greatest? I Don't Know. I'm the Greatest That *I* Can Be.'" *Glamour*, June 7, 2016. Retrieved July 17, 2017, from https://superselected.com/serena-williams-covers-glamour-magazine-with-interview-by-melissa-harris-perry/.

———. *Sister Citizen: Shame Stereotypes, and Black Women in America*. New Haven, CT: Yale University Press, 2013.

Harwood, E. "Serena Williams Will Wear Virgil Abloh at the U.S. Open." *Vanity Fair*, August 13, 2018. Retrieved January 28, 2018, from https://www.vanityfair.com/style/2018/08/serena-williams-will-wear-virgil-abloh-at-the-us-open.

Haskell, R. "Love All." *Vogue*, February 1, 2018. Retrieved February 26, 2018, from https://archive.vogue.com/article/2018/2/1/love-all.

———. "Serena Williams on Motherhood, Marriage, and Making Her Comeback." *Vogue.com*, January 10, 2018. Retrieved January 23, 2018, from https://www.vogue.com/article/serena-williams-vogue-cover-interview-february-2018?verso=true.

Hazell, R. "Maria Sharapova's Book Reveals Her Fear of a Serena-Led Tennis Planet." *Shadow League*, September 11, 2017. Retrieved December 27, 2017, from https://www.theshadowleague.com/story/maria-sharapova-s-book-reveals-her-fear-of-a-black-tennis-planet.

Healy, J. "Serena Williams U.S. Open Breakdown Blow-by-Blow." *Australian Broadcasting Company*, September 9, 2018. Retrieved February 1, 2018, from https://www.abc.net.au/news/2018-09-09/serena-williams-us-open-breakdown-blow-by-blow/10218962?section=sport.

Henderson, J. "Sensational Sharapova Is a Russian Revelation." *Guardian*, July 3, 2004. Retrieved January 30, 2018, from https://www.theguardian.com/sport/2004/jul/04/wimbledon2004.wimbledon4.

Hewitt, B. "Fatal Volley." *People.com*, September 19, 2003. Retrieved January 23, 2018, from http://people.com/archive/fatal-volley-vol-60-no-13/.

"Hingis, Williams Feud Is Over." *CBS News*, September 4, 1999. Retrieved December 15, 2017, from https://www.cbsnews.com/news/hingis-williams-feud-is-over/.

Hodgkinson, M. "Custody Battle for Williams Family." *Telegraph*, January 23, 2004. Retrieved January 23, 2018, from http://www.telegraph.co.uk/sport/tennis/australianopen/2371726/Custody-battle-for-Williams-family.html.

———. "Serena: From Queen of Tennis to Fashion Menace." *Telegraph*, January 14, 2005. Retrieved February 4, 2018, from https://www.telegraph.co.uk/sport/tennis/australianopen/2353735/Serena-from-queen-of-tennis-to-fashion-menace.html.

Hui, S. "Queen Elizabeth II Makes First Visit to Wimbledon in 33 Years." *Christian Science Monitor*, June 24, 2010. Retrieved February 1, 2018, from https://www.csmonitor.com/From-the-news-wires/2010/0624/Queen-Elizabeth-II-makes-first-visit-to-Wimbledon-in-33-years.

Hunt, D. "Traci Green Leads Harvard Tennis Program to Ivy League Title." *Philadelphia Tribune*, May 16, 2017. Retrieved February 3, 2017, from http://www.phillytrib.com/ap/sports/traci-green-leads-harvard-tennis-program-to-ivy-league-title/article_ff1447d1-cc5e-528e-a2a1-0777d0f06377.html.

"Indian Wells, Women." *ASAP Sports*, March 21, 2001. Retrieved December 15, 2017, from http://www.asapsports.com/show_interview.php?id=22089.

"IPTL Draft: Serena Williams Goes to Manila Mavericks." *ABS/CBN Sports*, April 12, 2015. Retrieved February 1, 2018, from https://sports.abs-cbn.com/tennis/news/2015/04/12/iptl-draft-serena-williams-goes-manila-mavericks-1745.

Jacobs, R. "Nike Names World Headquarters Building after Serena Williams." *Black America Web*, December 7, 2017. Retrieved December 27, 2017, from https://blackamericaweb.com/2017/12/07/blackgirlmagic-nike-names-its-biggest-and-newest-building-after-serena-williams/.

Jacques, M. "Tennis Is Racist—It's Time We Do Something about It." *Guardian*, June 25, 2003. Retrieved July 17, 2017, from https://www.theguardian.com/sport/2003/jun/25/wimbledon2003.tennis11.

Jones, L. "Shocked Wimbledon Fans Slam BBC after It Shows Serena Williams's 'Distracting' Nipples." *Sun*, July 7, 2016. Retrieved February 18, 2018, from https://www.thesun.co.uk/news/1402901/angry-viewers-slam-bbc-as-serena-williams-flashes-her-nipples-during-wimbo-quarter-final/.

Kreidler, M. "There's No Evidence to Prove Sisters Tanked." *ESPN*, March 20, 2002. Retrieved January 29, 2018, from http://www.espn.com/columns/kreidler/1158786.html.

"Kuznetsova 10 Years at Sanchez-Casal Academy in Barcelona." *Sanchez-Casal Academy*. Retrieved January 31, 2018, from https://www.sanchez-casal.com/public/assets/pdf/playersAtp/c8bcddc1-2959-43eb-a453-15d753a4a9a9.pdf.

Kyle-DeBose, C. H. *Charging the Net*. Chicago: Ivan R. Dee, 2007.

Lapchick, R., B. Jessica, S. J. Baker, C. Lahey, S. Martin-Tenney, H. Ruiz, and R. Sleeper. *100 Trailblazers: Great Women Athletes Who Opened Doors for Future Generations*. Morgantown, WV: Fitness Information Technology, 2009.

Lawrence, J. "U.S. Open Ticket Prices Climbing with Serena Williams Looking to Win a Grand Slam." *Forbes*, July 13, 2015. Retrieved February 1, 2018, from https://www.forbes.com/sites/jesselawrence/2015/07/13/2015-u-s-open-ticket-prices-climbing-with-serena-williams-looking-to-win-grand-slam/#3d710dd72b2a.

Lefton, T. "Penalty Drop: Tiger Woods Plummets on Sports Q Scores List." *Sports Business Daily*, June 7, 2010. Retrieved January 30, 2018, from https://www.sportsbusinessdaily.com/Journal/Issues/2010/06/07/Marketingsponsorship/Penalty-Drop-Tiger-Woods-Plummets-On-Sports-Q-Scores-List.aspx.

———. "Some of the Interest in New Sports Scores Isn't at the Top." *Sports Business Daily*, June 29, 2009. Retrieved January 30, 2018, from https://www.sportsbusinessdaily.com/Journal/Issues/2009/06/29/Marketingsponsorship/Some-Of-The-Interest-In-New-Sports-Q-Scores-Isnt-At-The-Top.aspx.

Leibenluft, J. "Why Don't Jehovah's Witness Vote?" *Slate*, June 26, 2008. Retrieved July 17, 2017, from http://www.slate.com/articles/news_and_politics/explainer/2008/06/why_dont_jehovahs_witnesses_vote.html.

Lemoncelli, J. "Serena Williams Body Shamed for Nipples at Wimbledon: Fans Come to Her Defense." *Hollywood Life*, July 7, 2016. Retrieved February 18, 2018, from http://hollywoodlife.com/2016/07/07/serena-williams-body-shamed-wimbledon-2016-nipples-fans-defense/.

Li, D. K. "Williams Sisters Funeral Too Tragic for Dad." *New York Post*, September 20, 2003. Retrieved January 23, 2018, from https://nypost.com/2003/09/20/williams-sis-funeral-too-tragic-for-dad/.

"The Lipton Championships." *ASAP Sports*, March 28, 1999. Retrieved December 15, 2017, from http://www.asapsports.com/show_interview.php?id=22315.

Luigi, G. "Patrick Mouratoglou: 'Serena Williams Plans to Come Back in Indian Wells.'" *TennisWorld*, January 21, 2018. Retrieved January 31, 2018, from http://www.tennisworldusa.org/tennis/news/Serena_Williams/51124/patrick-mouratoglou-serena-williams-plans-to-come-back-in-indian-wells-/.

Lupica, M. "Serena Williams's First U.S. Open Title." *New York Daily News*, September 9, 2016. Retrieved December 15, 2017, from http://www.nydailynews.com/sports/more-sports/great-day-tennis-long-time-coming-article-1.2014993.

Majendie, P. "Serena Williams Promises Curtsy Queen Will Never Forget." *Reuters*, June 22, 2010. Retrieved February 1, 2018, from https://www.reuters.com/article/us-tennis-wimbledon-serena-queen-idUSTRE65L43D20100622.

"Major Matches between Venus and Serena Williams." *ESPNW*, January 2017. Retrieved December 15, 2017, from http://www.espn.com/espnw/news-commentary/slideshow/13206202/2/1998-australian-open-second-round-venus-wins-7-6-4-6-1.

McCarvel, N. "Is Sloane Stephens the New Serena of American Tennis?" *Daily Beast*, January 22, 2013. Retrieved February 3, 2018, from https://www.thedailybeast.com/is-sloane-stephens-the-new-serena-of-american-tennis.

McCluskey, M. "Serena Williams's Inspiring Sportsperson of the Year Acceptance Speech." *Time*, December 16, 2015. Retrieved January 30, 2018, from http://time.com/4152274/serena-williams-sportsperson-of-the-year-acceptance-speech/.

Minton, M. "Nike Headquarters Names Building after Serena Williams." *Architectural Digest*, December 7, 2017. Retrieved January 30, 2018, from https://www.architecturaldigest.com/story/nike-headquarters-names-building-after-serena-williams.

"The Mother behind the Williams Sisters." *Daily Nation*, November 25, 2008. Retrieved July 17, 2017, from https://www.nation.co.ke/lifestyle/living/1218-494902-p4mbdbz/index.html.

Newman, P. "Mad, Dad, and Dangerous to Know: The Strange World of Tennis Parents from Hell." *Independent*, March 11, 2006. Retrieved May 2, 2018, from https://www.independent.co.uk/sport/tennis/mad-dad-and-dangerous-to-know-the-strange-world-of-tennis-parents-from-hell-6106941.html.

———. "Sloane Stephens Sets Up Test for Serena Williams's Mentoring." *Independent*, January 22, 2013. Retrieved February 3, 2018, from https://www.independent.co.uk/sport/tennis/sloane-stephens-sets-up-test-of-serena-williams-mentoring-8460940.html.

"Neymar, Serena Williams, and Kolo Touré Join UNICEF and the Global Goals Campaign to Launch the World's Largest Lesson." *UNICEF*, November 2015. Retrieved July 25, 2017, from https://www.unicef.org/media/media_83097.html.

"Nike Assembles All-Star Cast for Equality in Women's Sports." *Nike.com*, August 24, 2007. Retrieved July 17, 2017, from https://news.nike.com/news/nike-assembles-all-star-cast-calling-for-equality-in-womens-sports.

Nordstrom, L. "Serena Williams Hopes 'S' Means Success." *WWD*, May 30, 2018. Retrieved April 10, 2018, from http://wwd.com/eye/people/exclusive-serena-williams-launches-serena-line-1202683280/.

Norman, J. "Football Still America's Favorite Sport to Watch." *Gallup.com*, January 4, 2018. Retrieved February 1, 2018, from http://news.gallup.com/poll/224864/football-americans-favorite-sport-watch.aspx.

Ogus, S. "Serena Williams Announces Her VC Firm on Instagram after Five Years Investing in Diverse Companies." *Forbes*, April 19, 2019. Retrieved May 20, 2019, from https://www.forbes.com/sites/simonogus/2019/04/19/serena-williams-announces-her-vc-firm-on-instagram-after-five-years-investing-in-diverse-companies/#2d7ceadf7bac.

Okudaira, H., Y. Kinari, N. Mizutani, F. Ohtake, and A. Kawaguchi. "Older Sisters and Younger Brothers: The Impact of Siblings Preference for Competition." *Personality and Individual Differences* 82 (August 2015): 81–89.

Olson, L. "Spirlea Stays on Bumpy Road No Apology for Venus." *New York Daily News*, November 14, 1997. Retrieved December 15, 2017, from http://www.nydailynews.com/archives/sports/spirlea-stays-bumpy-road-no-apology-venus-article-1.772890.

"Oprah Talks to Venus and Serena Williams." *Oprah.com*, March 2003. Retrieved January 31, 2018, from http://www.oprah.com/omagazine/oprahs-interview-with-venus-and-serena-williams/2.

Parsons, J. "Williams Bows Out to Boos." *Telegraph*, June 6, 2003. Retrieved July 17, 2017, from https://www.telegraph.co.uk/sport/tennis/frenchopen/2405480/Williams-bows-out-to-boos.html.

Perry, D. "Serena Williams Isn't 'America's Sweetheart,' but She Is America's Greatest Champion." *Oregon Live*, February 23, 2015. Retrieved February 3, 2018, from https://www.oregonlive.com/the-spin-of-the-ball/index.ssf/2015/02/serena_williams_isnt_americas.html.

Perry, P. "Past as Prologue: Where Serena Williams's Philanthropy Comes From." *Inside Philanthropy*, September 2016. Retrieved July 17, 2017, from "https://www.insidephilanthropy.com/home/2016/9/15/past-as-prologue-where-serena-williamss-philanthropy-comes-f.html.

Phelps, S. *Contemporary Black Biography*, vol. 20. Farmington Hills, MI: Gale Research, 1999.

Philip, R. "Sister Act 'Sad for Women's Tennis,' says Mauresmo." *Telegraph*, July 5, 2002. Retrieved January 29, 2018, from https://www.telegraph.co.uk/sport/tennis/wimbledon/3030608/Sister-act-sad-for-womens-tennis-says-Mauresmo.html.

Price, S. L. "Father Knew Best." *Sports Illustrated*, September 20, 1999. Retrieved December 15, 2017, from https://www.si.com/vault/1999/09/20/8110667/father-knew-best-with-her-galvanizing-win-at-the-us-open-serena-williams-proved-dad-righthe-predicted-that-she-not-older-sister-venus-would-be-the-better-playerbut-may-have-created-family-tension.

Puma, M. "Venus Defeats Serena in 2001 U.S Open Final." *ESPN Classic*, September 8, 2004. Retrieved December 15, 2017, from http://www.espn.com/classic/s/add_williams_venus_and_serena.html.

Ramadan, L. "What Were They Like? Coach Recalls Venus, Serena's Youth in Delray." *Palm Beach Post*, July 21, 2017. Retrieved December 27, 2017, from https://www.palmbeachpost.com/news/what-were-they-like-coach-recalls-venus-serena-youth-delray/rRyl6bQmy2xLnoI9hYn5UJ/.

Ramsey, A. "Williams Sisters Fear Umpiring Conspiracy." *Telegraph*, September 9, 2004. Retrieved January 31, 2018, from http://www.telegraph.co.uk/sport/tennis/usopen/2386415/Williams-sisters-fear-umpiring-conspiracy.html.

Rankine, C. "The Meaning of Serena Williams." *New York Times Magazine*, August 25, 2015. Retrieved July 17, 2017, from https://www.nytimes.com/2015/08/30/magazine/the-meaning-of-serena-williams.html.

Reason, M. "Serena Williams Just a Little Too Black to Be Accepted in the United States." *Stuff*, February 4, 2015. Retrieved February 3, 2018, from https://www.stuff.co.nz/sport/opinion/65740611/reason-serena-williams-just-a-little-too-black-to-be-accepted-in-united-states.

"Record Crowd Sees Clijsters Beat Serena Williams." *BBC Sports*, July 9, 2010. Retrieved February 1, 2018, from http://news.bbc.co.uk/sport2/hi/tennis/8803116.stm.

Reed, A. "Serena Williams Backs Nike's Powerful Statement." *CNBC*, September 5, 2018. Retrieved February 1, 2018, from https://www.cnbc.com/2018/09/05/serena-williams-on-nike-colin-kaepernick-advertising-campaign.html.

Riddell, D. "John McEnroe: 'Attlia the Hun' of Tennis." *CNN*, February 21, 2013. Retrieved February 3, 2018, from https://edition.cnn.com/2013/02/20/sport/tennis/john-mcenroe-tennis/index.html.

Rimm, S. "The Effects of Sibling Competition." *Family Achievement Clinic*. Retrieved January 31, 2018, from http://www.sylviarimm.com/article_sibcomp.html.

Roberts, E. "Serena Williams Posts Loving Tribute to Sister Venus." *Today.com*, January 29, 2017. Retrieved January 31, 2018, from https://www.today.com/news/serena-williams-posts-tribute-sister-venus-after-australian-open-win-t107526.

Roberts, J. "Williams Sisters' Rare Bond Produces Problems." *Independent*, June 24, 2002. Retrieved December 15, 2017, from https://www.independent.co.uk/sport/tennis/williams-sisters-rare-bond-produces-problem-181338.html.

Roberts, S. "Serena Williams Wins as Boos Pour Down." *New York Times*, March 18, 2001. Retrieved December 15, 2017, from http://www.nytimes.com/2001/03/18/sports/tennis-serena-williams-wins-as-the-boos-pour-down.html.

———. "Serena Wins Match, Then Takes Shot at Hingis." *New York Times*, September 2, 1999. Retrieved December 15, 2017, from http://www.nytimes.com/1999/09/03/sports/u-s-open-serena-williams-wins-match-then-takes-a-shot-at-hingis.html.

Robin, M. "Serena Williams Is Reportedly Launching a Beauty Brand." *Allure*, March 12, 2018. Retrieved January 31, 2018, from https://www.allure.com/story/serena-williams-beauty-brand.

Robson, D. "Mouratoglou: The Man behind Serena's Latest Surge." *USA Today*, September 2, 2013. Retrieved January 30, 2018, from https://www.usatoday.com/story/sports/tennis/2013/09/02/us-open-2013-serena-williams-patrick-mouratoglou-partnership/2755659/.

Roenigk, A. "Serena Williams Hasn't Lost Focus—She's Gained Perspective." *ESPN*, July 15, 2019. Retrieved February 1, 2018, from https://www.espn.com/tennis/story/_/id/27191585/serena-williams-lost-focus-gained-perspective.

Rosenberg, E., and C. Boren. "You're Hastening the Hell You Wish to Avoid'; Controversial American Delivers a Shot and Is Called Out by Serena Williams." *Washington Post*, January 22, 2018. Retrieved February 1, 2018, from https://www.washingtonpost.com/news/early-lead/wp/2018/01/22/meet-americas-new-tennis-sensation-tennys-sandgren-he-should-never-have-tweeted/?utm_term=.abca0d391d5e.

Rothenberg, B. "Tennis's Top Women Balance Body Image with Ambition." *New York Times*,
   July 10, 2015. Retrieved July 17, 2017, from https://www.nytimes.com/2015/07/11/sports/
   tenniss/tenniss-top-women-balance-body-image-with-quest-for-success.html.
Royce-Greensill, S. "Serena Williams on Exercising While Pregnant and Why Fashion Is
   Harder Than Tennis." *Telegraph*, August 21, 2017. Retrieved January 28, 2018, from http://
   www.telegraph.co.uk/luxury/jewellery/serena-williams-exercising-pregnant-fashion-harder-
   tennis/.
Sambu, P. "Serena to Visit Kenya." *Capital FM*, November 10, 2008. Retrieved July 17, 2017,
   from https://www.capitalfm.co.ke/sports/2008/11/10/serena-to-visit-kenya/.
Sappenfield, M. "Serena Williams Foot Fault: What Did She Say and Why Did She Say It?"
   Christian Science Monitor, September 13, 2009. Retrieved January 30, 2018, from https://
   www.csmonitor.com/USA/2009/0913/p02s01-usgn.html.
Satenstein, L. "It Took Serena Williams's Professional Bedazzler 24 Hours to Customize Her
   Wedding Sneakers." *Vogue*, November 22, 2017. Retrieved June 10, 2018, from https://
   www.vogue.com/article/serena-williams-bedazzled-wedding-nike-sneakers.
"Selling the Sisters." *Guardian*, January 9, 2005. Retrieved January 23, 2018, from https://
   www.theguardian.com/sport/2005/jan/09/tennis.features.
"Serena and Venus Williams Join Advisory Board of the Billie Jean King Leadership Initiative,
   Nonprofit Focused on Promoting Equality and Inclusion in the Workplace." *PRNewswire*,
   April 10, 2018. Retrieved January 12, 2019, from https://www.prnewswire.com/news-
   releases/serena-and-venus-williams-join-advisory-board-of-the-billie-jean-king-leadership-
   initiative-bjkli-non-profit-focused-on-promoting-equality-and-inclusion-in-the-workplace-
   300626837.html.
"Serena Goes for Another First in Bastad." *Women's Tennis Association*, July 2013. Retrieved
   February 1, 2018, from https://www.wtatennis.com/news/serena-goes-another-first-bastad.
"Serena Williams Ass Shakin' and Servin' Aces . . . in Front of Private Jet." *TMZ*, January 10,
   2018. Retrieved February 1, 2018, from http://www.tmz.com/2018/01/10/serena-williams-
   dancing-private-jet-lemon/.
"Serena Williams Completes Her First 5K Run." *South Florida Times*, December 18, 2014.
   Retrieved July 25, 2017, from http://www.sfltimes.com/sports/florida-sports/serena-
   williams-completes-her-first-5k-run.
"Serena Williams Fined $2,000 for Umpire Rant." *BBC Sports*, September 11, 2011. Retrieved
   February 1, 2018, from https://www.bbc.com/sport/tennis/14876919.
"Serena Williams Flaunts Million-Dollar Bump . . . at Dollar Tree!" *TMZ*, May 4, 2017.
   Retrieved February 4, 2018, from http://www.tmz.com/2017/05/04/serena-williams-dollar-
   store-baby-bump/.
"Serena Williams in Tears after Triumph." *Evening Standard*, June 21, 2011. Retrieved Febru-
   ary 1, 2018, from https://www.standard.co.uk/sport/tennis/serena-williams-in-tears-after-
   triumph-6413685.html.
"Serena Williams Reveals She Designed the Garish Yellow Tennis Ensemble Slammed as
   'Hideous' by Australian Open Spectators—to Bring 'Pop Culture and Fun' to the Courts."
   Daily Mail, January 22, 2016. Retrieved February 2, 2018, from https://
   www.dailymail.co.uk/femail/article-3411920/Serena-says-new-outfit-pops-Australian-
   Open.html.
"Serena Williams Suffers the Worst Defeat of Her Career." *CNN*, August 1, 2018. Retrieved
   August 8, 2018, from https://www.cnn.com/2018/08/01/tennis/serena-williams-johanna-
   konta-silicon-valley-classic-spt-intl/index.html.
"Serena Williams through to Wimbledon 2018 Final after Victory over Julia Georges." *Mirror*,
   July 12, 2018. Retrieved July 17, 2018, from https://www.mirror.co.uk/sport/tennis/serena-
   williams-through-wimbledon-2018-12906380.
"Serena Williams Vows to Never Stop Fighting for Equality." Wimbledon Press Conference,
   ESPN, July 13, 2019. Retrieved July 28, 2019, from http://www.espn.com/videohub/video/
   clip/_/id/27181898.
"Serena Wins 18th Slam." *ESPN*, September 8, 2014. Retrieved February 1, 2018, from http://
   www.espn.com/tennis/usopen14/story/_/id/11484243/2014-us-open-serena-williams-beats-
   caroline-wozniacki-win-3rd-straight.

Shultz, E. J. "Serena Williams's New Gatorade Spot Includes Her Baby's Double." *Ad Age*, November 20, 2017. Retrieved January 31, 2018, from http://adage.com/article/cmo-strategy/serena-williams-gatorade-spot-includes-baby-s-body-double/311356/.

Spain, S. "Serena Williams Focusing on Business, Charity, Family While Away from Tennis." *ESPN*, June 23, 2017. Retrieved January 30, 2018, from http://www.espn.com/espnw/voices/espnw-columnists/article/19719611/serena-williams-focusing-business-charity-family-away-tennis.

Stump, S. "Serena Williams on Motherhood, Return to Tennis: 'I Feel Like I've Already Won.'" *Today*, September 7, 2018. Retrieved September 17, 2018, from https://www.today.com/parents/serena-williams-motherhood-i-feel-i-ve-already-won-t137064.

Sullivan, M. "Double Fault in Article on Serena Williams and Body Image." *New York Times*, July, 13, 2015. Retrieved July 17, 2017, from https://publiceditor.blogs.nytimes.com/2015/07/13/double-fault-in-article-on-serena-williams-and-body-image/.

Swisher, S. "Serena Williams Is Joining SurveyMonkey Board." *Vox*, May 24, 2017. Retrieved January 30, 2018, from https://www.vox.com/2017/5/24/15683476/serena-williams-joins-survey-monkey-board.

Talarico, B. "Serena Williams on Designing Her Line in between Tennis Tournaments: 'It Was a Lot.'" *People*, September 17, 2015. Retrieved February 4, 2018, from http://people.com/style/serena-williams-on-designing-her-line-in-between-tennis-tournaments-it-was-a-lot/.

Tandon, K. "Conventional Ways of Serena." *ESPN*, September 4, 2012. Retrieved February 3, 2018, from http://www.espn.com/tennis/usopen12/story/_/id/8333931/us-open-conventional-serena.

———. "IPTL Spends Nearly $24 Million on Inaugural Teams." *Tennis.com*, March 3, 2014. Retrieved February 1, 2018, from http://www.tennis.com/pro-game/2014/03/itpl-spends-nearly-24-million-inaugural-teams/50789/.

"Tennis Ace Serena Williams Appointed UNICEF's Newest Goodwill Ambassador." *UNICEF.org*, September 2011. Retrieved February 1, 2019, from https://www.unicefusa.org/press/releases/tennis-ace-serena-williams-appointed-unicef%E2%80%99s-newest-goodwill-ambassador/8071.

"Tennis Legend Serena Williams Aces with Sell Out of Exclusive New Collection on HSN." *Home Shopping Network*, May 5, 2009. Retrieved January 30, 2018, from https://corporate.hsn.com/newsroom/pressrelease/tennis-legend-serena-williams-aces-with-sell-out-of-exclusive-new-collection-on-hsn/.

"Tennis Star Serena Williams Becomes UNICEF's Latest Goodwill Ambassador, with a Focus on Education." *UNICEF*, September 2011. Retrieved July 25, 2017, from https://www.unicef.org/people/people_59874.html.

Thomas, D. "Why Everyone Is Saying 'Black Girls Are Magic.'" *Los Angeles Times*, September 9, 2015. Retrieved July 17, 2017, from https://www.latimes.com/nation/nationnow/la-na-nn-everyones-saying-black-girls-are-magic-20150909-htmlstory.html.

Thomas, L. "Serena Williams Joins Online Retailer Poshmark's Board of Directors." *CNBC*, February 20, 2019. Retrieved January 28, 2018, from https://www.cnbc.com/2019/02/20/serena-williams-joins-online-retailer-poshmarks-board-of-directors.html.

"Ticket Prices for U.S. Open Women's Final Plunge after Serena's Loss." *Reuters*, September 11, 2015. Retrieved February 1, 2018, from https://www.reuters.com/article/us-tennis-open-tickets/ticket-prices-for-u-s-open-womens-final-plunge-after-serenas-loss-idUSKCN0RB2MI20150911.

Tignor, S. "Mariana Alves's Missed Call Ushers in Hawk-Eye." *Tennis.com*, November 19, 2015. Retrieved January 31, 2018, from http://www.tennis.com/pro-game/2015/11/2004-mariana-alves-missed-call-ushers-hawk-eye/56853/.

———. "Tennis through the Lens." *Tennis.com*, September 11, 2013. Retrieved February 4, 2018, from http://www.tennis.com/photos-video/2013/09/tennis-through-lens/49128/.

"Tops of 2017: Pro Athlete Marketability." *Nielsen*, December 21. 2017. Retrieved January 30, 2018, from http://www.nielsen.com/us/en/insights/news/2017/tops-of-2017-pro-athlete-marketability.html.

Tresniowski, A. "Serena, Serene." *People.com*, March 19, 2007. Retrieved July 17, 2017, from https://people.com/archive/serena-serene-vol-67-no-11/.

Tsang, J. "Serena Williams Rules in Women's Tennis while Also Making Her Mark in Fashion." *South China Morning Post*, July 2, 2015. Retrieved February 2, 2018, from http://www.scmp.com/magazines/style/article/1826481/serena-williams-rules-womens-tennis-while-also-making-her-mark.

Tsuji, A. "Naomi Osaka Had the Greatest Reaction to Beating Serena Williams at Miami Open." *USA Today*, March, 21, 2018. Retrieved September 17, 2018, from https://www.usatoday.com/story/sports/ftw/2018/03/21/naomi-osaka-had-the-greatest-reaction-to-beating-serena-williams-at-miami-open-omg/111141426/.

Ubha, R. "End of an Era for Serena Williams." *CNN.com*, March 6, 2015. Retrieved February 1, 2018, from https://www.cnn.com/2015/03/06/tennis/serena-williams-bajin-tennis/index.html.

"The Unique Way Serena Williams Is Giving to Charity." *Rolling Out*, March 8, 2019. Retrieved February 1, 2018, from https://rollingout.com/2019/03/08/the-unique-way-serena-williams-is-giving-to-charity/.

Vallego, J. J. "Serena and Venus: Sisters in Arms." *Rolling Stone*, September 9, 2015 Retrieved February 1, 2018, from https://www.rollingstone.com/sports/features/serena-and-venus-williams-sisters-in-arms-20150909.

"Venus Beats Sister at Lipton." *CBS News*, March 28, 1999. Retrieved December 15, 2017, from https://www.cbsnews.com/news/venus-beats-sister-at-lipton/.

Voepel, C. C. "Is Serena Williams the Best Female Athlete Ever?" *ESPN*, July 22, 2015. Retrieved March 20, 2017, from http://www.espn.com/espnw/news-commentary/debate/13462699/is-serena-williams-best-female-athlete-ever.

Wagner, L. "Serena Williams Calls on Tennys Sandgren to Apologize." *Deadspin*, January 24, 2018. Retrieved January 31, 2018, from https://deadspin.com/serena-williams-calls-on-tennys-sandgren-to-apologize-1822373452.

Waldman, A. "How Hospitals Are Failing Black Mothers." *ProPublica*, December 27, 2017. Retrieved February 17, 2018, from https://www.propublica.org/article/how-hospitals-are-failing-black-mothers.

Waldstein, D., and B. Rothenberg. "Serena Williams Accuses Official of Sexism in U.S. Open Loss to Naomi Osaka." *New York Times*, September 8, 2018. Retrieved February 1, 2018, from https://www.nytimes.com/2018/09/08/sports/serena-williams-vs-naomi-osaka-us-open.html.

Wertheim, J. "Four Days Later, Reassessing the Serena–Ramos Controversy." *Sports Illustrated*, September 12, 2018. Retrieved February 1, 2018, from https://www.si.com/tennis/2018/09/12/serena-williams-carlos-ramos-us-open-controversy-umpire-penalty.

———. "Serena Williams Wins Australian Open, 19th Major Title, in Championship Form." *Sports Illustrated*, January 31, 2015. Retrieved February 1, 2018, from https://www.si.com/tennis/2015/01/31/serena-williams-beats-sharapova-wins-australian-open-title.

———. "The Two and Only the French Open Removed All Doubt: Serena and Venus Williams Are in a Class by Themselves." *Sports Illustrated*, June 17, 2002. Retrieved January 31, 2018, from https://www.si.com/vault/2002/06/17/325325/the-two-and-only-the-french-open-removed-all-doubt-serena-and-venus-williams-are-in-a-class-by-themselves.

———. *Venus Envy: A Sensational Season Inside the Women's Tennis Tour.* New York: Harper, 2001.

Whack, E. "Why Serena Williams Is the Definition of #BlackGirlMagic." *ESPN*, September 11, 2015. Retrieved December 27, 2017, from http://www.espn.com/espnw/athletes-life/article/13625369/why-serena-williams-definition-blackgirlmagic.

"Wheaties Scores an Ace with Serena Williams Wheaties Box." *General Mills*, June 25, 2019. Retrieved July 7, 2019, from https://www.generalmills.com/en/News/NewsReleases/Library/2019/June/Wheaties-scores-an-ace-with-Serena-Williams-Wheaties-box.

Whyte, D. "Serena Prepares for Acting Career." *Independent*, August 10, 2002. Retrieved August 12, 2009, from https://www.independent.co.uk/sport/tennis/serena-prepares-for-acting-career-172763.html.

Wiggins, D. K. *Out of the Shadows: A Biographical History of African American Athletes.* Fayetteville: University of Arkansas Press, 2006.

Williams, J. "Serena's Husband's Net Worth Revealed after the Wedding." *Newsweek*, November 17, 2017. Retrieved February 1, 2018, from http://www.newsweek.com/serena-williams-alexis-ohanian-wedding-714738.

Williams, R., with B. Davis. *Black and White: The Way I See It*. New York: Atria Books, 2014.

Williams, S. "The Ball Is in Your Court." *Wired*, October 2015. Retrieved July 17, 2017, from https://www.wired.com/2015/10/serena-williams-guest-editor-race-gender-equality/.

———. "Serena Williams: How Black Women Can Close the Pay Gap." *Fortune*, July 31, 2017. Retrieved July 17, 2017, from http://fortune.com/2017/07/31/serena-williams-black-women-equal-pay/.

Williams, V. "Wimbledon Has Sent Me a Message: I'm Only a Second-Class Champion." *Times*, June 26, 2006. Retrieved July 17, 2017, from https://www.thetimes.co.uk/article/wimbledon-has-sent-me-a-message-im-only-a-second-class-champion-f056h05hmzq.

"Williams Apologizes for Abusing Line Judge." *Guardian*, September 14, 2009. Retrieved January 30, 2018, from https://www.theguardian.com/sport/2009/sep/14/serena-williams-us-open-kim-clijsters.

"Williams Comeback Stuns Sharapova." *BBC Sport*, January 27, 2005. Retrieved January 30, 2018, from http://news.bbc.co.uk/sport2/hi/tennis/4207687.stm.

"Williams Hurt by Jeers." *BBC*, June 3, 2003. Retrieved January 31, 2018, from http://news.bbc.co.uk/sport2/hi/tennis/french_open_2003/2967190.stml.

"Williams Sisters to Star in Reality Show." *Guardian*, March 29, 2005. Retrieved May 2, 2018, from https://www.theguardian.com/media/2005/mar/29/broadcasting.realitytv.

Yotka, S. "Serena Williams Is Launching Her Own Direct-to-Consumer Fashion Collection." *Vogue*, May 30, 2018. Retrieved June 10, 2018, from https://www.vogue.com/article/serena-williams-launches-serena-fashion-collection?verso=true.

Zinser, L. "Serena Williams to Face Wozniacki, Who Wants to Be Next Big Thing." *New York Times*, September 9, 2011. Retrieved January 30, 2018, from https://www.nytimes.com/2011/09/10/sports/tennis/serena-williams-to-face-wozniacki-who-wants-to-be-next-big-thing.html.

———. "Titan of Tennis vs. the Next Big Thing." *New York Times*, September 10, 2011. Retrieved February 1, 2018, from https://www.nytimes.com/2011/09/10/sports/tennis/serena-williams-to-face-wozniacki-who-wants-to-be-next-big-thing.html.

Zivlak, M. "All Nike Dresses Serena Wore during Her 78 Match Wins and 11 Trophy Lifts in 2013." *Women's Tennis Blog*, November 27, 2013. Retrieved February 4, 2018, from http://www.womenstennisblog.com/2013/11/27/all-nike-dresses-serena-wore-during-her-78-match-wins-and-11-trophy-lifts-in-2013/.

———. "World-Record Crowd Watches Kim Clijsters Beat Serena Williams." *Women's Tennis Blog*, July 9, 2010. Retrieved February 1, 2018, from http://www.womenstennisblog.com/2010/07/09/world-record-tennis-crowd-watches-kim-clijsters-beat-serena-williams/.

INDEX

ABOUT THE AUTHOR

Merlisa Lawrence Corbett is a sports journalist who writes about tennis and sports in society. She is a former tennis columnist for *Bleacher Report* and reporter for *Sports Illustrated*. She also covered sports for the *Pittsburgh Press*, *Staten Island Advance*, *Tampa Tribune*, and *Tampa Bay Times*. Lawrence Corbett wrote the foreword for Arthur Ashe Jr.'s *A Hard Road to Glory: A History of the African American Athlete: Track and Field*. Currently a contributor to *Tennis View* and *Black Tennis* magazines, she lives in Central Florida, where she competes in local tennis leagues. She wields a mean one-handed backhand and takes pride in being called the "Evil Backhand Lady."

www.Merlisa.com
Twitter: @merlisa